D1321383

RULING ROMAN BRITAIN

RULING ROMAN BRITAIN

Kings, Queens, Governors and Emperors
from Julius Caesar to Agricola

David Braund

London and New York

First published 1996
by Routledge
11 New Fetter Lane, London EC4P 4EE

Simultaneously published in the USA and Canada
by Routledge
29 West 35th Street, New York, NY 10001

© 1996 David Braund

Typeset in Garamond by BC Typesetting, Bristol

Printed and bound in Great Britain by
Biddles Ltd, Guildford and Kings Lynn

British Library Cataloguing in Publication Data
A catalogue record for this book is available from the British Library

Library of Congress Cataloging in Publication Data
Braund, David, 1957–
  Ruling Roman Britain: kings, queens, governors and emperors
from Julius Caesar to Agricola/David Braund.
    p.   cm.
  Includes bibliographical references (p.) and index.
  1. Great Britain–Politics and government–55 BC–449 AD
  2. Great Britain–History–Roman period, 55 BC–449 AD
  3. Romans–Great Britain–Kings and rulers. 4. Romans–Great
Britain–Queens. 5. Governors–Great Britain. 6. Emperors–Rome.
I. Title
DA145.B835 1996   95-52388
936.2′04–dc20   CIP

ISBN 0-415-00804-2

FOR DIANE

CONTENTS

List of figures	viii
List of abbreviations	x
Preface	xi
Acknowledgements	xiii
Map of Roman Britain	xiv
INTRODUCTION: READING ROMAN BRITAIN	1
1 THE CONQUEST OF OCEAN	10
2 KINGS, GOVERNORS AND EMPERORS	24
3 CAESAR: THE EXCITEMENT OF INVASION	41
4 ARTFUL COMMENTARIES: CAESAR ON HIMSELF	55
5 COINS AND DYNASTIES	67
6 FROM COMMIUS TO CUNOBELINUS	76
7 CALIGULA, CLAUDIUS AND CARATACUS	91
8 BOUDICA AND CARTIMANDUA	118
9 AGRICOLA AND TACITUS, TRAJAN AND THE FLAVIANS	147
EPILOGUE	177
Notes	182
Bibliography	204
Index	212

FIGURES

Map of Roman Britain. xiv
1 The 'Battersea Shield'. 13
2 The 'Waterloo horned helmet'. 14
3 Reconstruction of the head of Lindow Man. 14
4 Water-deity from the Roman fort at Chesters, Hadrian's Wall. 16
5 Altar to Neptune, Newcastle-upon-Tyne. 16
6 Altar to Oceanus, Newcastle-upon-Tyne. 16
7 The temple-pediment from Bath. 17
8 Panel from the Withington mosaic (Glos.). 17
9 'Great Dish' from the Mildenhall Treasure. 18
10 'Great Dish' from the Mildenhall Treasure (detail). 18
11 Reconstruction of a British chariot. 47
12 Chariot-burial, Garton. 47
13 Bronze coin of Cunobelinus (obverse): VA 2089. 70
14 Bronze coin of Cunobelinus (obverse): VA 2095. 70
15 Bronze coin of Cunobelinus (reverse): VA 2095. 70
16 Gold quarter-stater of Verica (obverse): VA 501. 71
17 Gold quarter-stater of Verica (reverse): VA 501. 71
18 Gold quarter-stater of Verica (obverse): VA 527. 71
19 Gold quarter-stater of Verica (reverse): VA 527. 71
20 Gold stater of Epaticus (reverse): VA 575. 71
21 Silver coin of Eppillus (obverse): VA 415. 73
22 Silver coin of Eppillus (reverse): VA 415. 73
23 Silver coin of Prasutagus (obverse): VA 780. 75
24 Silver coin of Prasutagus (reverse): VA 780. 75
25 The silver Augustus-medallion, Lexden Tumulus (Colchester), diam. 25mm. 98

26 An elite Late Iron Age burial, Welwyn Garden City
    (reconstructed).   98
27 Imported silver cup from the burial at Welwyn Garden
    City.   99
28 Claudius and Britannia (Aphrodisias, south-west
    Turkey).   104
29 Silver didrachm of Claudius (obverse), Caesarea
    mint: BMC 237.   105
30 Silver didrachm of Claudius (reverse), Caesarea
    mint: BMC 237.   105
31 Lead ingot from Blagdon (Som.), bearing the name
    Britannicus.   105
32 Silver coin of Prasutagus (obverse): recently discovered
    hoard, south-west Norfolk.   133
33 Silver coin of Prasutagus (reverse): recently discovered
    hoard, south-west Norfolk.   133
34 Tomb-monument of C. Julius Classicianus.   140

ABBREVIATIONS

AJPh	*American Journal of Philology*
ANRW	*Aufstieg und Niedergang der römischen Welt*
ASNP	*Annali della Scuola Normale di Pisa*
BAR	British Archaeological Reports
BMCRE	*British Museum: Coins of the Roman Empire*
CIL	*Corpus Inscriptionum Latinarum*
CPh	*Classical Philology*
CQ	*Classical Quarterly*
CW	*Classical World*
HBMCE	Historical Buildings and Monuments Commission for England
ILS	*Inscriptiones Latinae Selectae*
JHS	*Journal of Hellenic Studies*
JRS	*Journal of Roman Studies*
LIMC	*Lexicon Iconographicae Mythologicae Classicae*
LSJ	*Liddell-Scott-Jones, Greek-English Lexicon*
OJA	*Oxford Journal of Archaeology*
OUCA	Oxford University Committee for Archaeology
PBSR	*Papers of the British School at Rome*
Proc. Camb. Phil. Soc.	*Proceedings of the Cambridge Philological Society*
PSAS	*Proceedings of the Society of Antiquaries of Scotland*
RIB	*The Roman Inscriptions of Britain* (2nd edn by R. S. O. Tomlin; Stroud, 1995)
TAPA	*Transactions and Proceedings of the American Philological Association*

PREFACE

A Preface offers its author many opportunities to indulge himself. On this occasion, I shall restrict myself to sincere expressions of thanks. The task is simple and pleasant, but also difficult because so many people have contributed to this book, often unwittingly. As I wrote it, my teachers often came to mind, particularly Dick Whittaker, Ray Van Dam and Joyce Reynolds, who also (yet again) gave me specialist advice. Re-reading the books and articles of Elizabeth Rawson, I have been reminded both of her wisdom and of her unfailing kindness to me from undergraduate days, though formally I was never her pupil. Among others from whom I have learnt (or tried to learn) a lot over the years, I will single out two scholars for special acknowledgment: Tony Woodman, who has had no involvement with this book, but whose impact on my thinking (and reading) has been enormous; and Peter Wiseman, whose influence has been much greater than he knows, and whose comments have made this a much better book than it would otherwise have been.

At the same time, I have often had cause to recall the generosity with which many friends in Romano-British studies have allowed me a place at their particular conference table over the years, and indeed a place in the Pilgrimage of 1989: I shall not risk embarrassing them by name, for I am sure that they know who they are, and I am not at all sure what they will think of this foray into Roman Britain. The sources of my illustrations are acknowledged elsewhere: I am grateful to those who have helped me gather them together from various parts of the country.

The idea for this book emerged some ten years ago in the course of conversation with Richard Stoneman, in the aftermath of the publication of my *Rome and the friendly king: the character of client kingship* (London, 1984), wherein I touched upon Britain from time to time. In the intervening years, the notional book went through many forms without ever being committed to paper, while I devoted my attention to the less familiar lands of Transcaucasian Georgia. It was my work in Georgia that convinced me of the need to explore together literary texts which may have little in common save their relevance to the same geographical area. Meanwhile, Richard Stoneman exhibited a patience that never seemed to be a lack of interest.

I began to commit my long-churned thoughts to paper at the end of 1994, inspired and encouraged by my wife, Diane Braund. Early drafts flowed quickly at Holywell, Cornwall, in a coastal retreat which made Ocean come alive. It was Diane who first took me there. Without her support I would not have written this book or, as it once seemed, anything else. And without her perceptive questions and sense of style, my writing would have been still more opaque in thought and word. The dedication of this book to her is a completely inadequate expression of my gratitude and love.

ACKNOWLEDGEMENTS

I would like to acknowledge the help of the following individuals and institutions with regard to illustrations. The British Museum provided nos. 1–3, 8–24, 26–7, 29–31 and 34. English Heritage provided no. 4. Lindsay Allason-Jones provided nos. 5–6, from the collection of the University of Newcastle. Jane Bircher and Stephen Bird of Bath Museum Services provided no. 7. The staff of Colchester Museum furnished no. 25, while no. 28 is published courtesy of the Aphrodisias Archive (my thanks to Bert Smith). I am particularly grateful to John A. Davies of the Castle Museum, Norwich, for the newly discovered nos. 32–3 (photograph: David Wicks, Norfolk Field Archaeology Division). Philip de Jersey of the Institute of Archaeology, Oxford, was unfailingly helpful during my search for numismatic illustrations.

CALEDONIA

OCEANUS

Castlecary
●
Antonine Wall

Birrens   Chesters
●   ●
Hadrian's Wall ●●●   ● Newcastle
Carlisle Vindolanda

BRIGANTES

● Stanwick

● Aldborough

● York

● Chester

ORDOVICES

CORIELTAUVI

ICENI

DOBUNNI

TRINOVANTES

CATUVELLAUNI

SILURES

Verulamium ●   ● Camulodunum

● Bath

ATREBATES   ● London   CANTIACI

BELGAE   REGNI

DUROTRIGES

DUMNONII

● Chichester

OCEANUS

OCEANUS

HIBERNIA

0   150 km

GAUL

INTRODUCTION:
READING ROMAN BRITAIN

A new book on Roman Britain requires explanation and perhaps justification, since the island has been the subject of many a book already. The purpose of this book is to offer a significantly different perspective upon the history of Roman Britain from the middle of the first century BC to the end of the first century AD. Its focus is primarily upon the literary evidence. Its aim is not only to complement the mass of archaeological evidence and analysis that has accrued over recent decades, but to provide a more nuanced historical framework within which Romano-British archaeology can be situated and understood. In my view, this book is necessary because the literary sources for early Roman Britain have not yet been subjected to the intense and rigorous scrutiny that has been applied to our archaeological evidence by students of Roman Britain. It is in that sense that this book is to be understood: this is a 'reading' of Roman Britain as it appears in the quite numerous and various texts that have survived from antiquity.

The key issue is context. The chapters that follow are designed to explore the broad patterns of Roman thought, literature and practice within which the history of Roman Britain was enacted and, most important, within which that history was thought and written about in antiquity. A fundamental contention throughout this book is that Roman Britain cannot be understood without a firm and expansive grasp of the ideology of Roman imperialism at large, and particularly of the principal concerns and outlooks of Roman writers and decision-makers at the centre of power in Rome, for it is they who shape our perception of the history of the island.

Of course, history does not write itself, whether in antiquity or today. In writing this book I have chosen themes which seem to me important and indicative. I have selected the questions that seem to me to be most interesting. And in so doing I have also omitted much, though nothing that seems to me to be germane to my arguments, whether for or against. At the same time, I have shaped this work of history so as best to convey my own reading of Roman Britain from Julius Caesar to Trajan. Throughout I am aware of the different and (in a sense) competing accounts of other modern writers: indeed, where I consider it necessary, I engage with such other versions through the book. There is nothing unusual or special about my procedure, except that I have decided to discuss it explicitly here in the Introduction. History is always, and can only be, written like this: in the process, historians usually see themselves as providing an account which embodies their understanding of the truth. However, the process is rarely acknowledged, because it is at once a banal commonplace and an admission that may seem shameful to those who believe themselves to be propounding a truth which is absolute, when they are in fact presenting no more than their own versions of the truth.

In antiquity, historical writers were no less concerned with truth than their modern counterparts, but, as today, they preferred usually to ignore or conceal the ultimate subjectivity of their particular versions of truth. This book will focus again and again on that subjectivity: on the various viewpoints, assumptions and strategies of the historical writers whose works form the bulk of the material that we use to construct histories of Roman Britain. The purpose of that recurrent concern in this book is not to find untruth in those works, but to develop an understanding of their writers' attitudes to Britain and of the uses made of Britain in their different accounts. It is through the exploration of those viewpoints, assumptions and strategies that we shall be able to trace and assess the shifting evocations and significances of Britain in Roman thought. In that sense, a principal objective is to understand Roman conceptions of and attitudes towards Britain. In modern works on Roman Britain it is usual to bemoan the paucity of Roman literary sources. By contrast, this book will consider why Romans wrote about Britain at all and how they wrote about it.

A basic assumption in the chapters that follow is that the accounts of Caesar, Tacitus and the rest are not simply reportage, but analytical and selective explorations of issues. And those issues were at least as much defined by the concerns of the Roman centre as by experience at the British periphery: as we shall see, the point is well illustrated, for example, by our sources' difficulties with queens, or by their obsession with freedom and slavery under the Principate. Accordingly, there is much to be gained from the study of sources which do not seem historical in the familiar sense: in particular, we shall see that Roman poetry often provides insight into Roman thought about Britain and about the changing significance of the island from period to period.

This is a book about Roman Britain, but it is also a book about how to read texts of various sorts, especially historical and poetical works. The reading of any such text may be considered an act of translation, but the reading of texts written in Greek and Latin makes particular demands. To produce an English version of the original text is straightforward enough, perhaps, but to capture all its nuances in translation is at least very difficult and perhaps impossible. But those who would understand the history of Roman Britain must strive for such nuances. Accordingly, although no great claims are made for the perfection (beyond basic accuracy) of the translations of the many passages quoted in this book, attention will be drawn from time to time to important nuances in the original languages which have been either overlooked or misconstrued hitherto. If we are to understand our sources, we must first listen to them and be sure as to what they are saying.

Three further and related strands run through the book and are worth identifying at the outset. First, issues of imperialism: we shall see that Britain offered particular attractions to imperialist Romans, while it could also disappoint, and later could be used by Roman writers as a theatrical setting for the exploration of the negative consequences of imperialism. Second, issues of geography: it was Ocean that gave Britain much of its appeal to the Roman imperialist and moralist, cutting it off from the rest of the empire as 'another world', to be conquered and perhaps corrupted: the conquest of the island entailed the conquest of Ocean, imagined as the divine father of the rivers which divided the world and, in the persons of the Rhine, Danube and Euphrates, marked the frontiers of the empire. Third, issues of monarchy in its various forms, encompassing kings (with kinglets, dynasts, chiefs, etc.), queens, governors and emperors: although the list is heterogeneous, it derives a strong unity from the long tradition of Graeco-Roman thought on monarchy within the framework of which all its members were located and understood. Indeed, the multiple polarities which distinguish members of the list of monarchs (e.g. Roman/barbarian; male/female; long-term/short-term) can also serve to bind them together, for different writers not only employ these polarities to pursue comparisons and make judgments (as, for example, Tacitus on Agricola and Domitian in the *Agricola*, and by implication on Cartimandua and Boudica in the *Annals* and *Histories*), but also locate different individuals at different poles: for example, we shall see that Tacitus' Boudica is rather Roman (and probably a Roman citizen), while Dio's is strikingly barbarian.

The first chapter begins the discussion of imperialism and geography that runs through the book. This chapter is designed to explore the role of Ocean in attracting Roman imperialism to Britain and contributing to the discourse in which victory in Britain could be claimed as something very special. Imperialism was much more than a scramble for booty and the prestige of conquest to which booty contributed: more broadly, it was a world-view within which conceptions of geography occupied key positions. Ocean was a river and a god, the father of the rivers of the world, the boundary of the inhabited world itself. The conquest of Britain required the crossing and thus the conquest of this mighty supernatural force, a vast undertaking which could be claimed as a first for mankind and human culture against the ultimate force of nature. In this way the conquest of the island could be elevated from the almost mundane to the epic.

The second chapter introduces issues of monarchy. Its particular purpose is to explain how and why not only conquest but also the administration of the provincial regime of a Roman governor mattered in Roman thought and politics. A direct line is traced from the ideas of Greek philosophers on kingship (not only the likes of Xenophon and Plato, but also the thinkers of the Hellenistic world), through the Roman Republic, to the writings of Tacitus. As often in Roman history, the survival of so many of the works of Cicero makes his outlook the most rewarding point of reference in the late Republic. And in Cicero we find an active acceptance both of the influence of Greek ideas on kingship and of their application in the Roman society and politics of the late Republic to the role of the provincial governor. Provincial governorship is seen to be a profoundly moral issue, centred upon knowledge and self-control, like kingship. At the same time, that moral issue was a pressing one, for much of the social and political conflict of the late Republic was conducted in and around the subject of governorship, good and bad. The impression that might be gained from Cicero's speeches, for and against governors, is confirmed by his own provincial letters as governor of Cilicia in 51–50 BC and, still more powerfully, by a treatise on governorship which he addressed about 60 BC to his brother, Quintus Cicero, then praetorian governor of the rich province of Asia and subsequently Caesar's legate in Britain.

In that treatise, Cicero forcefully reminds Quintus that his position is monarchical and that his conduct of his temporary monarchy in Asia will have major repercussions, for good or ill, not only for himself upon his return to Rome, but also for his associates and relations (not least his brother). The province is a theatre, with the governor on-stage, says Cicero: the governor's act may not be seen in far-off Rome, but the reaction of the audience will certainly be heard. In short, the exercise of governorship was the ultimate test of character in a society which, for all its imperialism, preferred to imagine its empire and provincial administration as moral, and beneficial to its provincial 'allies'. As we shall see, an appreciation of that approach to provincial governorship is fundamental to any understanding of Roman writing about the provinces, most obviously Tacitus' *Agricola*.

The third chapter explores the intellectual and political atmosphere within which Caesar mounted his invasions of Britain in 55 and 54 BC. The invasions were controversial, not only because Britain represented a further step into the unknown, into a fantastic 'other world', but also because Caesar's explosive consulship of 59 BC had placed his every act at the centre of political conflict. In the late Republic, Caesar's invasions of Britain constituted a particularly striking part of his closely scrutinized and hotly debated decade of governorship. In this case, in particular, we can see very clearly how imperialism and administration on the frontier were enmeshed with the society and politics of the centre of power at Rome. And Cicero's correspondence indicates that such interaction functioned also on a cultural and literary level: Cicero himself now chose to write a poem on Britain in which Caesar, also an active writer, took a personal interest while on campaign. Of course the poem was an epic, a genre appropriate to the grandeur of Caesar's undertaking.

Caesar's *Commentaries*, often known as his *Gallic Wars*, were not only an account of his campaigns on the continent and in Britain, but also an integral part of those campaigns and in a sense their objective. An ultimate goal for the Roman commander was a place in Roman history: through his *Commentaries* Caesar sought to carve out the place he wanted. We shall see in the fourth chapter how the *Commentaries* were a polemical work of self-justification, anticipating and engaging with the objections and criticisms levelled at Caesar by his detractors and opponents in the political conflicts of the late Republic. This chapter attempts to show how Caesar the writer draws his readers into viewing events from his perspective, according to which he was an upright Roman striding into the unknown and there struggling manfully against dangerous, perfidious barbarians, against the strange elements (principally Ocean) and against the brevity of the time available for campaigning there. These are artful *Commentaries*, all the more beguiling through their apparent lack of guile.

The fifth chapter pauses to consider coins, for coins represent our principal hope if we wish to construct the history of the rulers of Britain, especially between the invasions of Caesar and of Claudius. They are a source which was generated from the island itself, by contrast to the literary versions of Romans. However, it is their mixture of Roman and local Celtic features that particularly attracts attention: they offer some evidence of the absorption of Roman culture among the ruling British elite, though they may not be typical of the broader pattern of cultural interaction. Coins also indicate family connections, so that we can attempt to trace dynasties among the rulers of Britain. Yet great caution is required: as the fifth chapter stresses, there are disappointing but firm limits to the historical usefulness of numismatic studies, and, for all its attractions, the temptation to compose historical accounts on the basis of coins alone is best resisted, not least in view of uncertainties in dating, the problems of assessing the status and often the relationships of the individuals featured on the coins, and the existence of homonymous rulers.

The sixth chapter traces and seeks to explain the shifting attitudes to the invasion of Britain that are discernible at Rome through the reigns of the emperors Augustus, Tiberius and Gaius (Caligula). Under Tiberius in particular, the analysis of the geographer Strabo seems to play down the achievement of Caesar and to validate the decision not to invade Britain again. Diplomacy was the preferred course, it seems: British rulers came to Rome, acknowledged as friends and allies of the empire. A close reading of Strabo's text shows his understanding of the problem of Britain to be much more coherent and indeed sophisticated than is commonly imagined.

However, the emperor Gaius chose to re-enact the campaigns of his ancestor, Julius Caesar. In the seventh chapter we shall see that

there was nothing insane about Gaius' plans and actions with
regard to Britain, though they have often been dismissed as the
incomprehensible doings of a madman. However, no special pleading is needed to make sense of Gaius' undertakings, including his
conquest of Rhine and of Ocean. While Gaius needed the prestige
of military success, the diplomatic strategy that Rome had pursued
in Britain had started to fall apart, not least through turmoil in the
realm and family of King Cunobelinus, who shortly died. The very
fact that the emperor Claudius soon mounted his own invasion of
Britain in AD 43, only two years after his tumultuous accession, does
much to show that Gaius had had good reasons to consider an
invasion of his own. We shall see in detail how Claudius used his
British campaigns as the running theme of his imperial regime until
his death in AD 54. We shall see also how the regime of Claudius had
a strong interest in denigrating the campaign of his predecessor,
generating the hostile tradition that has come down to us.

At the same time, Tacitus' account of the rulers of Roman Britain
after the Claudian invasion shows how the island offered scope for
moralizing on themes of broader imperial interest. On the one
hand, we find King Cogidubnus, loyal to the flawed empire and
therefore servile; on the other, Caratacus, a son of Cunobelinus, the
champion of freedom against the Roman empire, an enemy of
Rome and a barbarian, but also admirable in his cause and dignity, a
contrast to Claudius. At Rome as in the empire at large, freedom
and slavery are dominant polarities in the outlooks of our sources.
It is in that context that we must understand the treatment of
powerful women in literary accounts of Britain.

Queens form the subject of Chapter 8. There we shall see the
largely negative picture of Cartimandua of the Brigantes, very much
a queen in Tacitus' account. For Tacitus and, more broadly, the
Roman society of the Principate, her power and her gender are irre-
concilable: it is in that light that Tacitus' narrative and analysis
should be read. By contrast, the Boudica of Tacitus' *Annals* is never
described as a queen: rather, she is a wife and mother, wronged by
corrupt Romans of low status. Thus, in the *Annals*, Tacitus offers a
strong contrast between the immoral Cartimandua and the moral, if
ultimately misguided, Boudica. However, in his *Agricola*, written
some twenty years earlier, Tacitus encourages a distinctly less sympathetic approach to Boudica, while almost a century after the
Annals the historian Cassius Dio provides an influential depiction
of Boudica which makes her more monstrous even than Tacitus'

Cartimandua. Such judgments tell us much more about attitudes to powerful women as a type than about the individual women portrayed, with the image of Cleopatra in particular looming in the background. Accordingly, we shall read the so-called 'rebellion of Boudica' (very much not Tacitus' phrase) as an imperial morality tale, not as a narrative of what actually happened.

Finally, the ninth chapter sets Tacitus' *Agricola* in the context of Flavian and Trajanic attitudes towards Britain. Vespasian and his family sought to appropriate the glory of the conquest of Britain which had featured so prominently in the regime of Claudius. Vespasian's participation in the Claudian adventure gave an opportunity: his role was duly magnified and extended. A continuity was suggested from the Claudian invasion (appropriated for the Flavians) into the reign of Vespasian himself and on into that of Domitian. It was the Flavians, it could be claimed, who had conquered Britain. However, in the aftermath of Domitian's assassination in AD 96 and the emergence of the emperor Trajan in AD 98, when Tacitus produced his *Agricola*, such a claim was insufferable: Domitianic success could not be permitted and must be explained away as a sham or as contrary to the emperor's evil wishes. It is in that context that the *Agricola* is to be read.

The *Agricola* suggests that the conquest of Britain was achieved not by Domitian, but despite him. It seeks to convince its readers that Agricola was the conqueror and the just administrator, who by his example highlighted the tyranny of Domitian. Tacitus suggests that in the 'other world' of Britain Agricola had wielded monarchical power in the way that Domitian should have wielded it at Rome. The fact that Agricola could not have continued to advance north through Britain without at least the acquiescence of the emperor Domitian is quietly ignored, for the thought immediately disrupts the central argument of the work by indicating that Agricola was not so much Domitian's counterpoint as his agent.

The conquest of Caledonia at the battle of Mons Graupius dominates the account of Britain in the *Agricola*, which itself takes up an enormous part of the biography. Victory at Mons Graupius is presented as the pinnacle of Agricola's achievements; his rational speech before the battle exemplifies his virtues. At the same time, the long tirade of the leader of the Britons, one Calgacus (possibly a Tacitean invention), shows the disastrous effects of unjust Roman government. Calgacus' speech has won much modern admiration, but, as the reader of the *Agricola* should understand, Calgacus has miscalculated in his irrational barbarian passion: his immediate opponent is not the unjust Domitian or earlier unjust governors, but the just and rational Agricola. Tacitus invites sympathy with Calgacus and the cause of freedom, but through the earlier sections of the *Agricola* he has shown his readers repeatedly that, in directing such sentiments against this particular Roman governor, the Caledonians have made a fatal error.

Of course, in evoking sympathy for the Caledonian cause, if only it were properly directed, Tacitus is treating a principal theme of the *Agricola* which he was later to treat again in the *Histories* and *Annals*: namely, the problematics of imperialism and Romanization when the Roman state has already been so corrupted. The main problem can be stated simply: if Rome has gone bad, how can Romanization be good? Is there not something positive about the extremes of freedom that have survived outside the empire?

Tacitus' *Histories*, completed about AD 110, provided a detailed year-by-year narrative of the Flavian regime from its beginnings under Vespasian in AD 69 to the assassination of Domitian in AD 96. The *Histories* must have contained a great deal about Britain, including, we may presume, another Tacitean account of Agricola's campaigns there. Unfortunately, only the opening books have survived; in consequence, that narrative is lost. However, the very beginning of the *Histories* offers a summary of its contents which make clear enough the line that Tacitus took there about the conquest of Britain: Domitian's role had been to neglect the island, though it had been completely conquered (no doubt by Agricola, as he will have stressed). Such an approach was consistent with the argument of the *Agricola* (and indeed of the *Germania*) and was doubtless welcome to the emperor Trajan, whose regime defined itself substantially in contrast with the regime of Domitian (as the sustained contrast in Pliny's *Panegyricus* indicates). No glory was left for Domitian in Britain (nor in Germany, whose fate was often linked with it after Caesar), only the opprobrium of neglect.

Each of these nine chapters is both a reading of the evidence and a presentation of an argument. The three strands of imperialism, geography and monarchy are to be followed throughout the book. I hope that these chapters, their running themes and their subsidiary arguments amount to a reading of Roman Britain from Julius Caesar to Agricola that is new enough to justify the production of yet another book on the subject.

1

THE CONQUEST OF OCEAN

IMPERIALISM

Of course, Britain offered glory to its Roman conquerors. From Julius Caesar at the beginning of this book to the Flavian emperors at its end, Roman generals and emperors strove to gain the prestige of military success in Britain and to broadcast it to the rest of the Roman elite, to the Roman populace and to the empire at large. So much was not only possible but necessary, because the ideology of Roman society was so militaristic as to require military glory from its leaders. Each Roman emperor and general was caught up in a determining competition not only with present rivals, but also with the high achievers of the past and even the prospective successes of the future. Claudius was the emperor who made the most of military success in Britain: in need of military prestige, he made his successful invasion of Britain in AD 43 the leitmotiv of his reign, evoked and celebrated in Rome and the provinces until his death in AD 54. The Claudian adventure, like Caesar's before, continued to resound long after the event: while Nero all but denied it, the Flavians subsequently sought to appropriate the prestige of Claudius' achievement for Vespasian, a participant and continuator. Thereafter, the regime of Nerva and Trajan could only deprive Domitian of the glory of British conquest, which could be given safely to the dead Agricola.

Competition with past, present and future entailed literature. A central aim was the attainment of a place in history: so Gallus longed to read of Caesar (probably Octavian) in the history books. To establish a place for oneself in Roman history was to become part of tradition itself, an example for the future, to be admired and emulated.[1] And as major conquest might be enshrined in the highest form of prose literature – historiography – so it was also appropriate to the highest form of poetry, epic. Cicero's epic poem on Caesar's invasion of Britain was history of a sort, evidently designed to curry favour with Caesar by presenting his campaigns in a medium which suggested his place among the heroes of Homer. Caesar will have enjoyed the offer of such a place, and, as will be argued, he may well have sought it for himself in the deceptively straightforward presentation of his *Commentaries*.

The more particular attraction of Britain as a field of glory was its very novelty. In the desperate search for military glory, to be first was to gain a special prestige: Britain offered plenty of scope for the conqueror to be first. In the context of Roman social and political ideology, which made such a fetish of tradition, there was a particular *frisson* surrounding a new departure, a first, albeit a breach of tradition in traditional manner.[2] From Caesar in his *Commentaries* to Tacitus in his *Agricola*, Roman writers stress that Britain was unknown, in whole or in part; once southern Britain had become familiar, Caledonia (and even beyond) became the object of imperialist desire. A principal function of the conqueror was to make known the conquered and to redeem them for humanity, to create knowledge by constructing the geography of the hitherto unkown and writing a history for peoples considered too barbarous to have written their own. From a Roman perspective this was not simply the discovery of Britain: it was the creation of Britain and the Britons. Prior ignorance had generated excitement. What were Britons like? How long did they live? Where and how did they live? What was the shape of Britain? Was it an island? What was to be found there?

Of course, exploration was not disinterested. Not only was it part of imperial conquest and the extension of personal and imperial prestige, but it was also a search for profit, the investigation of an imagined El Dorado. When Caesar's forces crossed to Britain there were hopes of riches, soon dashed. When another invasion was considered under Augustus and Tiberius, emperors with no need for further military prestige, the wealth (or lack of it) that could be extracted from the island was a central issue for some at least. At the same time, the conquest of peoples adjudged impoverished and uncivilized offered the conqueror not only fewer potential riches, but also less prestige: the conquest of the menial was not the stuff of triumphs. Accordingly, glory and booty are best treated together, for they are not sharply divisible: so much is indicated, for example, by the prominent display of booty in the triumphal parade through Rome that was the ultimate celebration of a Roman's military glory.[3]

OCEAN

Two small plaques of bronze, once silvered, were discovered in the nineteenth century at York. Each bears an inscription punched in Greek, evidently dedicating offerings which have not survived. The inscription on the larger plaque (3 × 2 in.) reads: 'To the gods of the governor's headquarters, Scribonius Demetrius', while that on the smaller reads: 'To Ocean and Tethys, Demetrius'.[4] The use of Greek, and the official association of the former inscription, support the identification of Scribonius Demetrius, the dedicator, with the Demetrius who spoke with Plutarch at Delphi upon his return from Britain to Tarsus early in the 80s AD, fresh from a mission ordered by the emperor to explore Britain's offshore islands.[5]

At the same time, Demetrius' explorations of the islands suggest a particular reason for his dedication to the god Ocean and his divine sister-wife Tethys: the support or at least acquiescence of these deities might well be considered vital to Demetrius' mission. However, Demetrius' was not the only dedication to the god Ocean to be made in Britain, as we shall see. Indeed, the Britons themselves seem to have venerated water-deities: it has been suggested that at least some of the objects recovered from rivers were not lost, but deposited there as offerings: as, for example, the so-called Battersea Shield and Waterloo horned helmet in the Thames.[6]

From a Roman perspective, Britain lay both in Ocean and beyond Ocean, so that the conquest of Britain was also the conquest of Ocean itself, as celebrations of the British achievements of Caesar, Claudius and the Flavians were at pains to demonstrate. Such a conquest was familiar in the discourse of Greek and Roman imperialism, wherein the rivers of the world and their father Ocean, the great river thought to encircle the world, were seen as powerful divine forces that must be won over or defeated in the process of military conquest.[7]

Accordingly, it is no surprise to find Ocean in the developing epigraphy and iconography of Roman Britain, not least as Roman attitudes towards Ocean coalesced with those of indigenous populations. The evidence, often difficult to date precisely, is later than the first century AD. On Hadrian's Wall the reclining statue of a river-deity occupied a prominent place in the bath-house of the

Figure 1 The 'Battersea Shield'.

commanding officer of the fort at Chesters: it may be significant that a key bridge was also located there, as we shall see. Further east, at Newcastle-upon-Tyne, a pair of inscribed altars was dedicated by Legion VI Victrix to Neptune and to Ocean respectively: here too a bridge was important, as the Roman name Pons Aelius indicates. In fact the altars, which were found in the nineteenth century during construction of the Swing Bridge across the Tyne, may even have belonged to a Roman bridge: a narrow bridge-location might account for their unusual lack of depth from front to back. To the south, at Bath, the famous moustachioed head on the pediment of the temple of Sulis Minerva has been identified by some as Ocean: the tritons which occupy the lower corners of the pediment would be appropriate enough. He could also be Neptune, whose realm might include inland waters too, as his appearance inland at

Figure 2 The 'Waterloo horned helmet'.

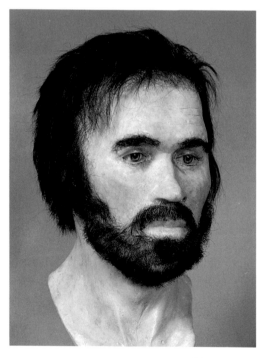

Figure 3
Reconstruction of the
head of Lindow Man.

14

Castlecary on the Antonine Wall has been taken to indicate. Neptune and Ocean are not always distinguished easily. Indeed, they may not have been distinguished sharply in antiquity: an apparent Ocean on the mosaic from Frampton, Dorset, is revealed by an accompanying inscription to be Neptune, while a Neptune on the mosaic from Withington, Glos., complete with trident, is shaggy enough to recall Ocean. Again, and also much later than our period, from the fourth century, the head that occupies the centre of the so-called Great Dish in the Mildenhall treasure could be Neptune or Ocean.[8]

Throughout classical antiquity, rivers (not least Ocean himself) were seen as deities. In Homer, for example, rivers visit Olympus to participate in the councils of the gods; they have their own priests and receive sacrifices; they can procreate, speak and fight, not least to defend their own land.[9] River-cults were a reality both in the Greek and in the Roman world, as Cicero observes: a letter of the Younger Pliny illustrates the point for Italy in the first century AD, while extant inscriptions indicate as much for the Rhine and Danube amongst other rivers. Accordingly, the Elder Pliny describes the Tiber as *religiosus*.[10]

River-gods are characterized by a selection from a fairly consistent set of criteria. They are regularly perceived as paternal, often with the epithet *pater*.[11] Their role as fathers accords with the great antiquity invariably accorded them; they are often depicted as aged men. And these ancient fathers are regularly accorded great wisdom, including prophecy. Moreover, in so far as they are ancient fathers, they are commonly accorded a role in the creation of their lands and peoples; on coins they are symbols of their communities.[12] Despite their age, they remain rampantly sexual and procreative: often they are bulls or, more commonly, bull-men.[13] They change their shapes at will; they also harbour man-eating beasts.[14] Rivers constitute the principal divisions of the world into continents, while the river of Ocean constitutes its outer limit.

Accordingly, to channel rivers, to bridge them, to sail on them or to cross them was a mighty undertaking. As to channelling, Tacitus mentions a senatorial discussion on controlling the floods of the Tiber: a delegation from Reate reminded the Senate of the religious implications of such work and claimed that 'Tiber himself would be altogether unwilling to be deprived of his neighbour streams and to flow with less glory'.[15] Diodorus equates channelling a river and fighting it. And the greatness of such undertakings is further

15

Figure 4 Water-deity from the Roman fort at Chesters, Hadrian's Wall.

Figure 5
Altar to
Neptune,
Newcastle-
upon-Tyne.

Figure 6
Altar to
Oceanus,
Newcastle-
upon-Tyne.

16

Figure 7 The temple-pediment from Bath.

Figure 8 Panel from the Withington mosaic (Glos.).

17

Figure 9 'Great Dish' from the Mildenhall Treasure.

Figure 10 'Great Dish' from the Mildenhall Treasure (detail).

18

THE CONQUEST OF OCEAN

indicated by the recurrent desire of kings and emperors to cut great channels.[16] To bridge a river was to chain it, like Virgil's Araxes.[17] Accordingly, Rome's first bridge across the Tiber, the Pons Sublicius, was very much a sacred entity, constructed by oracular design. The bridge was the locus of regular ritual, performed by the Vestals and pontifices, whose name was commonly explained as 'bridge-makers'.[18] As to sailing, Arrian, as governor of Cappadocia, writes to the emperor Hadrian that those sailing into the River Phasis appease the river by pouring overboard any water held on ship.[19]

Of course, bridging and sailing are forms of crossing. From Hesiod onwards, sources observe the religious significance of the crossing of rivers. Crossings were regularly preceded by sacrifice or other ritual: ancient explanations stress the need to propitiate the river and to discover the future that lies across it.[20] Cicero states that auspices are to be taken at the crossing of rivers, though he complains that this is not sufficiently done in his own day. Servius offers more detail: it seems that to cross water was to break the force of a previous augury.[21]

For Romans, rivers were indeed natural boundaries: not because they separated territories (although they might, like the Tiber itself, which formed a boundary of Latium),[22] but because they were features of a world-order within which they bounded and divided – to cross them was a major step, a religious act, quite literally a rite of passage.[23] For that reason Lucullus sacrificed a bull to the Euphrates when he took his army across. And Cassius Dio describes the unfavourable sacrifices performed by Crassus as he led his army across the Euphrates to destruction at Carrhae, together with the portents that occurred during crossing. Although Crassus' case was evidently special, Dio mentions his sacrifices on crossing as if they were entirely normal practice. Julius Caesar dedicated horses at his crossing of the Rubicon, another river boundary. The religiosity of boundaries is well enough understood: as these instances serve to illustrate, rivers are to be counted among such boundaries.[24] In this way, broad conceptions of rivers predisposed Rome to their use at the frontier and to perceive frontiers in terms of rivers, for Roman conceptions of space and geography played a fundamental part in the construction of Roman military and bureaucratic decision-making.[25]

As the Roman empire expanded to east and west, the notion of a world-empire gained currency, often couched in terms of an empire which stretched from Ocean to Ocean, connecting across land the world-encircling river. Nicolaus of Damascus, a contemporary of Augustus, claims that Caesar was preparing a Parthian campaign at the time of his death in 44 BC in order to reach the Ocean in the east as he had reached it in the west during his conquest of Gaul and invasions of Britain.[26] Caesar's empire was to be a world-empire that was bounded only by Ocean, which was itself to be conquered.[27] Under Augustus the objective of world-empire bounded by Ocean became a literary and ideological commonplace.[28] And in view of the location of Britain, which might be seen either as in or across Ocean, it is no surprise to find that the island bulks large in the discourse of world-wide imperialism from Ocean to Ocean. Indeed, it may well be that Caesar's British adventures had given a great stimulus to the notion of an empire bounded only by Ocean.[29]

The second of the two plaques of Demetrius from York expresses a dedication to Ocean and Tethys. In his small way Demetrius echoed, consciously perhaps, the dedication which Alexander the Great was said to have made at the edge of the Indian Ocean.[30] Alexander offered a key example of world-wide conquest, to be emulated by Roman commanders and discussed by Roman writers and orators. Although the historicity of his concern to extend his conquests to Ocean has been challenged,[31] there can be no doubt about the power of his example to encourage the notion at Rome. Ocean itself was to be explored; its islands and the very nature of its waters presented a substantial challenge: Ocean was not simply to be reached, but revealed and opened up.[32]

It is in the context of rhetorical declamation upon the conquests of Alexander that a fragment has survived from a poem composed by Albinovanus Pedo on the expedition in AD 16 of Germanicus, with whom Pedo had served:[33] Tacitus describes the disaster suffered by that expedition in AD 16, while he also hints at Germanicus' concern to emulate Alexander.[34] Pedo's fragment tells how, having entered the North Sea from the Ems, Germanicus' ships fell victim to the dangers of Ocean:

Now at their backs day and sun abandoned,
and now they see, driven from the known bounds of earth,
through unpermitted shadows daring to go
to the turning-points of things and the farthest shores of the
    world,
the one who bears huge monsters beneath his thick waves,
Ocean, who has vicious whales all around

and sea-hounds, rise up, ships in hand
(the din itself piles on the fear), as the ships sink
in mud and the fleet loses its following breeze,
and they think themselves abandoned to the wild
sea-beasts, becalmed, to be torn apart, a wretched fate now.
And someone high from a lofty deck struggling to break
    through
the sightless air with battling vision,
when he failed to make out anything, the world snatched from
    him,
forced out such words from his blocked chest:
'Where are we carried? Day itself is in flight and
the end of nature closes the abandoned world with endless
    shadows.
Is it beyond, to peoples under another pole and to
another world untouched by war that we are going?
The gods call us back and forbid mortal eyes to know
the end of things. Why do we violate alien seas with our oars
and sacred waters? Why disturb the settled
home of gods?'

(Albinovanus Pedo, ap. Sen. Suas. 1.15)³⁵

Pedo acknowledges the divinity of Ocean, as does Tacitus in the
Germania.[36] Further, he gives lavish epic treatment to the significance of the boundary that is Ocean: beyond Ocean is another
world beneath another sky, where Roman conquest has not reached.
The very seas become alien as Germanicus' fleet is carried across
Ocean. The journey is a rupture of the bounds of nature, a challenge
to the limits imposed on man by the gods and, of course, a distur-
bance of the gods themselves. Small wonder that the hazards of the
voyage entail not only a sea that is fierce, packed with savage man-
eaters, and muddy, thick to row, but also an atmosphere that blocks
the breath and blinds the eyes of sailors, while it fails to fill their
sails. Ocean closed off the world and was itself closed; the Roman
conqueror could hope to open it up and find another world.

Ocean was not simply a limit, but also an object of conquest and
exploration: not only Alexander, but also the more evidently mythical Dionysus and Hercules, were explorers and breakers of such
limits.[37] None had reached Britain: its invasion and conquest offered
a ready means to excel them. In so far as Britain lay *beyond* Ocean,
its conquest fulfilled the abandoned ambition famously accorded to

Alexander of crossing Ocean into another world, breaking the boundaries of nature as known to mankind.[38] In the first century AD an adviser of Alexander the Great, the ultimate conqueror, was imagined as urging the king to stop at the shores of Ocean:

> To whatever Nature gave greatness she also gave a limit: nothing is endless save Ocean. They say that fertile lands lie in Ocean and that beyond Ocean other shores, another world are born again, that Nature stops nowhere, but where it seems to have stopped it rises afresh. Such stories are easily invented, since Ocean cannot be sailed. Let Alexander be satisfied to have conquered thus far, as far as the world is illuminated. It was within the limit of these lands that Hercules earned a place among the gods. The sea stands motionless, like an inert mass of nature failing at its own limit: new and horrendous forms, portents great even for Ocean, which that vast deep feeds; light shrouded in deep fog and a day enveloped in darkness; the sea itself heavy and motionless: no stars or none known. That, Alexander, is the nature of things. After everything, Ocean; after Ocean, nothing.
>
> (Sen. *Suas.* 1.1.1)

It is in this context that we should understand Caesar's claim to have found another world when he landed in Britain, as reported in an imperial panegyric of late antiquity. He had excelled not only Romans, but also Alexander and Hercules, pushing back the limits of man:

> When Caesar, he the author of your name, entered Britain, the first of the Romans, he wrote that he had found another world, thinking it of so great a size that it seemed not to be surrounded by Ocean, but to embrace Ocean itself.
>
> (*Paneg. Lat.* 8.11.2)[39]

However, Caesar was not to be allowed all the glory: it was too great a prize to be left to a single dead man. Even after Caesar, Horace could imagine Britons as 'untouched', ripe for Augustus' attention. Britain remained another world.[40] Not only Claudius, but also Agricola, could be said to have 'opened up' Ocean. The conquest of Britain could be imagined and presented readily enough as much more than another successful imperialist endeavour. It could be seen, rather, as an unparalleled extension of human (especially Roman) experience, a challenge to the gods themselves.[41] It may be more than coincidence that it was in the aftermath of Caesar's British invasions that Lucretius chose to speak of the achievement of the philosopher Epicurus in much the same terms.[42] Caesar by his invasions, and Epicurus by his philosophy, had broken the bonds set upon humankind. Small wonder that Ocean, like lesser rivers, might be paraded in triumph at Rome.[43]

2

KINGS, GOVERNORS
AND EMPERORS

In so far as Britain was 'another world', it offered a realm not only distinguishable from the rest of the Roman empire, but even parallel to it. Accordingly, in Britain there was particular scope for familiar utopian fantasies, notably about its long-lived inhabitants or the power of women there.[1] As we shall see in the final chapter of this book, Tacitus' extended comparison in the *Agricola* between the regime of the bad emperor Domitian at Rome and that of the good governor Agricola in Britain is all the more effective when Britain is seen as a world alternative to that of Rome. However, even without that interpretative refinement, Tacitus' comparison is telling enough in any event, for it emerges principally from a matrix of traditional ideas about the rule of one man, whether as emperor or as governor or as king. Under the Republic, Rome had absorbed key ideas which Greek philosophers had developed around the issue of monarchy. Such ideas offered Rome an intellectual framework within which not only kings and dictators, but also Roman governors, could be understood. And with the advent of a *princeps* in the person of Augustus, a further focus had been created for the application of the philosophy of monarchy.

The single most important text on the theory of Roman governorship is Cicero's first letter to his brother Quintus, dated to 60 BC, when Quintus had already been governor of the province of Asia for two years and was about to begin a third. The considerable length of this text, and the theoretical nature of the disquisition it embodies, combine to give the impression that it is not so much a letter as a treatise on governorship. Such 'letters' were well enough understood at Rome: later, Cicero was to wrestle with the problem of writing another treatise on good government in the form of a letter to Caesar during his dictatorship.[2] In his first letter to

Quintus, Cicero makes explicit the relevance to Roman governors and governorship of discussions of monarchy in Greek philosophy. Xenophon is given particular attention:

> how welcome, I ask you, must the courteousness of a praetor be in Asia, where so vast a multitude of citizens and allies, so many cities and communities, concentrate their gaze upon the nod of a single man, where there is no succour for the oppressed, no facility for protest, no Senate, no popular assembly? It must therefore ever be the privilege of some great man – and a man not only instinctively self-controlled, but also refined by learning and the study of all that is best in the arts – so to conduct himself in the possession of so vast a power that the absence of any other power may never be regretted by his subjects.
>
> The great Cyrus was portrayed by Xenophon not only in accord with historical truth, but as a model of just government, and the impressive dignity of his character is combined in that philosopher's description of him with a matchless courtesy. And indeed it was not without reason that our great Africanus did not often put those books out of his hands, for there is no duty belonging to a painstaking and fair-minded form of government that is omitted in them. And if Cyrus, destined as he was never to be a private citizen, so assiduously cultivated those qualities, how carefully, I ask, should they be preserved by those to whom supreme power is only given on the condition that it must be surrendered, and given too by those very laws to the observance of which those rulers must return?
>
> And my personal opinion is that those who govern others must gauge their every act by this one test – the greatest possible happiness of the governed.
>
> (Cic. *Ad Q. fr.* 1.1.22–4)

Cicero stresses the strongly monarchical position enjoyed by the provincial governor, albeit temporary, and vulnerable to censure and subsequent prosecution. He offers the view, familiar in Greek thought, that the good ruler (whether king or governor) requires instinctive self-control honed by proper education: the key test of the goodness of the ruler is the benefit of those whom he rules. Elsewhere in this letter-cum-treatise Cicero draws attention to Plato, whose ideal of philosopher-kings accords very well with that position. But here it is Xenophon's *Cyropaedia* that is warmly recommended, an account of the development of an ideal ruler in the person of Cyrus the Great. Quietly, Cicero deals with the potential hostility that a Roman audience might have towards Greek philosophy by indicating that the *Cyropaedia* was good enough for the younger Africanus, sacker of Carthage, and very Roman friend of philosophers. Africanus, claims Cicero, had found the *Cyropaedia* to be of practical value in the daily exercise of supreme authority: the text and the ideas it presented had been adopted as part of Roman practice by the best of examples. At the same time, Cicero also dismisses the obvious objection – that Roman governors are not kings *stricto sensu* – by the telling observation that if a king might see fit to cultivate good government, though an absolute ruler, how much more valuable would such concern be for a Roman governor who would shortly abdicate his temporary monarchy and become subject to the rigours of the law. Implicit is an identification of morality and utility which Cicero was later to develop in his *On duties*.

In the Greek world the problematics of monarchy were a standard feature not only of specialized philosophy, but also of social and political thought at a more general level. Monarchy was an issue which was a prime concern not only to the likes of Plato, Xenophon, Isocrates and Aristotle, but to a wide range of writers. In particular, the Athenian tragedians display a recurrent interest in exploring monarchy which seems best understood as a reinforcement and reaffirmation of the superiority of the democracy within which they wrote and competed.[3] Similarly, Athenian comic playwrights, more overtly engaged with contemporary events, also show a substantial concern with the issue.[4] Historians too offer not only narratives, but also analyses which indicate a concern with monarchy, in pursuit of an understanding of power and its role in causation.[5] Indeed, Herodotus' presentation of an alleged debate among leading Persians might reasonably be claimed as the earliest extant treatment of the philosophy of monarchy.[6] Thereafter, from the fourth century BC, as ruling kings became still more important in the Greek world, the issue of monarchy became all the more pressing a concern. Accordingly, it is no surprise to find Hellenistic philosophers giving the issue at least as much attention as their predecessors. Even Epicurus recognized the value of royal patronage, and the limited merits of monarchy which permitted philosophical expression, when he wrote his *On kingship*, though he rejected political involvement.[7]

26

Therefore, Roman writings on monarchy, among which Cicero's treatise-cum-letter occupies an early and influential place, followed a long and very substantial tradition of Greek thought. And that tradition was strikingly homogeneous. Although writers as diverse as Thucydides and Plato approached monarchy in very different ways and contexts, they and other writers on monarchy are in fundamental agreement. The key to good rule was broadly recognized as the acquisition, development and rational application of knowledge, however variously understood. It was knowledge that underpinned the beneficial 'rule' of Thucydides' Pericles, while Plato's philosopher–kings were defined and distinguished by their knowledge. The bad rulers who regularly feature in Athenian tragedy share a profound lack of knowledge and understanding, which is their undoing. There is a broad agreement that it is knowledge that permits good rule, though the viewpoint was not without challenge (as exemplified by Plato's Thrasymachus in the first book of his *Republic*). Good rule in that sense is characterized by the self-control of the wise ruler in the common interests of himself and his subjects. In his wisdom the good ruler abstains from the standard vices, which are manifestations of a lack of the self-control that knowledge brings: namely, the killing, sexual abuse and robbing of subjects. While the good ruler pursues the benefit of himself and his subjects, the bad ruler in his ignorance is the enemy of his subjects, whom he keeps at bay with corrupt advisers and a bodyguard that constitutes a private army which wages war on them.

Roman thought on the various forms of monarchy developed along very much these lines, as Cicero's allusions to Plato and Xenophon serve to indicate. Cicero urges upon his brother the fundamental importance of the governor's knowledge and self-control, both innate and acquired:

> For what trouble is it to control those whom you rule, if you control yourself? For others, I grant, that may be a great and difficult thing to do, and it is indeed most difficult. But for you it has always been the easiest thing in the world, and indeed was bound to be so, since your nature is such that I think it would have been capable of self-restraint even without education; but you have had such an education as might well ennoble the most depraved nature.
>
> (Cic. *Ad Q. fr.* 1.1.7)

Subsequently he summarizes much of his case:

> Let these therefore be the foundations of your public position:
> first of all your own integrity and self-restraint; second, the
> respectful treatment of those about you, an extremely cautious
> and careful choice, in the matter of intimacy, of both pro-
> vincials and Greeks, and a strict and consistent system of
> discipline in dealing with slaves.
>
> (Cic. *Ad Q. fr.* 1.1.18)

The good governor must control himself and his entourage, particularly the slaves among the latter. As we shall see, there is much
here that would later recur in Tacitus' *Agricola* and in his and other
analyses of the regimes of the emperors, not least with regard to
Britain.[8]

Cicero's treatise constituted a major formulation of concepts of
governorship which recur through many of his speeches, both in
prosecution and in defence. Such concepts had also been central to
the political debates and struggles of the past at Rome: Cicero's
claim that Africanus made heavy use of the *Cyropaedia* may well
reflect his awareness of how much his own thinking owed to the
Romans who had engaged with Greek ideas in the previous century.
Although little enough has survived from Latin writers of the
second century BC, it is clear, for example, that the speeches of the
Elder Cato and of Gaius Gracchus had foreshadowed much that we
find in Cicero's speeches on the subject of governorship, while
Cicero seems to have drawn upon the satirical writings of Lucilius
for some of his more aggressive denunciations of a governor's
impropriety. It is a considerable pity in this regard that we have lost
the satirical writings of Sp. Mummius, written in the entourage of
L. Mummius at Corinth in 146 BC; Cicero knew them.[9]

And, of course, the very issue of proper and improper governorship had long had a direct bearing upon well-known controversy
about the justice of Roman imperialism, at least as early as the
second century BC, for Roman governors were key agents of that
imperialism. Cicero chose to present his engagement with that
controversy in the third book of his *De republica*, a dramatic dialogue set in the mid-second century BC. Rome, like her provincial
governors, should show herself to be morally superior to the
subjects of her empire and to be ruling in their best interests.[10]
When Romans ruled in such a fashion, collectively and individually,
they did so in accordance with nature, an incontestable good: as

Dionysius of Halicarnassus has it, the Romans were superior to Greeks and non-Greeks not only in war, but also in justice, piety and self-control.[11] Ideally, at least, Roman rule was a beneficial exercise in patronage: Cicero could claim that the extortion law was itself an embodiment of patronage, protecting Rome's subjects against the potential maladministration of her governors.[12] For Rome as for her individual governors, the interests of morality and utility could be seen conveniently to coincide, though they were often treated as standards of the past, now less regarded in the present.

Cicero's prosecution of Verres is founded upon the familiar characteristics of the bad ruler. For Cicero's Verres displays a consistent lack of self-control, born of ignorance and moral turpitude, while he fails conspicuously to exercise proper control over his subordinates. His regime, claims Cicero, far from the beneficial ideal, operated very much against the interests of his subjects in Sicily, whether provincials or Roman citizens. As was to be expected of the stock bad ruler, Cicero's Verres duly murdered, raped and pillaged. So far from giving benefits to his realm, he took and devoured all he could without regard to law, whether human or divine. Rather than suppress pirates as the champion of proper order, he was in league with them, a pirate himself. He was the enemy of his subjects, not their beneficent protector. Throughout, Verres' regime in Sicily is characterized by Cicero as an uncontrolled and irrational pursuit of false and base pleasure in the mistaken belief that he would obtain for himself real benefit at the expense of his subjects.

The very fact that Cicero could construct a case in these terms, closely akin to Greek concepts, is but one illustration of the acceptance and currency of such ideas by the early decades of the first century BC.[13] There can be no real doubt that Sulla's controversial dictatorship had given a new relevance and dynamic to Roman thought on the problematics of monarchy and the abuse of power at Rome and in the provinces, which in turn entailed an assessment of the good and bad kings of early Roman 'history'.[14] Indeed, the very origins of the Roman Republic were conceived and discussed in terms of the possible value but ultimate perils of monarchical rule. In that sense the Roman Republic constructed its very identity within a framework of ideas on monarchy, themselves incorporated and adapted from Greek models. Subsequently, even Augustus presented his regime, however monarchical, as the redemption of republican freedom in the face of an internal chaos that threatened to generate monarchy, and against the external threat of a female monarch in the person of Cleopatra.[15] But it was the growth of empire that offered an abiding and ever more pressing focus for concern with issues of monarchy at Rome. It was not only outside Italy, but even in Rome itself, that Romans encountered ruling kings.[16] Such encounters raised large questions about the nature of Romans' dealings with kings. An anecdote concerning the Elder Cato illustrates the point:

> During King Eumenes' visit to Rome, when the Senate received him lavishly and the leading men struggled and strove to be about him, Cato stood out in being suspicious and cautious towards him. And when someone said, 'But he is a fine man and a friend of Rome!' Cato replied, 'Indeed, but by nature the creature that is king is flesh-eating.'
>
> (Plut. *Cato Maior* 8.8)

Attractive but dangerous, kings threatened insidiously to infect the traditional moral values which the Roman Republic liked to claim for itself. In his *Jugurthine War*, Sallust's account of Jugurtha's exploitation of weaknesses in that republican moral order combines such anxiety about foreign rulers with a committed analysis of internal Roman failings; Sallust's Jugurtha can subvert Roman values because they are ripe for subversion, entrusted to untrustworthy nobles, enemies within. Under the Principate, the malign impact of a Jugurtha could only be imagined as an influence upon the *princeps*: two counterparts of Jugurtha under the Principate were Antiochus IV and Agrippa I, who were reckoned responsible for much of Gaius' lack of self-control, like 'tyrant-trainers'.[17]

In the provinces Roman magistrates could expect both to meet monarchs and to become monarchs: in particular, it was the potentially absolute power of the provincial governor that made monarchy a pressing issue. Even in Sicily Verres dined with Syrian princes; in other provinces kings were key factors in the governor's military and administrative thinking, as Cicero's letters from his province in Cilicia show very clearly.[18] Moreover, at Syracuse the governor's residence was the erstwhile royal palace of King Hiero.[19] Governors may even describe their position and their actions by reference to their royal predecessors, as did Cornelius Gallus, the first Roman prefect of Egypt after the death of Cleopatra:

Gaius Cornelius Gallus, son of Gnaeus, Roman *eques*, first prefect of Alexandria and Egypt after the defeat of the kings by Caesar, son of a god, put down the uprising of the Thebaid in fifteen days, in which he defeated the enemy, having won two pitched battles and taken five cities by storm – Boresis, Coptus, Ceramice, Diospolis Magna and Ophieion; the leaders of these uprisings were captured and our army was led beyond the [first] cataract of the Nile, whither neither the arms of the Roman people nor those of the kings of Egypt had previously advanced; the Thebaid, a source of fear for all the kings alike, was subdued, and envoys of the kings of the Ethiopians were given audience at Philae, and that king was received into protection, and a ruler of the Ethiopian Triakontaschoenus was established. He made this dedication to the ancestral gods and to Nile, his helper.

(ILS 8995)

Gallus stresses not only that he is the successor to kings, but also that he has excelled them: the governor was engaged in permanent competition even with his royal predecessors. Further, he proclaims that he has received kings and even appointed a ruler. At the same time, in a fashion that should now be familiar enough, he presents the river-god Nile as his helper, a recipient of his dedication, and an ally in his military campaigning up the river's course.

In view of the relevance of monarchy on a wide front to the theory and practice of Roman provincial governorship, the relationship of L. Piso and Philodemus of Gadara has a particular interest. Piso, consul in 58 BC, was given the province of Macedonia in 57, where he governed until 55. Cicero's excoriating attacks upon his governorship have survived, particularly in his *On the consular provinces* and his *Against Piso*. Although these attacks seem to have been generated principally by the demands of republican power politics, Cicero presents and denounces Piso's regime in Macedonia, after the fashion of his treatment of Verres' regime in Sicily some fifteen years before. He chose the discourse of monarchy as a medium appropriate to the use and abuse of absolute power, for Piso, for Verres and for other governors, whose regimes were made an issue not only in speeches of attack and prosecution, but also in those of defence. The key theme of that discourse was the abuse of absolute power: Cicero portrays a Piso who as governor of Macedonia sold himself to the Thracian King Cotys, as his associate

31

Gabinius sold himself to Ptolemy Auletes while governor of Syria. He failed not only to control himself, but also to control his subordinates: his slaves were in charge. Cicero portrays Piso as the stock tyrant, slaughtering the best and advancing the worst.[20]

Cicero's monstrous portrait notwithstanding, Piso was the patron of Philodemus of Gadara, an eminent Epicurean philosopher, whose many works have survived, largely in the damaged papyrus rolls which were discovered in the library of the family of Piso at Herculaneum, preserved by the ash of Vesuvius' eruption in AD 79. The relationship presented Philodemus with no ethical problem, for, despite the Epicurean rejection of political involvement, Epicurus himself seems to have advocated a philosophical life led in the patronage of a great man, a king, wherein the sage's peace of mind, his $\dot{\alpha}\tau\alpha\rho\alpha\xi\acute{\iota}\alpha$, could be achieved and maintained. However, the relationship was something of a problem for Piso, whose association with a 'Greek' philosopher, worse an Epicurean, offered Cicero a convenient line of attack upon the returned governor. Not for the first time, Cicero's own deep engagement with Greek philosophy was no obstacle to his criticism of other Romans who showed an active interest in Greek thought.[21] Cicero sarcastically suggests that Piso's governorship gave no sign that he had benefited from his concern with Philodemus' teachings: Cicero's Piso is 'our Epicurus, product of the sty, not the school'.[22] On this occasion it suits Cicero to denounce not so much Epicureanism as Piso himself, who has shown his warped character by misconceiving Epicureanism's basic tenets.[23]

Of particular relevance among Philodemus' writings is his *On the good king according to Homer*, which was dedicated to his patron, Piso.[24] Unfortunately, the work survives only in fragmentary form. While at least some of its principal concerns can be identified with confidence on the basis of the larger fragments, we cannot be sure as to any particular purpose in its creation, still less as to the date of its production. It is clear that Philodemus drew upon the Homeric poems for instances of the use and abuse of monarchical power: he discusses such instances to underpin a broadly Epicurean treatment of the theory of monarchy which seems closely to resemble the concerns and arguments more familiar in non-Epicurean discussions of monarchy. Extant fragments stress the importance of the monarch's self-control.

According to Philodemus, the good king must control his passions, sexual and homicidal.[25] The good king must be especially controlled at banquets and must use his leisure for edifying exercise, not fripperies. He must eschew greed for the goods of others.[26] The good king must develop benevolence, calmness, clemency and kindness.[27] In military matters, he must maintain discipline by appropriate treatment of officers and ordinary soldiers; he must be warlike, but not aggressive. In particular, he must avoid civil war by promoting concord among his subjects: it is concord, argues Philodemus, that is the foundation of peace and prosperity in a state.[28] The good king needs wise advisers.[29] He must eschew arrogance and show due respect for gods and men: the stability of a regime depends upon the goodwill of its subjects.[30] The good king should be physically attractive and impressive, but should conduct himself without undue ostentation.[31] After death the good king will be rewarded with the fine reputation that his reign has earned him.[32]

There is nothing here with which Cicero would quarrel, save in committed pursuit of a rhetorical point: the arguments espoused by Philodemus (as far as we can recover them) seem to accord well enough with those of Cicero's treatise on governorship or the *Cyropaedia* of Xenophon, which he there recommends. For that very reason, there is no need to imagine any very particular impetus to Philodemus' composition: to write on monarchy was a familiar (though not necessary) part of the philosopher's lot. No doubt, Philodemus' *On flattery* also included discussion of monarchical themes, not least on the relations between a king and his advisers. At the same time, the search for precepts in the Homeric poems was familiar enough even among the Romans of the late Republic, as Cicero's letters serve to indicate.[33] Indeed, the exercise of monarchical power by a governor in his province, often complete with actual warfare, constituted an elevated experience suitable for epic comparisons and epic compositions, as we shall see in the case of Caesar.[34]

Yet there might also be a very particular reason for Philodemus' composition. It is a pity that, despite much scholarly endeavour, we cannot date Philodemus' *On the good king according to Homer* to a particular year or cluster of years in the late Republic. However, given its monarchical subject-matter and its dedication to Piso, it is tempting to speculate that it was composed in the early 50s BC, when Piso was a sort of monarch, first as consul in 58 and then as governor of Macedonia from 57 to 55.[35] Indeed, if this work on the proper use of absolute power had gained any currency by 55, there would also be a particular point to Cicero's repeated references to

Epicureanism in his condemnation of Piso's alleged abuse of such power in that year. If there are any grounds for such speculations, a passing reference to 'the father of the last Nicomedes' (that is, Nicomedes III, father of the last king of Bithynia, Nicomedes IV) may also be of interest: Bithynia and the family of Nicomedes were topical subjects in the politics, poetry and invective of the early 50s. Indeed, the poems of Catullus display a concern both with the Bithynians and with Piso's governorship in Macedonia.[36] Caesar was very much involved in the Bithynian question. Moreover, as consul in 59 BC he married Piso's daughter, Calpurnia. While Caesar's governorship in Gaul became ever more an issue through the 50s BC and offered occasional Homeric resonances, it may well be that the very literary Caesar too cast an eye over the work that Philodemus crafted for his father-in-law.

Caesar's account of his governorship demonstrates and embodies a governor's concern for his reputation in office. Of course, Caesar's governorship was exceptional, as was his account – but in degree more than in substance. That simple but important point is amply illustrated by Cicero's missives from his much humbler and much less controversial governorship in Cilicia in 51–50. Cicero's was a governorship which would hardly have troubled the historical record but for the chance that it was Cicero's: to govern Cilicia was no great honour, and it was of no great moment by comparison with the governorships of 'frontier' provinces with legions, such as Syria or Macedonia, or of peaceful Sicily or Asia, rich in history and in pickings. Nevertheless, Cicero displays an overwhelming interest in his reputation as governor there. Nor was this simply a personal idiosyncrasy: Cicero's predecessor as governor of Cilicia, Appius Claudius Pulcher, had much the same interest. Caesar, Cicero and Pulcher all shared the assumption that their conduct as governor in their province mattered, and mattered deeply. And it mattered most as perceived by the governor's peers at Rome, themselves erstwhile or potential 'monarchs' in their own right.

The governor was powerfully concerned to ensure that he would be considered by his peers at Rome to have been a 'good' governor. For he expected to return to Rome, where his reputation was key not only to his political success, but, more fundamentally, also to his position in society.[37] As Cicero's correspondence indicates, and as his speeches repeatedly demonstrate, governorship was a moral issue. In particular, the governor's absolute power could be seen as the ultimate test of his character. Despite the ready acceptance of the ideology of imperialism in late republican Rome, there were moral parameters within which the governor was expected to exercise his power. The absolute power of governorship reveals the foul character of a Verres (as Cicero would have it), while it gives the opportunity for a Cicero to show his moral rectitude. Accordingly, Cicero stresses in the treatise he addressed to his brother Quintus that the conduct – and fundamentally the moral conduct – of the governor has a profound impact at Rome not only upon the standing of the governor himself, but also upon that of his associates (not least his brother):

> We are in such a position that all good men, though they support us, at the same time demand and expect of us every devotion to duty and every virtue, whereas all the worse elements – since with them we are engaged in an endless conflict – seem to be satisfied with the most trivial pretext for censuring us.
>
> Since therefore you have been assigned a theatre such as this, crowded with such multitudes, so ample in its grandeur, so subtle in its criticism, and by nature possessed of such an echo that its manifestations of feeling and words reach Rome itself, for that reason, I implore you, struggle and strive with all your might not merely to have proved yourself to be worthy of the task allotted to you, but also to prove that by the excellence of your administration you have surpassed all that has ever been achieved in Asia . . .
>
> Finally, you should also bear in mind that you are not seeking glory for yourself alone . . . but you have to share that glory with me, and bequeath it to our children.
>
> (Cic. *Ad Q. fr.* 1.1.41–4)

It was not only military renown that was to be gained in the provinces, but also a broader reputation for moral rectitude that offered a context and an explanation for military success. Glorious achievement in war could be included among the virtues of the good ruler, as Philodemus' treatise indicates; it could plausibly be argued that true military success could only be achieved by the virtuous, true glory by the glorious. At the same time, as usual among the Roman elite, there was competition: Cicero urges Quintus to seek to surpass his predecessors, not only as Cicero was himself eager to surpass Pulcher, but also as Tacitus' Agricola surpassed his predecessors in Britain under the Principate.

Cicero compares the province of Asia to a theatre. The governor and his regime are on show there, while the audience is the diverse population of the province. From Rome, the show cannot be seen: it is too far away. But the theatre and its audience are such that, despite the distance, reactions to the show can be heard in Rome. The image is telling. The theatre was a principal locus of political action and expression in Cicero's Rome.[38] And in his province the governor was indeed playing a role, as Cicero's provincial letters indicate; indeed, much of his interaction with his 'subjects' will have been the dispensation of justice from an elevated tribunal. He was a king on-stage, who must avoid the hubris of the doomed kings of Athenian tragedy. In exceptional cases, at least, the Roman provincial commander might become the subject of an actual play at Rome, as did L. Aemilius Paullus in the *Paullus* of Pacuvius.[39] At the same time, it is worth noting that the idea that life itself was the performance of a role on stage was by now a commonplace of the philosophical writers who also wrote on monarchy.[40] The king on-stage, like the king in Homer, was the very stuff of thought on monarchy.

The image of the theatre was appropriate. It was also important in that it offered Cicero a means of dealing quietly with the problem of the distance of the province from Rome. By use of the image he acknowledges that the governor's regime will not be seen from Rome, but he stresses that Rome has ears as well as eyes. The issue had already featured significantly in Cicero's speeches on governors and was very probably central also to earlier Roman thought on governors and provinces in a world which lacked all but the most rudimentary telecommunications. Of course, in his speeches Cicero adopts an approach to the problem that best suits the particular case that he wants to support.

Much has been made of a particularly vivid and archly 'autobiographical' passage in Cicero's defence of Plancius. Cicero sets out to 'explain' why Laterensis' provincial record as quaestor in Cyrenaica did him no good in an election of 54 BC, when Plancius gained the office of *aedile*. Laterensis claimed that Plancius had used bribery to overcome his inferior qualities. The essence of Cicero's argument here is that Laterensis has overestimated the significance of his provincial post, for Rome is the place to be if one wishes to succeed in political life. One must be in the eye of the Roman people, for their ear is less effective:

You say that at Cyrene Laterensis was generous to the tax-farmers and just to the provincials. Who denies the fact? But in the bustle of life at Rome it is almost impossible to attend to what goes on in the provinces. I have no fear, gentlemen, of appearing to have too good an opinion of myself if I say a word about my own quaestorship [in western Sicily, based at Lilybaeum] . . .

At that time I can say with most assured confidence that I thought that my quaestorship was the sole topic of conversation at Rome. I had dispatched an enormous quantity of corn at a time of very high prices: the universal opinion was that I was civil to the financiers, just to the merchants, liberal to the contractors, never enriching myself at the expense of the provincials, and that I spared no pains in all my official duties. The Sicilians had contemplated the bestowal upon me of unparalleled honours. So I retired from the province filled with the notion that the Roman people would spontaneously lay all their distinctions at my feet.

It happened that on my way back from the province I had arrived at Puteoli, intending to make the journey thence by land, just at the season when the place was thronged with fashionable people. And I nearly swooned, gentlemen, when someone asked me on what day I had left Rome and whether there was any news. When I replied that I was on my way back from my province, he said, 'Why of course – you come from Africa, don't you?' 'No,' I replied, somewhat coolly, for I was now in high dudgeon, 'from Sicily.' Hereupon another of the party interposed with an omniscient air, 'What! Don't you know that our friend has been quaestor at Syracuse?'

To cut my story short, I dropped the dudgeon and made myself just one of those who had come for the waters.

This experience, gentlemen, I am inclined to think was more valuable to me than if I had been hailed with salvoes of applause. For, having once realized that the ears of the Roman people were somewhat obtuse, but their eyes keen and alert, I ceased henceforth from considering what the world was likely to hear about me. From that day I took care that I should be seen personally every day. I lived in the public eye. I frequented the Forum . . .

In this way, any reputation I possess – and for all I know it is but small – has been won at Rome and earned in the Forum.

(Cic. *Pro Plancio* 63–6)

Cicero deploys his rhetorical talents to such effect that his account has been challenged less vigorously than it should have been.[41] Of course, it is the very attractiveness of Cicero's embellishing anecdote that should warn the reader to be particularly critical: Cicero beguiles modern audiences as well as ancient ones. Elsewhere, with the opposite case to push, Cicero presents an argument which flatly contradicts that of the *Pro Plancio*, anecdote notwithstanding. Like Plancius, L. Licinius Murena was accused of electoral bribery. Unlike Plancius, Murena had a provincial reputation that outweighed that of his opponent, Servius Sulpicius Rufus, whose talents had been devoted to the law at Rome. Accordingly, Cicero stresses the importance of such a reputation in supporting Murena, where he had diminished it in his case for Plancius:

Asia is thrown in his [i.e. Murena's] teeth. But Asia was not deliberately coveted by him for purposes of riotous pleasure, but traversed in the course of military service. . . . And if Asia has about it some suspicion of laxity, it is cause for praise, not never to have seen Asia, but to have lived an honourable life in Asia. . . .

Servius here has enlisted with me for service in the city – a service full of giving legal opinions, of writing documents, of protecting interests, of anxiety and vexation; he has learnt the civil law, he has lost much sleep, he has assisted many. . . . It is a great service, highly appreciated by mankind, that one man should earnestly toil over that science from which many are to profit. What about Murena meanwhile?

He was an officer on the staff of that very brave and sagacious man, that very great general, Lucius Lucullus. On this mission he led an army, disposed his standards, joined battle, vanquished great forces of the enemy, captured cities. . . . That Asia you speak of, a rich and tempting morsel, he traversed without leaving any trace of greed or extravagance. . . .

Both Servius and Murena have the greatest reputation, the greatest worth, to which I, with Servius' permission, would give the same and equal honour. But he does not permit me. He harps on military matters, he attacks this whole mission, he thinks the consulship should consist of his constant presence and the performance of these everyday matters.

'So far as I can see, you've been with the army', he says, 'all these years. You've not touched the Forum. When you return after being abroad so long, do you put yourself on an equal footing with those who have been living in the Forum?'

First, this practice of ours, Servius, of being always at hand, you do not know how much dislike and disgust it sometimes brings to men. . . . To be missed would have harmed neither of us. . . . How can you doubt that distinction in war brings much more dignity to a canvass for the consulship than distinction in the civil law . . . ? He is engaged in extending the boundaries of the empire, you in regulating the fences of your clients.

(Cic. *Pro Mur.* 11–22)

And, later in the speech:

And finally you [Servius] were unwilling to take the government of a province. I cannot criticize in you a course of action which I followed both as praetor and as consul. But still his province brought Lucius Murena a very good reputation and much goodwill. . . . In Gaul too by his justice and energy he enabled our countrymen to collect debts which they had already written off. Meanwhile, you at Rome were of course of assistance to your friends, I admit that. Nevertheless, be assured that the enthusiasm of some friends usually grows cold towards those who, they know, scorn the government of a province.

(Cic. *Pro Mur.* 42)

The fact that Cicero could argue both sides of the case is not simply a tribute to his rhetorical talents, but also an indication that there was enough elasticity in the problem to permit either side to be explored. Who could say for sure and as a general principle whether it was better for the politically ambitious to take up or to avoid provincial appointments? However, the former seems to have been more the norm in a society in which innovation was deviation.[42]

The governor was on-stage: his act had to be a good one. But, crucially, it must also be a genuine one, for this was real life. There could be no pretence. A deadly charge against the governor was that his act was a sham, a misrepresentation: Cicero makes such a charge against Piso, returning from Macedonia:

When from that source and seed-bed of triumphs you brought back withered laurel leaves, when you left them cast aside at the gate, then you pronounced your own guilt. Given you had done nothing worthy of honour, what about the army? What about the costs? What about the command? And what about that province, abundant in thanksgivings and triumphs? But if you had hoped for something, if you had nursed the ambition that is declared by your imperatorial title, by your laurelled fasces and by those victory-trophies full of shame and ridicule, then who is more wretched than you, who more damned. You who dared neither to write to the Senate to announce the benefit you had gained the state nor to utter as much in person.

(Cic. *In Pis.* 97)

Cicero's claim is that Piso had taken the trappings of a successful governorship, not least military success (laurels, trophies, the title of *imperator*), but had not deserved to do so. The rhetorical strategy was as powerful as it was necessary: since the governor sought to claim that his administration had redounded to his credit and enhanced his reputation, his critics must diminish his claims by denying their substance, if not inverting it as Cicero does with Piso. As we shall see, Tacitus later contrasts what he claims as the mock triumph of the emperor Domitian with the substantial victories of the modest Agricola.[43] The triumph was the last possible act of the governor's administration, all the more prized because few would attain it. In triumph he could be seen in his monarchical pre-eminence at Rome, often displaying kings among those he had defeated. To be applauded, to be conveyed through Rome and to be seen – that was the point.[44]

3

CAESAR: THE EXCITEMENT OF INVASION

Great excitement surrounded Julius Caesar's invasions of Britain in 55 and 54 BC: Britain was still very much an unknown quantity at Rome. What was it like? Was it an island or not?[1] Some disputed the very existence of Britain, while others not only asserted its existence, but also imagined an El Dorado there. The extant fragments of Pytheas of Massalia, misguided but relatively sober, provide some insight into the claims that could be made. Indeed, such claims were not easily dispelled: the geographer Strabo considered it necessary to engage with Pytheas' views as late as the reign of Tiberius.[2] And the uncertainty surrounding Britain and any expedition there was not forgotten; by the end of the first century AD, Caesar's invasion of Britain, like the campaigns of Alexander, had become the stuff of rhetorical exercises, as Quintilian observes, doubtless influenced by the current Flavian concern with Britain:

> Matters of this type are treated from time to time in deliberative exercises: for example, if Caesar is deliberating whether to invade Britain, account must be taken of the nature of Ocean, of whether Britain is an island (for at the time that was not known), how much land it comprised and how many soldiers should be used for the assault.
>
> (Quint. *Inst. Or.* 7.4.2)

In the late Republic, not long before Caesar's invasions, his father-in-law's protégé, Philodemus of Gadara, had admitted a question as to the very existence of the Britons and had observed that, if living creatures exist at all in Britain, they are mortal. However, his purpose was to discuss not Britain as such, but types of argumentation, wherein Britain might figure as a convenient example:

41

We shall not therefore use the analogical argument:

'Since men in our experience are mortal,
men in Libya are mortal'

in preference to the argument:

'Since living creatures in our experience are mortal,
if there are any living creatures in Britain,
they are mortal.'

(*De signis* 5.29–36)[3]

He was probably alluding to a tradition of the longevity of the Britons. Before 91 BC Asclepiades of Bithynia had written that the Britons live to be 100, benefiting from the coldness of their climate:

Asclepiades says that Ethiopians swiftly grow old at 30 years because their bodies are overwarmed, heated right through by the sun. But that those in Britain grow to an old age of 120 years both because the region is chill and because they keep the fieriness in themselves covered. For the bodies of the Ethiopians are more porous, made loose by the sun, but the bodies of those in Britain are made tight by the north: for that reason too they endure for many years.[4]

Britain lay beyond the οἰκουμένη, the 'inhabited world', on the other side of Ocean: it was almost like another world.[5] To wage war in Britain was to achieve a major first in a Rome wherein firsts were becoming ever more exotic and ever more valued as the Roman empire was extended beyond the lands of the Mediterranean. Even the gods and heroes of Greek myth who were thought to have ranged far and wide around the periphery of the ancient world – Hercules, Dionysus and others – were not traced to Britain: Britain lay not only beyond the inhabited world, but even beyond the world of myth.[6] If Caesar could excel there, far to the west, he would surpass even the campaigns of Pompey in the distant east and open up a new world for Rome and for science.[7] As Cicero had claimed even of Caesar's less dramatic conquests in Gaul, this was the conquest of peoples hitherto unknown.[8] By conquering in Britain, Caesar would excel even the likes of Ulysses, the heroes of myth.[9] There was no need for conquest throughout the island, still less for annexation, though Caesar may have envisaged success on that scale and with that result. Conquest in another world was the key objective and thereafter was presented as the only objective.

Plutarch catches the excitement well in his brief summary of Caesar's British adventure:

> The expedition against the Britons entailed renowned daring. For he was the first to launch a fleet on the western ocean and to sail across the Atlantic with an army of invasion. And in attempting to seize an island incredible in size and the subject of great dispute among many authors (the claim being that it was a name and a story of an island which did not exist now and had not existed in the past), he extended the Roman empire beyond the inhabited world. After twice sailing to the island from the facing coast of Gaul, and having worsted the enemy in many battles while not benefiting his own men (for there was nothing worth taking from men who lived in wretched poverty), he put an end to the war of a sort that was not to his wishes. However, before he left the island he took hostages from the king and ordered tribute-payments.
>
> (Plut. *Caes.* 23.2–4; cf., in similar vein, Dio 39.50)

To cross the river of Ocean was still greater a first than to cross the River Rhine, another achievement that Caesar could boast.[10] Indeed, it was so great a first that much could still be made of the crossing when Claudius did it a second time: if Claudius' troops were later terrified at the thought of crossing, how much more terrifying was the first Roman crossing, by Caesar? After all, as we saw in the first chapter, Ocean was the father of all the great rivers, who, like him, were imagined and depicted as powerful and potent male gods, not to be crossed without care, attention and fear.

Plutarch wrote more than a century and half after Caesar's invasions, but he was well informed. Most important, he had read Caesar's own account, as can we. He had also read widely among authors contemporary with Caesar, of whose writings much has been lost: for example, he cites C. Oppius, an associate and admirer of Caesar, whose laudatory biography of his hero has survived only in tiny snippets, preserved in the works of other writers.[11]

Cicero offers further and contemporary glimpses of excitement at Rome about Caesar's invasions of Britain.[12] Since Caesar had attained such controversial prominence in Roman society and politics through his tumultuous consulship of 59 BC and his striking military successes in Gaul before 55 BC, we may be sure that anything he did – or even considered doing – was *ipso facto* important and interesting at Rome. All the more so because so much of the

Roman elite was caught up with his campaigns, and not least those who were on his staff.[13]

Cicero's younger brother, Quintus, was one of Caesar's key officers (a *legatus*) in Gaul and in Britain: he had already been a provincial governor for three years in his own right, albeit in the tranquil province of Asia. Cicero stresses his relief upon receipt of a letter from Quintus which brought news of his safe participation in Caesar's second invasion:

> I come now to the subject with which I should have begun. How welcome was your letter about Britain! I was afraid of Ocean, I was afraid of the coastline of the island. It's not that I despise what remains to be done, but it involves more hope than fear, and it's more the waiting than the worrying that bothers me. Indeed, I see that you have an excellent writing-project: what locations, what natural phenomena and places, what customs, what peoples, what battles and indeed what a general you have! I'll be delighted to help you, as you ask, in whatever ways you want, and I'll send you the verses you ask for, 'an owl to Athens'.
>
> (Cic. *Ad Q. fr.* 2.16.4)[14]

For Cicero, and apparently for his brother, the invasion was an opportunity for literature. For them such writing was both an expression and a consequence of the excitement of Caesar's invasions. Members of the Roman elite did not abandon their taste for culture and their literary aspirations when they went on campaign. For example, Quintus sent home a play entitled *Erigona*, perhaps from Britain.[15] In Gaul, Quintus translated Greek tragedies into Latin.[16] At Rome, Cicero set about writing a poem which had Caesar as its addressee.[17] That poem was probably the work on Caesar in Britain which Cicero began to write early in the summer of 54.[18] Meanwhile, on campaign, Caesar spent at least some of his time in reading Cicero's poetry; Cicero was anxious to know his opinion, very possibly on a section of the British poem upon which he was working, and in which Caesar would be most interested.[19] Indeed, Caesar himself was something of a poet: for example, in his early days he too had composed a tragedy, an *Oedipus*.[20] Caesar responded to Cicero's poetry with a grammatical work *On analogy*, which had much praise of Cicero in its preface.[21] No doubt by the time of his invasions of Britain Caesar had already sponsored the epic poem on his campaign of 58 BC against Ariovistus and the

Sequani which was composed by Varro Atacinus, the 'Sequanian War'.[22] By December 54 Cicero had finished his poem, an epic it seems, appropriately enough: as we shall see, there was more than a whiff of Homer's *Iliad* about Caesar's British adventures.[23]

Meanwhile, one of Caesar's key officers, L. Aurunculeius Cotta, managed to include in a work on Roman politics the claim that Caesar took only three servants with him to Britain, while his fleet was substantial. Since Cotta was killed by the Eburones in the winter of 54/3, there can be no doubt that he included the claim (and in all probability was engaged in writing on Roman politics) while Caesar's legate. The little we are told about his work confirms what might have been guessed from his presence on Caesar's staff: that his work praised Caesar. Cotta's claim that Caesar had very few servants seems part of a broader claim that Caesar eschewed luxury; perhaps Cotta was offering a defence against his general's detractors. Any work on Roman politics completed in the mid-50s must have been much concerned with Caesar. At the same time, Cotta seems further to have stressed that Caesar's expedition to Britain was very large: he seems to have mentioned a fleet of one thousand ships, an indication of his polemical exaggeration. He stressed also, it seems, that Caesar's crossing was a first, apparently referring to the invasion of 55. Cotta himself did not make the second crossing of 54, being left behind to deal with the Menapii; he is not mentioned with regard to the first crossing.[24]

The Roman elite on campaign not only strove to write and to overcome the vagaries and hazards of long-distance communication by energetic correspondence with friends and others at Rome, but also remained part of the social whirl of the capital, reproducing, as far as possible, the lifestyles it had enjoyed at home: it was said that Caesar went so far as to transport mosaic floors about with him on campaign.[25] From Caesar's staff one Titus Pinarius had sent a friendly letter to Cicero about Quintus, mentioning the great pleasure he took in Quintus' writing, conversation and dinners: Cicero reports the letter to his brother and urges him to pay Pinarius some attention.[26] And, of course, in such a context as this, the social was also the political. For Pinarius, Cicero wrote a letter of recommendation to Cornificius.[27] And it was Cicero who recommended to Caesar some of his entourage in Britain and in Gaul, most notably C. Trebatius Testa.[28] It was not only high literature, but also more practical matters, such as letters of recommendation, that absorbed the time and interest of the elite on campaign and at home.

45

However, excitement was soon dampened: Caesar's invasions established that the island was more than a story, but they also brought the disappointing news that it was not laden with riches. Britain was no myth, but the British El Dorado was. In summer 54, Cicero wrote to Atticus that he had had not only a letter from Quintus, but also a long letter from Caesar himself, both apparently written from Gaul, not Britain as often imagined.[29] Cicero expected and received his first letter from his brother in Britain around the end of August.[30] The novelty abided for a while: we should observe Cicero's excitement at receiving at the end of October further letters from Quintus and Caesar respectively dated to the end of September and despatched 'from the shores of nearer Britain'.[31]

Even before the invasion was launched in 54, it was already apparent that there was no silver on the island, and no hope of booty except in the form of slaves, and barbarous slaves at that. After all, Caesar should know: he had already been to the island in the previous year.[32] Cicero quips that such slaves are unlikely to know much about writing or music: they are not civilized poets like their Roman conquerors.[33] Nor does Britain boast experts in law: laws must come from Rome, for Britain is seen as an assemblage of disorderly barbarians who display their barbarism in their pervasive discord.[34]

Cicero also wrote to Trebatius:

> I hear there is not an ounce of either gold or silver in Britain. If that is true, my advice is to lay hold of a chariot and hurry back to us at full speed! But if we can gain our end even without Britain, contrive to make yourself one of Caesar's intimates. My brother will give you valuable assistance, and so will Balbus; but your greatest asset, believe me, is your own honourable character and hard work. You are serving under a very generous chief, your age is just right, your recommendation is certainly out of the ordinary. So the one thing you have to be afraid of is seeming to do yourself less than justice.
>
> (Cic. *Ad Fam.* 7.7)

Evidently Trebatius and Cicero had looked to Britain as an opportunity for enrichment, but all it could offer of note were curiosities: hence, Cicero's playful mention of a chariot, here and elsewhere.[35] Caesar offers a brief disquisition on the novelty and apparent effectiveness of the British chariot.[36] It is unlikely that any educated Roman could read of chariots without a thought of Homer's *Iliad*,

Figure 11 Reconstruction of a British chariot.

Figure 12 Chariot-burial, Garton.

47

by now so much a part of elite sensibilities at Rome.[37] Obligingly, Diodorus Siculus explicitly likens British use of chariots to that of the Greeks in the Trojan War.[38] Caesar's adventure was an epic affair, complete with epic accoutrements and fit for epic discourse – even for Cicero's epic poem. But there was little substance to the British bubble.

Disappointment is also evident, albeit tinged with relief, in Cicero's letter to Quintus a few months later, in September 54: Cicero had taken a letter of Quintus to show that there was no reason either for fear or for joy in the matter of Britain.[39] Excitement had been disappointed: Britain was backward and largely humdrum, at best another source of rough slaves.[40] The invasions of Britain could be trumpeted as a major and daring advance, in knowledge at any rate, but nothing significant and concrete had come of them. In 45 BC, Cicero found in Britain only a far-off place, a convenient pawn in polemic against Epicurean ideas about the nature of perception.[41]

CAESAR'S SELF-PRESENTATION

Caesar wrote and wrote. Plutarch states that in Gaul Caesar kept two scribes busy simultaneously by dictating letters on horseback: Oppius claimed that even two scribes were not enough for him. The Elder Pliny claims that Caesar used to dictate four letters at once, or as many as seven at a time, when he was not doing something else as well.[42] Accordingly, when travelling in a litter, Caesar kept a scribe beside him for dictation.[43] In Britain too he continued to write: Cicero can hardly have been the only Roman to receive a letter from him about affairs in Britain. We may be sure that much of Caesar's feverish writing was designed to present his own point of view to other Romans of influence.[44] We should regard such letters, together with Caesar's regular formal reports to the Senate, as distinct from his narrative account of his campaigns in Britain and Gaul, his *Commentaries*, though those formal reports to the Senate (presented in innovative form) were also available for reading.[45]

Caesar's *Commentaries* were published by 46, in seven books: notionally they were outlines, sketched on campaign, of material that could later be worked up into a literary history.[46] They seem to have been published book by book, not *en masse*, though complete certainty on the point is impossible.[47] However, the form is illusory:

these are artful outlines, as contemporaries observed, and as we shall see in the next chapter.[48] The cool reportage that characterizes Caesar's *Commentaries* may easily lead readers to forget the centrality and partiality of their author in the events which they purport to describe. Caesar presents himself not as a first-person 'I', but as a third-person 'he'. There is no introductory statement of the identity, purpose or antecedents of the author, such as might have been expected at the beginning of the work; nor do we find overt autobiography. Rather, an unidentified narrator recounts for the reader the thoughts and deeds of a Caesar who is a third party. It is not until the eighth book, composed by A. Hirtius before 43 BC to supplement Caesar's books, that we find the sort of introduction that might have been expected at the start of the whole work. Hirtius felt the need for the sort of introductory statement that Caesar had chosen to omit: Hirtius' decision to include such a statement highlights Caesar's decision to exclude one. Of course, concealed authorship (and the determined artlessness of style that accompanied it) should warn the reader of the resourcefulness (and the potential artfulness of composition) of the author. Any understanding of Caesar's campaigns in Gaul and in Britain requires not so much an appreciation of his military strategies as an awareness of his literary strategies.

In his introduction to the eighth book, Hirtius offers a partisan estimate of the significance of Caesar's seven books of *Commentaries*. That estimate encompasses an assertion of the uncomplicated truth of their narrative:

> For all agree that no work of others has been written with such attention that it is not surpassed by the elegance of these Commentaries. These have been published to ensure that writers do not lack the knowledge of matters so great. And they have been so universally approved that writers have not been given an opportunity but forestalled in one. However, my own admiration of that work is greater than others', for while they know how well and faultlessly he wrote, I know how easily and speedily he did it. There was in Caesar both the greatest facility and elegance of writing and the truest knowledge of his own plans, which he explicated.

In these words, Hirtius conveys the notion that Caesar's writing was forthright and disinterested and universally acknowledged as such. Caesar wrote, we are told, in the interests of knowledge alone.

His fine writing, we are told, was accomplished quickly and without the sort of pondering that might indicate literary strategy. Rather, Hirtius stresses, Caesar combined a natural flair for writing with the 'truest knowledge' (*verissima scientia*) of his own thinking.

In one sense we should not cavil at Hirtius' claims. It seems that Caesar did have a facility for writing, and he clearly wrote a great deal within a peculiarly busy schedule that involved matters of life and death, not least his own. Moreover, there can be no doubt, in one sense, that Caesar was best placed to know about his campaigns and about his own thinking in particular. But we cannot stop there. Caesar may have possessed the 'truest knowledge', but the concepts of knowledge and truth are too slippery, contentious and value-laden to permit the cosy acceptance of Hirtius' judgments. Indeed, the superlative implies a comparative: the very notion of 'truest' indicates the existence of degrees of truth and, perhaps, of contradictory versions. At the same time, before we choose to eschew the all-embracing problematics of epistemology, we should be warned by much of the writing on historiography that has survived from antiquity. Witness, for example, Cicero's very interested expressions of disinterest in his letter to Lucceius of 55 BC, wherein he strives to influence – in part, even to construct – the historical record of his suppression of the so-called Catilinarian conspiracy in 63.[49] Much as Cicero wrote about his suppression of that conspiracy (quite apart from his frequent passing allusions to it), so Caesar sought not only to guide events but also to guide the history of those events. And Caesar may have done so in full conviction of his own disinterested truthfulness: doubtless, for Caesar as for others, his own truth was the real truth, the 'truest knowledge'.

Of course, Caesar's account of his British adventures cannot sensibly be considered outside the context of the *Commentaries* as a whole, beginning in 58 BC with the campaigns against the Helvetii and Ariovistus. Caesar's consulship had confirmed and extended his place at the centre of political controversy at Rome. Whatever he did, he could expect biting criticism from his political opponents, akin to the abuse later heaped by Cicero upon Piso and Gabinius, which we observed in the previous chapter. And the very scale of his successes and of the honours he received for them at Rome ensured that his conduct in Gaul and Britain would be a principal target of his opponents' attacks. When, at the end of 57, Caesar sent a formal report to Rome on his defeat of the Belgae, a fifteen-day period of thanksgiving was officially decreed there. Caesar proudly notes that no man had received such an honour before.[50] We may be sure that there was not only eager support for the award at Rome, but also intense hostility to it, which can only have expressed itself in the criticism and devaluation of the successes which Caesar had claimed for himself in his report.

We happen to know that when the Senate debated the award of further honours to Caesar for his defeat of the Usipetes and Tencteri in 55, Cato went so far in his opposition as to argue that Caesar should be handed over to those peoples to do with as they pleased. Apparently, Cato based his argument upon the impropriety of Caesar's treatment of their envoys, which he claimed to be a religious pollution of the city, only to be assuaged by the surrender of Caesar to his enemies.[51] Success was not enough: detractors, such as Cato, had scope to object to the manner in which success was achieved. Curio's publication of a lengthy attack upon Caesar's consulship and subsequent governorship was sufficiently significant to attract Cicero's criticism in his Caesar-friendly *Brutus*.[52] As we saw in the previous chapter, the performance of military and administrative duties outside Rome was regularly a matter of keen dispute within the Roman elite, in general and in detail, even where minor figures were involved. How much keener was the dispute in the case of the controversial and high-achieving Caesar? Evidently Caesar replied in kind, attacking Cato for his maladministration of the annexation of Cyprus in 58, which Cato seems to have claimed as at least the financial equal of military conquests, and which Cato's enemies saw as an instance of his personal greed for money.[53]

Since Caesar's British adventures had raised excitement and then disappointed, they offered a prime target for criticism. What was their purpose, if any? Had they really been successful? Had they been properly conducted? What price had been paid for any success that might be claimed? Should something else have been done? Whether Caesar's opponents had made anything of the first British invasion in the debate of 55 is not known, though it seems unlikely that all their criticism was focussed sharply upon the Usipetes and Tencteri: they will have deployed every argument that they could muster. When Caesar's formal report on the second invasion reached Rome, there will have been another debate before the unprecedented honour of the previous year was exceeded by the decree of a thanksgiving of twenty days.[54]

The sources provide more specific hints of the criticisms that may have been levelled against Caesar at the end of 54 and thereafter.

Early in the first century AD, the geographer Strabo observes that Caesar returned from Britain in haste without achieving much of significance or penetrating far into the island: he cites commotion in Gaul and among Caesar's troops as a cause, besides the fact that Caesar had lost many of his ships.[55] About a century after Strabo, Suetonius relates a rationale for Caesar's British adventure which can only have come from its critics: namely, that it was inspired by the hope of finding pearls.[56] The amassing of wealth by any means, and its use to political ends, are recurrent and associated themes in the tradition about Caesar, both in the provinces and in Rome.[57] Criticism of his British adventure along such lines was plausible enough, and further enhanced by the shortage of worthwhile booty on the island in the event. As we have seen, Cotta's affirmation of Caesar's simple life on campaign may well have been designed to rebut such attacks.

A century after Suetonius, the historian Cassius Dio says that the second invasion was driven by Caesar's overwhelming desire to take the island: the failure of the Britons to send hostages as promised in the previous year was, he avers, no more than Caesar's excuse.[58] Dio proceeds to affirm the rightness of Caesar's decision to withdraw from Britain and not have his forces winter there in 54, but the very fact that the decision was evidently an issue for Dio may indicate that he found the withdrawal criticized in his sources.[59]

On the basis of these hints, the outline of a case against Caesar's invasions may be sketched. The crossing was no doubt a first, but for what purpose save the aggrandizement of the general and the satisfaction of his greed, ambition and love of luxury? No good had come of it for the Roman state; troops had been lost, and the whole force had been imperilled by the rash adventure. The invasion had been badly managed, for much of the fleet had been lost to Ocean: the general's foresight and luck had been wanting. And the absence of Caesar's army on this escapade in 54 BC had allowed a major uprising in Gaul which could have threatened even Italy itself. Alternatively, if it were claimed that real progress had been made in Britain, why had Caesar not pressed home his advantage? Why had he been so quick to retreat?

Inevitably, since we do not possess direct and detailed evidence of the arguments of Caesar's opponents in and outside the Senate, we are forced to speculate. However, we are on safe ground in so doing, for we know that Caesar had powerful and vocal critics, and we are told enough by our sources to suggest the broad nature of the case they might make against him and his British campaigns. At the same time, and most important, it is vital that we be aware of such criticisms, actual and potential, as we read the account upon which we (and our other sources) principally rely: namely, that of Caesar himself. For at every turn Caesar's narrative offers sound rationale, good cause and just decision-making, where critics might have inserted a stiletto. Of course, the aware reader should not assume that Caesar saw his actions as anything other than rational, reasonable and just. Self-justification does not require admission of guilt even to oneself.

Moreover, it should not surprise us to find that Caesar and his supporters stress the truth and the lack of embellishment in his *Commentaries*. In 46, as Caesar finally established himself as victor in the civil war with Pompey and the Pompeians, Cicero's *Brutus* offered gushing praise of Caesar's literary and rhetorical talents. In that dialogue, Cicero interjects excitedly at Brutus' mention of the *Commentaries*:

> Very much to be applauded! For they are unadorned, straight and graceful, stripped of all the apparel of rhetoric as if of their clothing. However, although it was his intention to give others a source for the writing of history (and perhaps he succeeded for the uncultured who like to scorch such material with their flourishes), he has deterred sensible men from writing. For in history there is nothing more sweet than pure, excellent brevity.
>
> (Cic. *Brutus* 262)[60]

Caesar's *Commentaries* offer, we are told, not only the unvarnished truth, but also the final truth, the last word. Although there was fine scope for epic paraphernalia, Caesar had nothing to say about myth and made very little of Ocean in the *Commentaries*.[61] Caesar has eschewed style, says Cicero, but in so doing has achieved the ultimate in style. The flattering paradox, all the more subtle through being couched in terms of Caesar's gentle failure, reconciles the potential opposition between art and truth. But the paradox was not new: when Cicero had approached Posidonius with the suggestion that the Greek historian might work up his own *Commentaries*, Posidonius had offered a similar reply, claiming to be deterred by the excellence of Cicero's outline.[62]

Cicero's assertion of the veracity of Caesar's account was topical in 46, the year of Caesar's triumphs, of which the first and the most spectacular was his triumph over Gaul (certainly including Britain). In the triumphal procession, Caesar's conquering crossings were illustrated with depictions of the Rhine, the Rhône and an Ocean of gold.[63] Suetonius indicates the scale of the Gallic triumph by mentioning that, at the final stage of the procession, Caesar mounted the Capitol through an avenue of forty lamp-bearing elephants, arrayed on either side of him.[64]

However, triumph and triumphalism could not establish beyond doubt or question the truth of Caesar's *Commentaries*. We happen to know of at least one historian of the late Republic who was able and willing to criticize Caesar's published version of events. According to Suetonius, Gaius Asinius Pollio, who composed *Histories* (now lost) which covered the period 60–42,

> thinks that the *Commentaries* were composed with little care and little untainted truth, since for the most part Caesar was too quick to believe others' accounts of their actions and gave a false account of his own actions, either on purpose or through forgetfulness. And he thinks that Caesar would have re-written and corrected them.
>
> (Suet. *Jul.* 56.4)

Pollio left himself a diplomatic exit: Caesar would have made major changes, he opines. Be that as it may, as they stand Caesar's *Commentaries* were not so much an account of his actions and successes as a key part of them.

4

ARTFUL COMMENTARIES: CAESAR ON HIMSELF

Caesar begins his *Commentaries* with his defeat first of the Helvetii, and second of the Suebi under King Ariovistus, together with their Sequanian allies. Both conflicts he presents as inevitable and undesired. At the same time, he repeatedly alludes to the Cimbri and Teutones, whose movements and military prowess had terrified Rome at the end of the second century BC. For Caesar it was no doubt a happy chance that they had been defeated finally by Marius, the husband of his aunt Julia and in many ways his paradigm. Sulla the dictator had famously described the young Caesar as one who had many Mariuses in him, while Caesar himself restored Marius' trophies for his defeat of the Cimbri and Teutones.[1] And, as the Caesarian Sallust stressed about 40 BC, relating the rise of Marius in his *Jugurthine War*, Gauls were especially difficult to defeat.[2]

While Caesar presents himself in his *Commentaries* as reasonable and pacific, concerned to defend Roman territory and Rome's allies, both the Helvetii and Ariovistus are shown as bent on causing trouble. In particular, they show wanton disrespect for Roman prestige and Roman rights in the region. The justice of Caesar's actions is thereby asserted, quietly and effectively.

The fact that Caesar, even on his own account, instigated the first clash with the Helvetii is casually and rationally explained: it seemed best not to wait.[3] And the Helvetian tribe which bore the brunt of his unexpected attack, the Tigurini, deserved all it got, for it was the very one, says Caesar, that had killed the Roman consul Lucius Cassius and subjugated his army in 107 BC. Caesar wonders whether their defeat at his hands was merely an accident or whether it was divinely ordained. If the latter, then Caesar was acting according to divine will, a further bulwark against criticism. Furthermore, Caesar had a personal claim to vengeance: with Cassius' army had died his legate L. Piso, the grandfather of Caesar's father-in-law.[4] Caesar's propriety is total. The Helvetii had given him no choice but to pre-empt them. Both Caesar and Rome had suffered prior wrongs (for so the defeat of Cassius is presented) at the hands of the Helvetii in general, and of the Tigurini in particular, for which they exacted revenge, perhaps by divine will. The narrative quietly makes a case which is strong but characterized by important details which were challenged in antiquity and which, if changed, would rob it of much of its strength.[5]

Next, the Helvetii compound their irrationality by threatening and insulting Rome and Caesar. To make that point, a speech is put in the mouth of their envoy, Divico, who had commanded the force that defeated Cassius some fifty years earlier (as we are told, improbably in view of his age but effectively). Caesar responds with righteous anger, denouncing Helvetian insolence and warning of divine reprisal. He offers peace, but on unfavourable terms: the Helvetii must give hostages to guarantee their word and must make amends to those Gauls they have harmed. Divico refuses angrily and reminds Caesar once more of the defeat of 107 BC.[6] But it is not long before the Helvetii themselves are defeated through the fine generalship of Caesar.[7]

It is in the context of apparent Gallic joy at Caesar's conquest of the Helvetii that King Ariovistus first appears in the *Commentaries*. We are shown that it was not Caesar's idea to engage with him. Rather, it is Rome's decent and faithful ally, Diviciacus of the Aedui, who brings his name to Caesar's attention on behalf of the other terrified Gauls. As their spokesman, he complains bitterly of Ariovistus' tyrannical empire-building. In particular, he complains that Ariovistus has started replacing Gauls with his fellow-Germans from beyond the Rhine. Caesar and the Roman people, he concludes, are the only hope for the Gauls. Caesar notices the particular silence of the Sequani, caused, we are told, by their particular terror at the retribution that Ariovistus might exact from them.[8] Their silence eloquently confirms the tyranny of the German king, as it was later to characterize the tyrannous regime of the emperor Domitian on Tacitus' account. It is worth noting that Caesar regularly has his enemies speak to him and about him; he thereby illustrates the open generosity of his regime, while he has his enemies damn themselves by the speeches he gives them. Ariovistus is an instance of precisely that.

Caesar reassures the Gauls that he can persuade Ariovistus to desist: he offers the reader a summary of his reasoning. First, he considers Ariovistus' domination of Rome's 'brothers and kinsmen', the Aedui, to be a disgrace to the Roman empire and to himself.[9] Second, he perceives in German migration a real threat to the Roman province and Italy: again, he recalls the Cimbri and Teutones. Third, Ariovistus' arrogance was not to be tolerated. In short, Caesar presents himself as reactive, not proactive. He has been begged to involve himself, and to do so is in keeping with Roman interests and Roman dignity, not to mention his own.[10]

Ariovistus' arrogance is immediately confirmed by his tart reply to Caesar's request for talks on neutral ground. Caesar's second invitation to talks stresses the injustice of Ariovistus' initial rebuff to him. This was fine thanks, he points out, for the formal recognition that the king had gained during Caesar's own consulship. Summarizing his requests of Ariovistus, Caesar concludes by reminding the king that the governor of the Roman province was required to protect the Aedui under the terms of a senatorial decree of 61 BC.[11] Final proof of Ariovistus' arrogance is contained in his second reply. Not only does he have the effrontery to equate his cruel treatment of the Aedui with Roman behaviour in the wake of military conquest, but he also mocks the notion of Aeduan kinship with Rome. He closes with the threat that Caesar is welcome to settle the matter by force, but he will regret the attempt.[12] Although the modern reader may be tempted to see a certain amount of justice in Ariovistus' position,[13] there can be no doubt that Roman readers would see only arrogance, ingratitude and a challenge to arms. At that point, says Caesar, he learnt from the Gauls that German progress was such that he must act immediately.[14]

The war had begun. But Caesar's account demonstrated (if it was taken at face value) that he had not sought a conflict, that he had behaved impeccably throughout, and that he was finally left no choice but to fight. The general's courage and the scale of his undertaking were demonstrated by the behaviour of those around him, not least those who hastened to leave his entourage and return to Rome. Thus Caesar deftly undermined the credibility of anyone from among his entourage who subsequently challenged his account or spoke against him at Rome: they had come to curry favour and had fled at the onset of danger.[15] Caesar, realizing what is needed, deploys his rhetorical talents and good sense to give new heart to his men (recalling again the Cimbri and Teutones).[16]

It is Ariovistus who wavers, his arrogance tested by the approach of Caesar's army: he agrees to the talks that he has twice refused. Caesar writes of his confidence that Ariovistus is coming to his senses and that he remembers his debt to Caesar and the Roman people. At the tense parley that ensues, Caesar relates the formal recognition that Ariovistus received in 59 BC and the generous gifts that he was given, stressing the beneficence and liberality bestowed upon the king. He next recounts the strength of the Roman bond with the Aedui and repeats his demands that Ariovistus desist from war against the Aedui and their allies and at least put a stop to German migration across the Rhine.[17]

Ariovistus is made to respond with the arrogance that we now know to be characteristic of him. Once more he equates himself and Rome: if Rome can have a Gallic province, why should not he? If Roman friendship requires that he weaken his position, then he will be glad to relinquish it. Finally, with consummate cheek, Ariovistus is made to state that if he were to kill Caesar, he would win gratitude from many of the Roman elite: he says that he has received messengers from such men, whose thanks and friendship he would gain by Caesar's death. If Caesar withdrew and left Gaul to him, he would give the general a fine reward and do any fighting that Caesar might wish done in the region.[18]

Caesar deals directly with Ariovistus' arguments. Romans do not abandon their allies. And Gaul does not belong to Ariovistus, for Rome had had a previous involvement there, earlier than Ariovistus', by 121, when Rome had declared Gaul to be free. The narrative proceeds with news of Ariovistus' treachery: his escort had started to attack Caesar's. Caesar's response is a fine indication of his awareness of criticism, however it is read, for Caesar claims that he instructed his escort not to return the missile-fire of the Germans because he did not want it to be said that they had been defeated by him in the context of a parley. In case the reader is in doubt, Caesar relates the outrage of his soldiers at the king's arrogance and treachery.[19] And that treachery is further illustrated by his subsequent abusive treatment of Caesar's envoys, C. Valerius Procillus and M. Mettius.[20] After the much-deserved defeat of Ariovistus, Caesar rescues both, while Ariovistus and the remnants of his army flee across the Rhine, out of Gaul to Germany.[21]

Caesar's whole account is replete with self-justification. Caesar's account of the Gauls' depiction of Ariovistus is amply borne out both by his actions and by the words that Caesar gives him: at best,

Caesar can only have had a very broad idea of what Ariovistus had actually said to him, and we may be sure that the king had not spoken in Latin. The reader is quietly persuaded that Ariovistus had forced Caesar to fight. By contrast, Caesar had proceeded with unusual tolerance, hopeful of a peaceful resolution, we are told. After all, the very fact that Ariovistus had been recognized at Rome meant that a war with him required caution and explanation. Arguably Caesar was in breach of his own *lex Iulia* of 59 by proceeding outside his *provincia*: his best defence was that he did so for the good of the state.[22] And a good defence was vital, for Caesar had enemies aplenty at Rome, and Ariovistus could not have gained recognition without important friends at the centre of power (then including Caesar himself, as consul). The point is confirmed by Caesar's claim that Ariovistus boasted of such connections.

Of course, anyone at Rome who decried Caesar's treatment of the king was left with a difficult case to make. How else could Caesar have responded to Ariovistus within the parameters of traditional Roman conduct and morality, when faced with such arrogance and tyranny? Caesar's account of Ariovistus' boast placed critics on the defensive. Would such critics have been happier if the German king had defeated a Roman army and killed its commander? Had they reckoned private disputes and civil in-fighting to be more important than the good of the state and the defeat of an arrogant foreign enemy?[23]

Caesar's accounts of his campaigns against the Helvetii and Ariovistus are worth surveying in this way because they show the rhetorical power and engagement of his apparently straightforward reportage. So much is characteristic of the *Commentaries* as a whole. Therefore, in reading Caesar's account of his invasions of Britain, we must be ever vigilant, aware of the arguments that underlie his account. We have already seen that, through the invasions of Britain, Caesar risked a fresh torrent of hostile analysis and criticism.

CAESAR AND BRITAIN: COMMIUS, CASSIVELLAUNUS AND MANDUBRACIUS

Caesar immediately presents his readers with justification for the brevity of his invasion of 55 BC: even as he left Gaul, winter was pressing. He does not demonstrate the need to invade at that moment, but he is at pains to convince readers both of the need and of the justice of an invasion before long. He knew, he says, that his enemies in Gaul had been supplied with help from Britain: that is, the British had already given grounds for war. He realized that little time was left for a campaign that year, but there was much to be gained by brief observation of the island and its population. We might add that since the very act of crossing the Channel offered vast prestige, it might have been enough for Caesar simply to have crossed; how long he stayed in Britain was less significant.

Caesar over-stretches his case. For, in stressing that Britain was an unknown quantity (which was indeed the case at Rome), he asks his readers to accept that the Gauls knew almost nothing about the nature of the Britons, their places, their ports and the approaches to the island – and that despite his earlier observation that the Gauls had received significant support from there, as had, for example, the Veneti.[24] He admits that traders made the crossing and did know about the coast and the part of Britain facing Gaul, but tells us that his diligent questioning of them failed to reveal the size of the island, the number and size of its tribes, the nature of their warfare and institutions, or the ports which were suitable for a fleet of large ships. On Caesar's account, Britain was a mysterious source of danger to Roman interests; it had to be explored and conquered.[25]

Such a claim may well have been accepted at Rome, where, as we have seen, Britain was very much a mystery. However, Caesar's own account indicates that it is an exaggeration. Elsewhere in his narrative, he tells us that the more committed among the Druids of Gaul regularly crossed to Britain and studied there.[26] Earlier he had had the Remi state that in recent memory King Diviciacus of the Suessiones (to be distinguished from his Aeduan homonym) had reigned simultaneously in Gaul and in Britain.[27] And he proceeds to explain his decision to send ahead to Britain King Commius of the Atrebates, on the grounds not only of his wisdom and fidelity, but also because Commius wielded great authority in Britain.[28] Commius can hardly have had such authority without significant knowledge of the Britons. Moreover, Caesar tells us that news of his projected expedition soon reached Britain (with telling speed and influence, it should be observed) and led to the despatch of envoys who proffered hostages and allegiance to Rome.[29] Perhaps it was at this point, if not earlier, that the young Mandubracius had come to Caesar from the state of the Trinovantes in search of refuge, when his father, their king, had been killed by King Cassivellaunus.[30]

Even without the arrival of British envoys and the likes of Mandu-bracius, there can be no doubt that Caesar had available to him in Gaul a great mass of first-hand information about Britain, with which he might have been satisfied. However, a quest for knowledge was a conveniently disinterested excuse for his British adventure, and one plausible enough at Rome. We are left to wonder about Caesar's other stated reason for the expedition: had British support for anti-Roman actions in Gaul been significant enough to prompt Caesar to cross the Channel? There is at least room for doubt that it had.

Despite the knowledge available to Caesar, and despite the recon-noitring he had entrusted to C. Volusenus, the landing in Britain was an uncertain affair on Caesar's account. It was only by virtue of his apposite commands and a soldier's bravery that the landing was accomplished in difficult conditions and against the armed opposi-tion of resourceful Britons, who used to the full their knowledge of the terrain.[31] So momentous a crossing was best completed in an atmosphere of heroism, fine generalship and success against the odds. With the British envoys who now sued for peace came King Commius of the Atrebates: his story confirmed the moral superior-ity of the upright Romans over the typically deceitful and immoral barbarians. The barbarous Britons had flouted civilized practice, for they had seized Commius and thrown him into chains, despite the fact that he had come to them as an envoy.[32]

Caesar showed tolerance, once more. He accepted their question-able excuse that Commius had been mistreated by the will of the masses, though he protested that they had attacked him without cause, despite the fact that they had sent envoys to him in Gaul of their own volition in search of peace. Caesar does not encourage readers to ponder that his invasion of Britain might itself be a cause of British aggression, or that the envoys who sought peace had not bargained upon invasion as the Roman response to their diplo-macy. Instead, Caesar reports that he pardoned the Britons but demanded hostages; they gave him some at once and promised to bring the rest from the hinterland in a few days. Meanwhile, the leading men of Britain gathered to present themselves and their tribes to Caesar.[33] By now, if they have read the first three books of Caesar's *Commentaries*, readers are sufficiently schooled in the ways of Western barbarians to suspect and expect that British per-fidy will soon show itself again, in particular that the promise of further hostages will not be fulfilled. The suspicion is duly and swiftly confirmed, though Caesar disingenuously observes that in this way peace was confirmed.

However, Caesar had still to cope with the forces of nature. First, the perils of the crossing were such that the ships bearing his cavalry proved unable to manage it in bad conditions. Second, high tides destroyed the ships which had brought across his infantry: this was a matter of chance and, we are left to suppose, not the fault of the commander. No food-supplies had been gathered to meet the eventuality, which was not an oversight, we are told, since Caesar had always intended to winter in Gaul (not a forced decision, we are casually informed). Being faithless and irrational barbarians, the British leaders who had gathered with Caesar turned to conspiracy: Caesar presents us with his version of their planning. The reader had suspected some such trickery, so had Caesar once his ships had been lost and the promised hostages failed to materialize. So far from being negligent, Caesar saw the problem early and energetically set about remedying the situation: food was steadily accumulated, the ships were resourcefully repaired.[34]

When the Britons (not Caesar) began hostilities afresh, Caesar was quick to see the danger and to order the right response. Though faced with unfamiliar and effective use of chariots against him, Caesar rescued his forces and by clever deployment of his very few cavalry inflicted a sufficient defeat upon a numerically superior enemy to inspire them to sue for peace once more.[35] Caesar doubled the number of hostages which he had earlier required and ordered that they should be brought to him in Gaul: winter was pressing, so he soon left for the continent.[36] Only the most optimistic Roman reader can have expected British hostages to be supplied at all, let alone sent to the continent. The more critical reader might wonder whether the imposition of half-baked conditions, destined to be flouted, was in keeping with the Roman imperial image: Caesar's only defence was the exigency of winter. In the event only two British tribes sent the required hostages to Caesar, who had also to deal with an uprising upon his return to Gaul. The Channel crossing itself had been the principal achievement of the year: Caesar's report of his campaigning in 55 BC led to the senatorial decree of twenty days of public thanksgiving.[37]

After settling affairs in Gaul among the Treveri, Caesar set off once more to invade Britain. The *Commentaries* offer no direct explanation of his reasons for invading Britain a second time. However, the predictable failure of most of the British tribes to send the requisite hostages gave him some grounds: as we have seen, at least one later source regarded that failure as an excuse, cloaking more straightforward lust for the conquest of Britain.[38] Caesar does not name the two tribes who did send him hostages and, more generally, has nothing to say about support he received from tribes in Britain before the defection of the Trinovantes at a late stage in the second invasion campaign. However limited, ready British compliance might have robbed him of some of the glory of conquest.

This time he took a large body of Gallic cavalry, including men of influence who could not safely be left to their own devices in Gaul during his absence: Caesar suggests that he had anticipated the revolt in Gaul that might be the price of his expedition to Britain. Dumnorix of the Aedui sought to escape Caesar and was summarily cut down, which duly encouraged others to obedience.[39] Again, we are told of the difficulties the Romans overcame in making the crossing, delayed by winds, blown off course and only reaching their destination by heroic hard work. The crossing of Ocean was no mean feat. This time, however, the landing was unopposed, for, we are told, the Britons took fright at the size of Caesar's fleet and withdrew to a fortified position just inland, thereby displaying the mixture of cowardice and irrationality characteristic of barbarians in Roman accounts. Superior Roman technique and controlled thinking soon won through against barbarian disorder: the fortified British position was quickly taken by use of the 'tortoise', without significant Roman losses, and the wisdom of the general prevented his troops from turning victory into defeat by unwise pursuit of the fleeing Britons.[40]

However, once more nature comes to the aid of the Britons. Although Caesar does not make the point, it is as if the river of Ocean – like many another river in antiquity – is incensed by his crossing and is eager to defend its people, the Britons.[41] It was an interesting coincidence that, also in 54, the Tiber flooded not only the lower levels of Rome, but even some of the higher parts of the city, causing much damage and loss of life. We are told that a supernatural cause was imagined by the majority at Rome. Some, at least, saw an affront to the gods in the current Egyptian Question. However, an easier explanation would have been in terms of Caesar's affront to Ocean: after all, Tiber was one of his many sons. In the absence of direct ancient testimony, we can only speculate, but if Caesar's enemies failed to make the connection between the flood and the crossing of the Channel, they missed a very obvious gambit.[42]

In the *Commentaries* Caesar has to report that, for a second time, the stormy sea wrought havoc with his fleet. Of course, this second mishap could be used to illustrate the difficulties of Caesar's enterprise, but it also offered an easy line of criticism for Caesar's opponents at Rome; Cato, Favonius and their friends must have had great fun with this repeated disaster, even if they failed to connect it with the Tiber's flood. Aware of actual or potential criticism, Caesar prepares his readers and excuses himself for the calamity to come immediately upon his landing in Britain: the position of the ships looked safe enough this time.[43] After the calamity – not only unforeseen but, as Caesar would argue, unforeseeable – Caesar shows himself taking decisive action to repair his ships and to protect them for the future.[44] Criticism was still possible: if Caesar had paid more attention to the writings of Posidonius, he could have avoided his losses through the tides.[45] But the defence was stout enough: Caesar's narrative constitutes a claim that he did everything that might reasonably be expected of him in the circumstances of this dangerous new land, before and after the second shipwrecks. In any case, even Alexander had difficulties with the tides of Ocean.[46]

While Caesar was building a stockade that may have evoked for some the Greek defences at Troy, a single named leader first appears among the Britons. Caesar gives his name as Cassivellaunus.[47] Cassius Dio, writing some 250 years later, describes Cassivellaunus as 'the man reckoned to be pre-eminent among the dynasts on the island', while Plutarch in about AD 100 writes of him, it seems, simply as 'the king'.[48] Caesar locates his kingdom on the other side of the Thames. He also offers some scant information on his earlier history. We are told that he had been continuously at war with the other British tribes.[49] Only one case of such conflict is specified: evidently Cassivellaunus had killed the ruler of the Trinovantes, 'one of the strongest tribes of those parts', and would have killed that ruler's son, Mandubracius, had he not taken refuge with Caesar in Gaul.[50] It seems that Cassivellaunus had brought the Trinovantes directly or indirectly under his control by the time of Caesar's invasion in 54. Such empire-building gave opportunities for self-justification to Caesar the writer: his Cassivellaunus echoes his Ariovistus, the tyrannical imperialist.

Cassivellaunus' expansionism also assisted Caesar the invader, as earlier in the case of Ariovistus. First, there were those leaders who escaped the empire-builder. As Diviciacus of the Aedui had escaped Ariovistus,[51] so the likes of Mandubracius could escape Britain to Gaul. Mandubracius is but the first attested royal refugee among several who feature in the early history of Roman relations in and around Britain. In subsequent cases, as we shall see, such men offered a potential just cause and practical help for Roman invasion: Tincommius and Dubnovellaunus for Augustus, Adminius for Gaius, Berikos (Verica?) for Claudius, not to mention an Irish princeling whom Agricola thought to use.[52] However, Caesar gives no indication that he deployed Mandubracius' plight as a justification for invasion, if only because his case was too obscure for a Roman elite public which had trouble enough locating the Nervii.[53]

Second, empires could be demolished at least as easily as they could be constructed. The Roman invader benefited not only from traditional hostilities and rivalries among the tribes of Britain and Gaul, but also from the fragility of the imperial structures created there. Cassivellaunus' pre-eminence brought him the leadership against Caesar at first. But after initial setbacks in pitched battle forced him to resort to guerilla tactics, his empire started to show its vulnerability. When the Trinovantes offered their submission to Caesar and called upon him (as Caesar has it) to install Mandubracius as their ruler and to protect him from Cassivellaunus, the empire-builder had lost a significant part of his domain. Caesar did as they asked in return for hostages, and grain to feed his army.[54] The example of the Trinovantes was soon followed by other tribes: Caesar calls attention in passing to the effectiveness of his policy of keeping the Trinovantes safe not only from Cassivellaunus, but also and particularly from the Roman troops. This was a key part of his strategy, designed to win defections, but it could also win dissent and criticism.[55]

From such defectors Caesar also gained valuable information, locating the principal stronghold of Cassivellaunus: again, British defences did not prove adequate to withstand Roman siege-tactics.[56] The king's last throw, we are told, was to summon his allies in Kent, where he wielded influence indirectly through four rulers; each had a portion of the area, and each apparently held the title of king. Caesar names them as Cingetorix, Carvilius, Taximagulus and Segovax. He also recounts their swift defeat and his capture of one of their generals, Lugotorix. Cassivellaunus now sought terms from Caesar, whose version of the king's rationale illustrates his own tactics. The king had suffered defeats, had had his lands ravaged and was, according to Caesar, 'especially influenced' to seek peace by the defection of tribes from his empire.[57]

As in 55, Caesar argues that it was the need to return to Gaul before the onset of winter that forced him not to press on: not much of the summer was left. Caesar demanded hostages and established that Britain should make annual payments to the Roman people.[58] Presumably, he received hostages before he left, by contrast with the fiasco of the previous year. He probably exacted money too, though how much was subsequently paid and for how long remain matters of speculation: Cicero notes the lack of booty.[59]

However, Roman forces had now set foot in Britain not once, but twice. It remained another world, but it was no longer entirely an alien world: the love-poet and proto-novelist Parthenius may offer an indication of the change in his own *Commentaries* (or ὑπομνήματα, as he terms them in Greek), story-outlines addressed at an uncertain date to Gaius Cornelius Gallus, himself a love-poet and the first prefect of Egypt:[60]

> It is said that Hercules, when he drove the cattle of Geryon from Erytheia, while wandering through the land of Kelts, came to Bretannos. The latter had a daughter named Keltine. She, enamoured of Hercules, hid the cattle and refused to return them until he slept with her. Hercules was eager to get the cattle, but was also and much more struck by the girl's beauty, so he obliged. When time had passed, a son was born to them, Keltos, from whom the Kelts take their name.
>
> (Parth. 30)

If the Celts took their name from Celtus (in Greek, Keltos), the name Bretannos becomes suggestive: was he not somehow the eponymous ancestor of the *Bretannoi*, in Greek 'the Britons'? Parthenius does not make the point explicit, but the occurrence of the name in this story of ancestry and naming can hardly be a matter of chance. It seems that a mythical link had been forged for Britain with Celtic Europe. Parthenius gives no hint of his source, though he often does elsewhere, so that we may have here his own creation: it cannot be dated closely, but would certainly be apposite in the aftermath of Caesar's campaigns in Gaul and Britain, where, as we have seen, there was a troubling lack of myth.[61] Parthenius, perhaps, had made his own contribution to the taming of the 'other world' across Ocean.

5

COINS AND DYNASTIES

The argument of the previous chapter centred upon the need to read Caesar's account of his British invasions with a cautious awareness of its particular artifice. There is a new problem in considering the rulers of Britain after 54 BC – or, rather, the return of an old problem: we do not have a literary narrative, even on the scale of Caesar's brief account. As will be argued in the next chapter, there is more to be gained from the brief surveys of Diodorus Siculus and Strabo than seems often to have been realized: the former, completed in the 30s BC, has simply been neglected, while the latter, completed in the 20s AD, has regularly been mistranslated and misunderstood. There is also coinage.

The coinage of the early rulers of Britain has been used to construct a chronology of their reigns, complete with historical sketches of their warfare, their relationships and even their thinking. The process has been influential: its principal appeal is its creation of a neat and known narrative outline where none otherwise exists. Accordingly, where only names of kings seemed to survive (and even those in varying and abbreviated forms), the use of coins proffers opportunities to assign years to their reigns. And once 'reigns' have been established, the modern scholar can proceed to weave hypotheses around them. Such a procedure has become standard in modern accounts of this shadowy period of British history. The more sober treatments give a brief caveat, before plunging in: for example, we are advised that 'information on this period of British history is based largely on coin evidence, and great caution must be exercised in drawing political conclusions from the discovery of particular coins in particular locations'.[1] However, even such a caveat is insufficient: the uncomfortable but incontrovertible fact is that we know almost nothing about the majority of the kings of Britain between the invasions of Caesar and Claudius, unless we have literary evidence. Further, it is probable enough that social and political traditions and structures varied significantly from one 'tribe' (the term may not be helpful) to another: and we know enough about Roman imperial practice to be quite confident that Rome would not have sought to establish uniformity, unless local systems had not seemed to work.[2]

Moreover, not only do we know nothing in detail of the lengths of the 'reigns' of those rulers who appear on coins, but we are also usually in the dark as to the extent and nature of their power. In particular, although modern accounts are usually couched in terms of tribal names – often located according to modern counties – there is very little about such tribes in our sources' accounts of the kings of early Britain. For example, although we often find in modern accounts statements like 'the chief opponents of Julius Caesar had been the Catuvellauni, located in the Hertfordshire area',[3] it is worth our reflecting that Caesar nowhere so much as mentions the Catuvellauni, and that nor do our other sources on his invasions. It is possible, as often assumed, that the imperialistic Cassivellaunus was king of the Catuvellauni (the similarity of the tribal and personal name is of some interest), but no ancient source says so; given our lack of evidence, we cannot even be sure that the Catuvellauni existed as an identifiable and distinct tribal grouping in Caesar's day.

Furthermore, the distribution of everyday artefacts tells us very little about the territorial parameters of a king's power. Rather, it tells us something about the range of use and acceptability of such artefacts. Of course, it is possible and tempting to develop histories where we have no history by using archaeological data to support top-heavy historical superstructures, but both author and reader should be aware that to do so may be to indulge in fantasy.[4]

However, we need not be completely pessimistic. For those who wish to write history can gain something valuable from the cautious and close study of extant coins, in particular, and of their distribution. As with other artefacts, the findspots of coins indicate primarily the places where they were deposited or lost, and thus suggest the range of their acceptability. At the same time, critical studies of coin distribution patterns – together with the construction of tentative hypotheses about the sequence of apparently related coin-types – offer the best hope of a fuller understanding of the history of British rulers between the invasions, particularly as coins continue to be found. However, despite important pioneering work, the close study of British coinage that is needed has only recently begun and remains fraught with difficulties.[5]

A general impression of Roman influence may be derived from the style of the coins of British rulers, though it would be unwise to assume that Roman influence through and upon coinage proceeded at the same pace and in the same fashion as in other areas of local material culture. In southern Britain a broad picture emerges, though encompassing great variety: an indigenous Celtic tradition, with highly stylized designs, survives strongly but comes to incorporate Roman designs, often copied from the types of the *denarii* of the Roman republic, of Antony and of the emperors.[6] The practice of copying offers some slight help in the vexed question of dating, providing a *terminus post quem* for the production of some British coins.[7]

Of particular interest are the heads which often occur on the obverses of the coins of British rulers, which occur in Romanized and Celticized forms: Cunobelinus' coins, for example, include both forms of obverse head, as do coins of Tasciovanus, his father.[8] The choice of a Romanized head, which must at least have been concordant with the ruler's wishes, was a significant development: the British ruler is presented in Roman guise, in the symbolic language of Roman power and Roman coinage. Further, and very broadly speaking, there are signs of a general development in British coinage away from Celticized forms towards Romanized ones, and the apparent development is used as a criterion for dating. But in this too, much caution is needed. Both father (Tasciovanus) and son (Cunobelinus) minted coins with both forms, while another ruler (perhaps a brother of Cunobelinus), whose name survives in the form ANDOCO, seems to have issued a small coinage in a short period, but he too presents both a Celticized and a Romanized head respectively on two of his coins.[9] At the same time, a Romanized head on the obverse is often wedded with a Celticized design on the reverse, as on a coin of Prasutagus of the Iceni.[10] In a few cases, heads look very like the heads of emperors: in particular, the head of the emperor Tiberius seems to appear on certain coins of Verica and Cunobelinus.[11] The use of imperial heads on rulers' coins is a phenomenon that is found elsewhere among the royal friends of Rome and is usually and very plausibly taken to indicate an expression of allegiance. Discussing the broad phenomenon under Augustus, Crawford must be right to conclude that rulers' use of imperial

13   14   15

Figure 13 Bronze coin of Cunobelinus (obverse): VA 2089.

Figure 14 Bronze coin of Cunobelinus (obverse): VA 2095.

Figure 15 Bronze coin of Cunobelinus (reverse): VA 2095.

heads on their coins indicates their awareness of the power of the emperor, though it is not the result of Roman direction.[12]

Of still more interest are the legends which appear on the coinage of these rulers. They constitute early examples of the use of Latin: despite many misspellings, the coins show a knowledge of the language that goes well beyond the alphabet in some cases. Presumably, those who minted these coins assumed that members of the British elite, at least, could read the legends: limited archaeological evidence suggests that in early Britain it was not only foreigners who could cope with a little Latin.[13] The use of filiation, with the appropriate genitive, is not uncommon: 'son of Commius' appears on the coins of three rulers (Tincommius, Eppillus and Verica), while 'son of Tasciovanus' appears on the coins of two more (Cunobelinus and Epaticu(s?)).[14] Further, some coins 'of Cunobelinus' seem to use the genitive of possession[15] and even a locative 'at Camulodunum', probably for the mint where many of his coins were produced.[16] The most complex Latin occurs on what seems to be a coin of Prasutagus, king of the Iceni: it shows SUBRIIPRASTO on the obverse (around a Romanized head), and ESICO FECIT on the reverse (around a Celticized horse). It is very tempting to interpret the obverse as SUB RI(CON) PRASUTAGO (UNDER KING PRASUTAGUS), with the reverse ESICO MADE [THIS COIN], apparently referring to a moneyer.[17]

Some rulers in Britain proclaim the title REX on their coins: namely, Eppillus, Verica and Cunobelinus.[18] These rulers had made the significant decision to present their authority explicitly in

Figure 16 Gold quarter-stater of Verica (obverse): VA 501.

Figure 17 Gold quarter-stater of Verica (reverse): VA 501.

Figure 18 Gold quarter-stater of Verica (obverse): VA 527.

Figure 19 Gold quarter-stater of Verica (reverse): VA 527.

Figure 20 Gold stater of Epaticus (reverse): VA 575.

Roman terms. As with every aspect of coin-types and legends, one wonders how far and in what sense the subjects of these rulers and others understood the title REX. Other rulers chose what is taken to be a Celtic equivalent to REX, namely, RIG or RICON(I): in addition to Prasutagus, these were Dubnovellaunus of Kent, and Anted of the Dobunni, who both seem to have had RIG as a title, while Tasciovanus used RICON, or RICONI.[19] Perhaps the Latin *rex* was readily assimilated to a local British term for king or chieftain. It is very tempting to interpret the term, whether in local or in Roman form, as a significant indication of a king's association with Rome: the Latin form in particular, *rex*, would seem to suggest a formal recognition of his rule by the Roman state, as we shall see in the next chapter.

Finally, coins also permit substantial knowledge about the family relationships between the rulers of early Britain, albeit in outline and with some residual doubt.[20] It is principally thanks to coins that we are able to trace dynasties in early Britain. Conventionally, these dynasties are located in tribal contexts: they are described as 'Atrebatic', or rulers of the Atrebates, or 'Trinovantian', rulers of the Trinovantes, and so on. By and large, the findspots of coins do much to support such attributions. However, it is worth remembering, none the less, that we know almost nothing about the nature of rulers' positions within particular tribes. For example, Caesar mentions four kings ruling simultaneously among the Cantii, somehow in alliance with or under the control of another king, Cassivellaunus.[21] It may well be that these kings each ruled a distinct and regional grouping within the Cantii, but we do not know that, and joint rule in some different form remains entirely possible. Moreover, there are indications in our evidence that ruling power was more transferable between tribes than might be imagined. A striking example is the apparent acceptance of the Catuvellaunian Caratacus, from the eastern half of Britain, as leader of the Silures of South Wales.[22] Certainly, the rulers of early Britain who struck coins with their names and images never included also an indication of their tribal affiliation, as far as we can tell. Even the very naming of tribes depends largely upon Roman authorities, who may simplify, and who give only vague indications of geographical location.[23] In consequence, we remain in a state of particular confusion even about the relatively well-attested Trinovantes and the nature of their relationship to the Catuvellauni,[24] with whom some would now identify them: elaborate stories of warfare and conquest have been woven around these tribal names, but few would now accept them.[25]

However, certain family relationships remain beyond much doubt. Coins present a Commios (conventionally Latinized as Commius) and three rulers who describe themselves as his sons on their coinage (conventional dates in parentheses): Tincom[mius] (ruled *c*. 30–10 BC?),[26] Eppillus (ruled *c*. 10 BC–AD 10?)[27] and Verica (ruled *c*. AD 10–40?). The Commius of the coins is normally identified with the Commius of Caesar's *Commentaries*. Caesar had made him king of the Gallic Atrebates in 57 BC and had sent him ahead to Britain on account of his standing there, but Commius had been thrown into chains, later to be released by Caesar. Commius had subsequently given some proof of his influence by brokering arrangements for peace between Cassivellaunus and Caesar, apparently at Cassivellaunus' instigation.[28] However, Commius had joined the Gallic uprising of Vercingetorix in 52 BC. His escape from its débâcle is recounted by Sextus Julius Frontinus in his *Stratagems*, which was completed under the emperor Domitian: Frontinus had been governor of Britain under Vespasian and no

21   22

Figure 21 Silver coin of Eppillus (obverse): VA 415.

Figure 22 Silver coin of Eppillus (reverse): VA 415.

doubt took a particular interest in the island's history. Frontinus'
account is anecdotal in flavour: Commius, though left high and dry
by the tide, raises his sails and deceives a pursuing Caesar into
thinking that he had successfully set sail for Britain and conse-
quently abandoning the chase.[29] The details are suspect, another
trope on the theme of the tides of Ocean, but there can be no real
doubt that Commius did return to Britain.

However, we cannot be sure that Caesar's Commius is the Commius of the coins that bear his name: Allen stressed as much half a
century ago.[30] Though our evidence is sparse, there are several
attested instances of the same name being held by different individuals, such as Cingetorix, Diviciacus, Dubnovellaunus and others.[31]
Indeed, a quite distinct Commius has been seen in the person of the
Dobunnic ruler whose coins give the name Comux.[32] As to Atrebatic Commius, there is a particular problem of chronology. Commius can hardly have been much less than 30 years old when Caesar
made him king in 57 BC, yet Verica his son seems still to have been
alive and fit enough to flee to Rome around AD 40. That is by no
means impossible, but the chronology is sufficiently stretched to
leave a doubt.[33] It might also be argued that 'son of Commius'
should not be taken too literally, but such an argument would seem
perverse in view of the limited amount of evidence available. If the
Commius of the coins is identified with Caesar's Commius, we are
left to imagine the process whereby he succeeded in establishing
himself in Britain, the founder of a dynasty there: it will have
required all his influence on the island. In taking power although
in flight Commius may have foreshadowed the establishment of
Caratacus among the Silures. At the same time, if the identification

is accepted, we can only wonder whether the hostility towards Romans that Commius had proclaimed in Gaul faded and even became friendship again during his subsequent reign in Britain; certainly, his sons seem to have enjoyed a friendly relationship with the Roman empire.

Among the Trinovantes (as it seems), we know the names of early rulers: Addedomarus (ruled *c.* 40–30 BC?)[34] and Dubnovellaunus, apparently distinct from his Kentish homonym (ruled *c.* 30–25 BC?);[35] he was followed, it seems, by a Vosenos (ruled *c.* 10–5 BC?).[36] Thereafter, the name of Tasciovanus predominates.[37] It occurs on the obverse of coins of Epaticu (ruled *c.* AD 35–43?), who is conventionally known to scholarship as Epaticcus;[38] only exceptionally does Epaticcus' coinage make it explicit that he was 'son of Tasciovanus'.[39] Several coins of Cunobelinus (ruled *c.* AD 10–40) name that king as 'son of Tasciovanus', including some which seem to have been minted relatively late in his reign.[40] Around the turn of the millennium, *c.* 10 BC–AD 10, a period of 'interregnum' is conventionally imagined among the Trinovantes, yet there is no real evidence of it. Rather, we have the name of Tasciovanus on the obverses of coins apparently minted by three distinct rulers, whose names (if names of rulers they are) occur as Sego, Andoco and Dias. It is clear that these individuals were seeking to associate themselves with Tasciovanus: none of them claims to be his son, but, since Epaticcus very seldom does so, while often presenting Tasciovanus' name without filiation, and since the coinage of these three rulers is so limited, the easiest inference is that they were indeed sons of Tasciovanus, or at least claimed to be.[41] If, as is now widely held, the Adminius of Suetonius is the Amminius of a small coinage in the region of Kent, then he was a son of Cunobelinus who saw fit to omit his father's name from his coinage: Suetonius mentions hostility between the two which might account for the omission.[42]

Among the other local coinages of early Britain, we cannot trace dynasties with any confidence. By and large, we have only names of rulers, for so they seem to be. Among the Iceni, in addition to King Prasutagus, there occur Anted, Ecen, Saenu and Aesu.[43] Among the Dobunni, we find Corio, Bodvoc, Anted (perhaps to be identified with his Icenian homonym), Comux, Eisu, Catti and Inam.[44] Among the Durotriges, it seems, we have only one name, Crab or possibly Crabos.[45] Among the Corieltauvi (once known as the Coritani), there are signs of dynastic development:[46] the earliest inscribed coins name a Vepocomes or Vepoccomes, who seems to

23   24

Figure 23 Silver coin of Prasutagus (obverse): VA 780.

Figure 24 Silver coin of Prasutagus (reverse): VA 780.

describe himself as son of Cor.[47] Thereafter, we find a practice which may be akin to that suggested among the Trinovantes: the name Volisios occurs on the obverses of the coins of three rulers, or so they seem, whose names occur on the reverses – Dumnocoveros, Dumnovellaunos and Cartivel. Further, Dumnocoveros occurs on the obverse of coins with Tigirseno on the reverse. Uncertainty prevails, but we may have here a dynasty in the person of Volisios, his three sons and his grandson Tigirseno: the link, if any, between Volisios and Vepoc(c)omes is a matter of further speculation.

The evidence of coins for the rulers of early Britain is at once both substantial and elusive, particularly where it cannot be supported by other sources of information. However, while constituting an example of contemporary material culture, coins have also preserved the names of an array of rulers, or at least prominent individuals, who are otherwise lost to history. In some cases, dynasties can be traced. But, encouraging and valuable as that may be, it seems most unwise to attempt to create speculative political and military histories from this meagre data, if only because such speculations may obstruct the course of more steady advances.

6

FROM COMMIUS TO CUNOBELINUS

Julius Caesar's invasions of Britain continued to dominate Roman thinking about the island for almost a century, until Claudius sought to emulate and surpass him with his own invasion of AD 43. Caesar's invasion had not only been a landmark in fact, a major stride into the shadowy northern periphery: it had also been presented and preserved – enshrined, perhaps – in writing and in the writing of Caesar himself. In so far as Caesar offered a principal source of legitimation for the very position and role of the emperors Augustus and Tiberius and for their families and descendants, everything that Caesar had touched had a special significance for the first emperors of Rome. However fleeting Caesar's British adventures might seem and might have seemed, they constituted significant progress in the imagination and in the process of diplomacy. Rome now had first-hand knowledge of Britain and of diplomacy and warfare there: the conquest of Britain no longer seemed so great an act of derring-do, while Britons knew that Rome was capable of an invasion to support its diplomatic enterprises.

AUGUSTUS

Caesar had broken the ice, so to speak. As we have seen, to applaud ice-breakers was typical of Roman social and political thought, for at Rome to be first in an achievement – not least in a military achievement – was to win special praise.[1] But Caesar's achievement both raised a question and presented a challenge. What happened next? Would the early emperors follow where Caesar had cut a path? Could they? There was much for those emperors to gain if Caesar could be followed and surpassed by more ringing military successes on the island. Britain still lay on the edge of the world, but it now seemed to be more a part of that world and to have a potential for inclusion within the Roman world-empire. That potential, which entailed the opportunity and even the need to trump the achievements of Julius Caesar, made a hot issue at Rome of a Britain which remained distant, marginal, little-known and unattractive, yet compelling.

It is in the historical context of that issue that early imperial writing on Britain should be read. The poets of Augustus' time trumpeted the imminent invasion of Britain as part of the emperor's glorious programme of imperial expansion, which was seen to include not only the distant west but also the distant east, as far as China. After all, he invaded so much else. Horace proclaims:

> We believed that Jove was ruler when he thundered
> in the heavens: a god amongst us will be held
> Augustus when Britons and dread Parthians
> have been added to the empire.
>
> (Hor. *Odes* 3.5.1–4)

Despite Caesar's invasions, the Britons are still the distant enemy of the west, matching the Parthians in the east: Horace prays that Apollo will visit war, famine and plague upon them, not upon the Romans.[2] The poet imagines himself, under the protection of the Muses, visiting the wild frontier: 'I shall visit the Britons, barbarous to guests . . . unscathed.'[3] Britain remains distant to Horace, as it had been for Catullus.[4] Let there be not civil war, but legitimate war, against foreign foes, urges Horace in the *Epodes*, completed about 29 BC in the wake of Actium:

> so that the untouched Briton might descend
> the sacred way enchained.
>
> (Hor. *Epodes* 7.7–8)

A triumph over Britons is the poet's desire: despite Caesar, they can be termed 'untouched'. Yet, for all that, there is an element of ambivalence: by about 13 BC, Horace can urge that Ocean at least already obeys the emperor, like its sons, the rivers:

> You the Nile obeys,
> who hides the sources of his springs,
> and Danube, and you headlong Tigris obeys,

and you the monster-filled Ocean,
which roars at the distant Britons.

(Hor. Odes 4.14.45–8)

While the Parthians require warfare by land, Britain means a
campaign by sea[5] and engagement with the characteristic British
chariots.[6] The *Panegyric of Messalla*, completed shortly after 31 and
preserved with the poems of Tibullus, presents Ocean as a ready
helper for Messalla's campaigning, and the Britons as still to be
conquered:

> Why do I hold back? Where Ocean holds the world within its sea,
> no region will oppose your oncoming arms.
> For you waits the Briton, unconquered by Roman Mars,
> for you the second part of the world, the sun between.

([Tibullus] 3.7.148–50)

Yet, even at the end of Augustus' reign, Ovid could write that
Caesar had 'conquered the water-girt Britons'.[7] On occasion so
much could be allowed, but we have seen that other contemporary
poets could describe the Britons as 'untouched' and 'unconquered
by Roman arms', and more generally as a conquest still to be
achieved. Ambivalence certainly, but the great weight of opinion
expressed by the Augustan poets is firmly of the view that Britain
remains an imperial military objective.

Yet how are we to assess such views? The key point must be that
the relative prominence of little Britain and its invasion in the
poetry written in these decades in itself provides a strong indication
of the new prominence of Britain as an issue in Roman thought.
Caesar's invasion had achieved that much at least. Looking back,
about a century later, Tacitus strikes the right note:

> So, first of all the Romans, the divine Julius entered Britain
> with an army: although he terrified its inhabitants with suc-
> cessful fighting and established control of the coast, he can be
> seen to have shown it to his descendants, not to have handed
> it down to them.

(Tac. *Agr.* 13.1)

What is less clear is the extent to which poets' imaginings of a new
invasion of Britain can be taken to indicate actual imperial decision-
making or objectives. Much later, Dio unequivocally stated that
Augustus planned to invade Britain on three separate occasions:

first, in 34 BC, when he only reached Gaul, whence unrest in the Balkans forced his return to Illyricum;[8] next, in 27 BC, when he again got as far as Gaul, from where he engaged in optimistic diplomacy with the island;[9] finally, in 26 BC, when the Britons proved intransigent and an invasion was only prevented (once more) by unrest elsewhere, now among the Salassi and in Spain.[10] The evidence of Dio should not be dismissed out of hand. It is true that the invasion of Britain seems an unlikely project in 34 BC, when Illyricum was surely enough.[11] Nevertheless, the campaigning of Caesar's heir in Illyricum may well have excited speculation fuelled by the memory of Caesar's own multiple and simultaneous involvements in Illyricum, Gaul and Britain. By contrast, Dio's account of Augustus' interest in Britain in 27/26 BC is hardly more than might have been expected: the emperor's presence in Gaul immediately offered an opportunity for diplomacy in Britain. And no doubt members of the British elite seized that opportunity for themselves by travelling to meet the emperor, as had happened before and would happen again in future. The notion of an invasion plan might be integral to Augustus' diplomacy, much as Dio presents it. Corroboration that we have more than a fantasy in Dio's account is furnished by Horace, whose poetic prayer to the goddess Fortuna suggests that an actual invasion of Britain was mooted:

> May you keep Caesar safe, about to go against
> the Britons at the end of the world.
>
> (Hor. *Odes* 1.35.29–30)[12]

We may be sure that Augustus thought about invading Britain: how often and how seriously are the questions that cannot be answered, but there is every reason to suppose that he came closest to it in 27/26 BC and perhaps again upon his subsequent sojourn in and around Gaul in 16–13 BC. We may be reasonably sure that Augustus would have been happy to be seen to be thinking about emulating Caesar's invasions.[13] In the event, when it came to action, his preferred course was not war, but diplomacy. While the possibility and threat of an invasion could only bolster imperial diplomacy in Britain, the impact of Roman culture became steadily stronger through the reign of Augustus.[14]

Augustus' account of his own achievements, as presented in the so-called *Res Gestae*, shows that there was glory in diplomacy as well as in military victory. In that inscription, military successes are catalogued for praise, but diplomacy is also given a great deal of space. In the *Res Gestae* diplomacy is presented rather as victory without the need for war, for the emperor's role there is to receive envoys who come not as equals, but as suppliants. Diodorus Siculus, who completed his work in the 30s BC, describes the rulers of Britain as being largely at peace with one another. It seems that Britain was relatively settled around the time of Augustus' consolidation of his grip on power at Rome. Diplomacy was relaxed and easy. It may well be that Augustus oiled the wheels of diplomacy with gifts, as Caesar claims to have done with Ariovistus, and as was regularly done later on the northern frontier and in Britain.[15] The bestowal of such gifts – or 'subsidies', as they are often called – might help to account for the sudden ability of at least one British ruler (Corio of the Dobunni) to issue a substantial gold coinage.[16]

Diplomacy was one face of the contemporary formulation of Virgil in the *Aeneid*, where the imperial mission of Rome is famously encapsulated as *parcere subiectis et debellare superbos*.[17] The formulation resists translation, but may be rendered as 'to spare those cast down and to bring down the haughty in war'. Those who came to seek the support of the emperor could readily be seen as among the *subiecti*, the 'cast down': they presented no resistance or threat to Rome and so were not among the rebarbative 'haughty', who were to be brought down in war. Whatever earlier notions Augustus may have entertained, his final answer to the question of a new invasion in the more cautious final decade of his life was that no invasion was necessary.

READING STRABO

By far the most important literary treatment of Britain between the invasions of Caesar and of Claudius is that of the geographer Strabo, who finished writing in the 20s AD under the emperor Tiberius. Strabo's geography is perhaps the single most valuable treatment of the Roman empire to have survived from antiquity. The work is substantial in scope and size, running to seventeen large books, which together encompass the full extent of the Roman world. Its interests are multiple and diverse: throughout, Strabo is concerned to give detail and to convince the reader, not least by source-citation, that he has got that detail right. Yet modern discussions of Britain between the invasions, though heavily reliant on Strabo's contemporary account of it, seldom give the author much thought, and still less often do they give him much credit.

Strabo tells us enough about himself in the course of his great geography to allow the outline of his life to be traced. His perspective was that of an easterner, in that he came from Amaseia in northern Asia Minor; his family had been important under Mithridates VI Eupator, king of Pontus. With the death of Mithridates and the creation of a province in his kingdom, Strabo reached Rome by 44 BC. Strabo will have regarded himself as a Greek, and his geography is written in Greek, accessible to a Greek-speaking public. However, Strabo spent much of his life in Italy, though he also travelled in the provinces. Accordingly, he had direct personal knowledge of the centre of power and moved among the Roman elite, a friend, for example, of the prefect Aelius Gallus, with whom he sailed the Nile *c.* 25 BC.

Strabo was no library-bound pedant. He brought to his writing a wealth of practical understanding – notably of kingship, of cultural differences, of the capital and of the provinces. When Strabo wrote of Julius Caesar, Augustus and Tiberius, he wrote as one who had personal experience of their regimes and very possibly of the men themselves. Geographers were very much in vogue at Rome. Caesar and Augustus fostered their art as a linchpin of the imperial bandwagon: now more than ever the conquest of the world was bound up with and inextricable from the mapping of that world. Moreover, this was mapping not simply in the sense of measuring and locating regions and places (important though that was), but also in ideological and intellectual terms as each corner of the world was tied into the culture and politics of the Roman centre through a share in Graeco-Roman myths and practices.

With all that in mind, we may start to consider Strabo's account of Britain. Of course, it is outstanding both in its qualities and in the very fact of its existence. If we did not have Strabo's account, 54 BC–AD 43 would be still more of a dark age in the history of Britain. However, his account looks quite meagre when set in the context of his seventeen-book geography as a whole. Evidently, Strabo made the decision to give Britain a cursory treatment, though he had significant sources of information: quite apart from Caesar's own account, Strabo had seen young Britons in Rome. And since much of his treatment of Britain is concerned to stress that its invasion is not worth considering, Strabo seems both to recognize that Britain was once an issue and to claim (polemically, perhaps) that it is not an issue any longer. Augustus' mention of his receipt of British kings, and Strabo's dismissal of any new invasion, together

suggest that by and during the opening decades of the first century
AD Julius Caesar's invasion exerted less strong an attraction than
earlier in the reign of Augustus. However, though the attraction had
receded it had far from disappeared, for Strabo shows the need to
make his case, and the emperors Gaius and, especially, Claudius
were soon to take the opposite view. Strabo's view was very much
that of his time, and probably that of his emperor.[18]

Strabo writes:

Britain is triangular in form, and its longest side lies parallel
to Keltike, being neither longer nor shorter. For each is some
4,300 or 4,400 stades ...

There are four ways which they usually employ to reach the
island from the mainland: these are from river-mouths, the
Rhine, the Sequana, the Liger and the Garumna. However,
those who put to sea from the vicinity of the Rhine do not sail
from the actual mouths of the river, but from the neighbours
of the Menapii, the Morini, in whose lands lies also Itium, the
port which the divine Caesar used in setting sail for the island.
He put to sea at night and on the next day made landfall about
the fourth hour, having accomplished a crossing of 320 stades.
And he seized grain in the fields. Most of the island is flat and
overgrown, but there are also many hilly places too. It bears
grain, livestock, gold, silver and iron. And these are exported
from there, as are hides, slaves and dogs well suited for hunt-
ing. And the Celts use both these and their own dogs for war.
The men are taller than the Celts, less fair of hair, but looser
in their bodies. This is an indication of their size: we ourselves
saw lads in Rome taller than the tallest here by as much as half
a foot, but they were bandy-legged and not graceful of figure
in any other respect either. Their customs are in part like
those of the Celts, in part simpler and more barbarous, so that
some of them do not make cheese in their ignorance, though
they have plenty of milk, and they are ignorant also of horticulture and other farming practices. There are dynastdoms
among them. For wars they mostly use chariots, like some of
the Celts. Their cities are the woods. For having fenced off a
large circular enclosure with felled trees, they make huts, and
stable their livestock there, temporarily. The weather is more
rainy than snowy. And on dry days a mist settles for a long
time, so that in the course of the whole day it is only for three

or four hours around noon that the sun is seen. This happens also among the Morini and the Menapii and their various neighbours.

Twice the divine Caesar crossed to the island, but he came back quickly, having achieved nothing significant, and not having penetrated far into the island, on account of uprisings which broke out among the Celts (both of the barbarians and of his own soldiers), and because most of his ships were destroyed when the ebb-tides and flood-tides were swollen at the time of the full moon. However, he won two or three victories over the Britons, although he had crossed with only two legions of his army, and he carried off hostages and slaves and much other booty. Now, however, some of the dynasts there, having arranged friendship with Caesar Augustus by embassies and by paying court, have set up dedications on the Capitol and made all but one with the Romans the whole island. And they tolerate heavy duties on exports from there to Keltike and on imports from Keltike (these are ivory chains and necklaces and amber-goods and glass-ware and other trinkets of such a sort), so that there is no need for a garrison on the island. For it would need at least one legion and some cavalry to exact taxes from them, a force which would cost as much as the sums thereby brought in. For the duties would have to be reduced if tribute were imposed, while dangers would also be encountered through the application of force.

(Strabo 4.5.1–3, pp. 199–201)

Although relatively brief, Strabo's account of Britain proceeds like many another of his treatments of a region. Location and extent are quickly followed by the fundamental question of access from the Graeco-Roman world, where Strabo's perspective is centred. The immediate prominence of Caesar's invasion should not surprise us. There follows a thumbnail sketch of Britons and British culture, whose principal function is both to inform and to allow the reader to gauge the position of the Britons on a Graeco-Roman scale of civilization.

Here, as usual, prominent among Strabo's principal (and for him uncontroversial) criteria are the practice of agriculture and the nature of civic settlement, if any.[19] Britain scores poorly on both counts. Although Caesar found fields of grain, there were Britons who knew nothing of agriculture or horticulture, while others are so backward that they do not know how to make cheese from milk. Their settlements are not proper cities, but crude enclosures in forest clearings. They dwell there with their livestock, human certainly but not so much more advanced than their animals. Still worse, their settlements are not long-term: for Strabo, who was cosmopolitan but confidently and militantly urban, the Britons bear the taint of nomadism. Strabo explicitly judges British customs to be akin to those of the Gauls, but less developed and more barbarous. On Strabo's account, the very nature of the land itself tends to the barbarous: though Britain produces metals and can support agriculture and herding, it is densely forested in great part and often shrouded in fog. Strabo's Britain is a land of semi-darkness, fenced by extreme and outlandish tides.

Strabo's assessment of Julius Caesar's invasions demands attention. It is very different from anything we know before him, though we may be sure that Caesar's political enemies and detractors had offered plentiful criticisms in his own day which have not survived. Strabo boldly states that Caesar did not accomplish anything great in Britain and that he did not proceed far into it. At the same time, although Strabo mentions that Caesar made the crossing twice, he gives no indication that to do so might be seen as a momentous achievement in itself. Moreover, he is interestingly vague as to quite what Caesar did achieve: having played down the significance of the invasions, he admits that Caesar won 'two or three' victories over the Britons although he had only transported two legions across the Channel. In that way, Strabo both records the fact of military victories and plays down the scale and significance of those victories and of the crossings themselves. Throughout Strabo's assessment of Caesar's invasions, the reader is encouraged to see them as a minor, almost half-hearted, affair. In Strabo's reckoning, there was nothing particularly compelling either about Britain or about Caesar's invasions of it: there was nothing special to be emulated.

Strabo's cool assessment of Caesar's invasion prepares his readers for the rest of his argument, which follows immediately: a better course has been found, claims Strabo, so that invasion would be both pointless and possibly counter-productive. The argument would not have displeased Tiberius, consonant as it was with Augustus' apparently anti-expansionist advice to his heir to 'keep the empire within its boundaries'.[20] Strabo tells how some of the British chieftains (literally, dynasts) worked hard to gain the friendship of the emperor Augustus. Dumnovellaunus and Tincommius may have been among the rulers he had in mind, for Augustus mentions them in the *Res Gestae* as kings of the Britons.[21] However, we know only a fraction of the story: Augustus states that these two kings came to him as suppliants, presumably in the context of upheavals or empire-building in Britain. Coins bearing each of these names were minted in Britain, and identification is tempting: Tincommius is presumably the son of Commius of that name, while Dumnovellaunus may well be one of the bearers of that name who appear on British coins.[22] Augustus' description of them as kings would tend to suggest that they had ruled there before they fled to him (together or separately?), but we do not know whether they ever returned to rule there. Nor do we know whether Dumnovellaunus and Tincommius were among those kings who made dedications upon the Capitol.

British kings' dedications upon the Capitol are major signs of their entrance into the Roman sphere, for so-called client rulers and other communities of the empire were permitted to make such dedications as a privilege.[23] Strabo may well have witnessed something of these British visits, for he had seen young Britons in Rome, and visiting rulers often brought a substantial retinue (including their families, not least their sons) with them to Rome.[24] However, Strabo does not give the number and dates of the British dedications. Nor does he say what form they took, though parallels indicate that an inscribed monument or object, dedicated with a sacrifice, is very probable. Most important, Strabo does not give any clue to the circumstances in which the dedications were made. In at least some other cases, dedications on the Capitol were made in the context of the recognition of a ruler by the Roman state; it is quite probable that British chieftains made dedications at the time of their recognition by the emperor. In that case, some will have been made under Augustus, but others could well have been made in the early years of Tiberius, between his accession in AD 14 and the completion of Strabo's work in the 20s AD. Strabo's Greek leaves open the possibility of dedications over a substantial period, not only under Augustus, but also after his death. Also uncertain is whether these dedications were made piecemeal or *en masse* by a group of chieftains: Strabo was not concerned to tell us, for it did not matter to his case. At any rate we may be sure that Augustus' preference for diplomacy was maintained by Tiberius: the point is illustrated by the decision of the British king Verica to mint coins bearing the imperial head of that emperor.[25]

Strabo's word for these rulers is 'dynasts', a term widely used for petty monarchs and civic grandees alike. Their realms he describes as 'dynastdoms'. He has chosen to withhold the terminology of kingship: for Strabo, these chieftains are too petty and too barbarous to deserve the name 'king'.[26] However, the Roman state had a formal terminology for such rulers that was applied to rulers great and small, adjudged barbarous or civilized: each was a king, a 'friend and ally and king' in the fullest formulation.[27] Petty and barbarous or not, to recognize British rulers as kings served Roman traditions and doubtless also the exigencies of successful diplomacy.

Cunobelinus has often been imagined as the creator and ruler of a substantial empire in south-east Britain in these years; the shortage of evidence for so firm and grand a vision has been observed only occasionally.[28] The notion that Cunobelinus was an implacable enemy of Rome was never supported by much evidence and is now usually rejected.[29] Certainly, Gaius' reception of Adminius in AD 39/40 suggests that his relations with Cunobelinus were at least cool, but that coolness cannot be taken as typical of Cunobelinus' entire reign: kings' relations with Roman emperors could and did fluctuate through their reigns.[30]

Cunobelinus was a son of Tasciovanus and is usually thought to have succeeded him c. AD 10: he chose to display his filiation on some of his coins,[31] while on others he presented his own name on the obverse, and Tasciovanus' name on the reverse.[32] Among the considerable variety of his coin-types occurs the head of the emperor Tiberius, surrounded by the genitive form of the king's name, CUNOBELINI (OF CUNOBELINUS); the reverse presents the king's filiation TASCIOVANI F(ILIUS) or F(ILII) (SON OF TASCIOVANUS or OF THE SON OF TASCIOVANUS).[33] Although the influence of Roman coin-types is extensive in early British coinage in general and in the coinage of Cunobelinus in particular, it is tempting to see Cunobelinus' use of the imperial head as an assertion of his bond with the emperor Tiberius, while the reverse presents his dynastic right to rule. Others of his coins have Romanized heads; and some of these bear the legend CUNOBELINUS REX.[34] Are these heads attempts to portray the king himself?[35]

Be that as it may, the closing sentences of Strabo's treatment of Britain have been the cause of much condemnatory comment by modern scholars, who have been quick to ridicule before achieving an accurate translation of his words. When properly translated, there is nothing ridiculous and much of interest in this closing passage. The two main criticisms levelled at Strabo have been, first, that he grossly exaggerates the extent of Roman control of the island in his day and, second, that he grossly minimizes the forces needed to conquer or dominate Britain militarily. However, although these criticisms have regularly been repeated in modern accounts, they do not withstand a close reading of Strabo's text.

As to the first criticism, it has often been supposed that Strabo goes so far as to claim that some of the British chieftains (as the Loeb translation has it) 'have also managed to make the whole of the island virtually Roman property'.[36] But Strabo says nothing of property, or even of control, in this sentence: the very fact that such a claim would be ridiculous should give the critic pause. Rather, Strabo asserts that these chieftains have made the whole island οἰκείαν σχεδόν τι to the Romans. Any appreciation of that phrase depends upon an understanding of the meaning of the adjective οἰκεῖος. It is true that in certain contexts the word can evoke a notion of property, but it usually does so in contexts where there is a contrast between private and public ownership or concern. However, in the context of inter-state relations it is very commonly used (not least in formal inscriptions) to indicate closeness, general affiliation and even kinship. The essence of the word οἰκεῖος is 'belonging', but not in the sense of property so much as in terms of relationship and association. Hence the use of the adjective (particularly in philosophical contexts) to denote the opposite of 'alien', whence the Stoic notion of the process of οἰκείωσις.[37] Given the context of Strabo's use of the adjective, and given the widely recognized inapplicability of any concept of property in his text, the adjective when applied to Britain can only be understood in the sense in which it is standardly employed in inter-state relations, viz. in terms of relationship. Strabo is claiming not that Rome has control of Britain, still less owns it, but that those kings who have entered into a relationship of friendship with Rome have made the whole island Roman-friendly, or akin to the Romans. Of course, even that was an exaggeration (though hardly as grotesque as in the Loeb version), so Strabo took the trouble to qualify the adjective with σχεδόν τι, 'all but', or even 'so to speak'. It would be pedantic to object that he should also have qualified his mention of the *whole* of the island: one qualification in the phrase was enough.

Accurately translated, a phrase that has regularly been reviled becomes a claim that is readily understandable in terms of the ideological milieu within which Strabo lived and wrote. Augustus himself is credited with the notion of bringing such rulers so close that they were made 'limbs and parts of the empire', an approach which accords well enough with Strabo's analysis of the impact of the British chieftains and with the discourse of Roman imperial power in general.[38]

The second criticism arises from the misreading of what follows: it is supposed that Strabo imagined that Britain could be conquered or controlled by one legion and some cavalry. Such a reading was never plausible, given his statement just before that Caesar had brought with him *only* two legions: Strabo was well aware that greater force was needed to conquer and control an island which he saw as murky and heavily forested.

The crucial point is that the Romanophile British chieftains remain the subject of the sentence which follows: when Strabo writes of 'they' and 'them' he is referring to these chieftains, not to the Britons in general. Strabo's language leaves no room for argument without special pleading: there is no indication whatsoever in Strabo's Greek that the subject has changed from the previous sentence, and without such an indication no change of subject can be supposed. All the more so since the sense of the passage would be lost if the subject changed. Accordingly, it is not the Britons in general, but the Romanophile chieftains, who endure heavy duties on imports and exports between Britain and Gaul: Strabo's language further suggests that the duties on both imports and exports were collected in Gaul, as might be expected. The exaction of direct taxes would usually entail the removal of the local ruler, for in most if not every case Rome did not demand taxes from client rulers. Strabo's estimate that at least one legion and cavalry would be needed to exact taxes in Britain refers not to the taxation of the whole of the island, but to the exaction of taxes in the area ruled by the chieftain or chieftains (who were evidently to be removed): that is, in part of the south and south-east of Britain. The larger the area to be taxed in this way, Strabo implies, the greater the military commitment: the cost of such intervention, the necessary concomitant reduction in import–export duties, and the fear of violent reaction combined to make such an enterprise uneconomic and foolhardy in his view.[39]

Strabo should not be criticized for claims he does not make. Far more to the point and far more interesting is the fact that he is so concerned to stress the advantage of the present arrangement to Rome. His account reads almost like an apologia for the failure of Augustus and Tiberius to realize the dreams of the poets and to repeat Caesar's adventure. In any case, both Augustus and Tiberius had earned elsewhere an abundance of the military glory that Roman culture so prized. They had no need to launch a new invasion of Britain.

TOWARDS INVASION

From a perspective in Rome under Augustus and Tiberius, the rulers of Britain were not a problem: thanks to its rulers, the island was well enough bound to Rome, as Strabo has it. The point is illustrated by a passing note in Tacitus' *Annals*, arising from the storm that shattered Germanicus' fleet in AD 16 on the coast of Germany. His ships were dispersed over a great area by the storm: those men who found themselves cast up in Britain were returned by the local 'kinglets', as Tacitus terms them.[40]

However, with the accession of a new emperor the situation changed markedly. In AD 37 the emperor Gaius ('Caligula') came to power without the military renown that his predecessors could proclaim. He, like Claudius after him, did need a spectacular military adventure. However, his need for military glory does not explain sufficiently his interest in Britain, for the frontier of the empire offered many opportunities for further conquest: why Britain?

The reign of Gaius is a major conundrum for the historian. The ancient writers who constitute our sources seem not to have felt the need to offer rational explanations of its key events: by and large, it was enough that the emperor was both tyrannical and unstable to the point of mental illness and insanity. Accordingly, to attempt to provide rational explanations of Gaius' decisions is to swim against the powerful and engulfing tide of our sources' judgments and of the narrative with which those judgments co-exist. Such attempts tend to sound like special pleading or to resemble the rationalization of myths.

However, we have one firm starting-point. However insane (or not) Gaius' interest in Britain may have been, his successor Claudius saw fit to go so far as to invade the island soon after his accession. Like Gaius, Claudius needed military renown, but, also like Gaius, he could have gained it (and at greater profit) elsewhere. There is a prima-facie case that Britain seemed to require imperial action now in the late 30s and early 40s AD, when it had not done so earlier. It would seem that something important had changed in Britain.

7

CALIGULA, CLAUDIUS AND CARATACUS

Under the emperor Gaius the invasion of Britain becomes an issue once more. After all, as was noted in antiquity, Gaius too was C. Iulius Caesar:[1] the new emperor's very name was perhaps enough to remind some of the abiding challenge of Britain. As we have seen, it was a challenge that Augustus, the imperial archetype, had not taken up, for all his conquests elsewhere; indeed, the notion may already have been current that he three times tried to launch an invasion of Britain but was distracted on each occasion.[2] The emperor who campaigned successfully in Britain would not only emulate Caesar, but also excel Augustus himself.

In AD 39 the emperor Gaius had a remarkable bridge of boats constructed from Puteoli across the northern sector of the Bay of Naples. The bridge and Gaius' parading along it have been seen by some as a clear sign of the emperor's madness. Gaius' most recent biographer observes that 'rational explanations are hardly needed',[3] but others have sensed method: Balsdon warns:

> that the building of the bridge was not a mere irrational caprice can be assumed safely from the fact that our authorities are at pains to give reasons for its construction and, especially, from its mention by Suetonius among the acts of the 'Princeps', not among those of the 'Monster'.[4]

Suetonius provides the earliest substantial account of the bridge and Gaius' parading on it. His testimony must carry particular weight: in addition to written sources, he also had the oral reminiscences of his grandfather, which he had heard in his boyhood.[5] The only other detailed treatment of the affair is that of Cassius Dio. His account shows signs of embellishment, particularly on the grandeur of the bridge itself, but it is Dio who provides a date and narrative context: Gaius constructs the bridge and parades on it in lieu of an ovation which the Senate had awarded him, 'as if he had defeated some enemies'.[6] Suetonius introduces the whole affair as a 'new and unheard-of kind of spectacle' which was the emperor's invention. And there can be no real doubt that it was indeed spectacle that was the prime function of both bridge and parading, apparently replacing the more sober celebration of an ovation.

The difficulty is to find and follow the evocations of that spectacle as described in our sources. Suetonius states that Gaius led two processions on the bridge, on successive days. On the first day, he rode a caparisoned horse and wore a crown of oak-leaves and a golden cloak; he also carried a sword and shield. On the second day, says Suetonius, he drove a small chariot with a team of famous horses; he was dressed as a charioteer. He carried before him the boy Darius, one of the hostages whom he had just received from the Parthians, while he was accompanied by a column of praetorians and by a group of his friends riding in chariots. Dio offers further details, of which some may be more than later embellishments: in particular, he has Gaius wear what the emperor claimed to be the breastplate of Alexander the Great, and he states that Gaius sacrificed, before mounting the bridge, to Neptune, Envy and some other gods. Dio also stresses the element of pseudo-warfare in the emperor's processing.[7]

Suetonius says that he found two lines of explanation in the sources he read.[8] The first explanation, which was evidently the view of the majority of Suetonius' authorities, held that Gaius was emulating Xerxes' famous bridge of boats across the Hellespont. And there can be little doubt that emulation of that sort was indeed part of the function of the bridge and the ceremonies: bridging the sea and major rivers (like channelling waterways and sailing upon them) was readily understood in antiquity as an act of conquest, either of the waterway itself or of peoples beyond, conducted with the alliance of the waters. As we have seen, this was the assertion of human authority over nature, with the sea or river often imagined in the form of a mighty deity.[9] We should give some weight to Gaius' reported sacrifice to Neptune and his observation, also in Dio's version, that the calmness of the sea upon which he rode demonstrated that even Neptune was afraid of him: even if these are no more than later embellishments, they embody a pattern of ancient thought which accommodates a cult of Neptune.[10]

The unheard-of spectacle was thus an assertion of imperial power over the sea, emulating the bridge of Xerxes. The choice of an Arsacid named Darius as his companion further drew attention to the Persian precedent, while a sacrifice to Envy was no more than appropriate in the context of the expression of such god-like power (not least, perhaps, for a reader of Herodotus, the key account of Xerxes' bridge). At the same time, the presence of the Parthian, who had not long arrived from the east, amply illustrated the successful diplomacy of L. Vitellius in AD 37, which had led to Darius being sent with other Parthian hostages to the emperor. Moreover, the negotiations between Vitellius and the Parthian king had been conducted on a specially constructed island in the middle of the River Euphrates:[11] Gaius may have intended to recall and to appropriate for himself the context of the negotiations on man-made ground above the waters. All such evocations were well suited to the triumphal, military tone of the proceedings.

The second explanation reported by Suetonius is also replete with military evocations, this time looking forward to future success in the west, not backwards to success achieved in the east. This second explanation has it that Gaius' purpose in the construction of the bridge and parading upon it was to strike fear into the Germans and Britons when they received reports of the grand scale of the work involved in the spectacle, since Gaius was already threatening them. But why should the Germans and Britons be terrified of the bridge at Baiae? Again, as with the first explanation, the significance of water-crossing seems to be the central point: to cross to Britain entailed the crossing of Ocean, while the Rhine must be crossed to reach Germany. The potential message for the Germans and Britons was direct enough: an emperor who can make it possible for his men to walk on water will have no difficulty in bringing an army into Britain or Germany.

In short, the two explanations which Suetonius found in his sources are not so much alternatives as two aspects of the same broad interpretation of the bridge, of Gaius' parading and of their evocations: namely, militarism to east and to west, with the emperor overcoming the significant religious and strategic obstacle of major bodies of water. Elsewhere, we hear of Gaius' concern with such water-cult and water-deities, though, as is usual in Gaius' case, his concern is couched by our sources in the discourse of insanity. We are told that Gaius decided upon an expedition to Germany, that is, to cross the Rhine, when he visited the remarkable and prophetic cult-centre of the River Clitumnus.[12] He once had a dream, we are told, wherein an 'image of the open sea' appeared to him: was this Ocean?[13] We shall observe the prominence of Ocean not only in Gaius' British campaign, but also in that of Claudius: we should also recall that a golden image of Ocean was carried in Julius Caesar's triumph of 46 BC.

It is Julius Caesar's campaigns that make immediate sense of the apparently over-ambitious (though hardly insane) plans of Gaius, which have caused so much perplexity among modern writers.[14] As with Suetonius on the bridge, so too our sources on Gaius' actual campaigning in the west mention a German campaign and a British campaign in the same breath. Caesar had set the example, for he had crossed the Rhine and the Ocean to Britain in the same year, 55 BC: together the Rhine and Britain were the 'monuments of great Caesar'.[15] There is a strong case for interpreting Gaius' actions in terms of his homonymous ancestor's: even the much-repeated charges that Gaius achieved nothing on either the British or the German front and that these campaigns were hardly more than ritualized sham-warfare might be mitigated, if not explained away, by Gaius' apparent desire to reproduce the achievements of Julius Caesar. For when Caesar had crossed the Rhine and the Channel in 55 BC, he too had achieved nothing substantial beyond the significant crossings themselves. Indeed, it may be that Caesar's detractors presented those adventures in much the same terms as our hostile tradition presents Gaius' expeditions.

Rather as Caesar's British invasions had inspired poetry, so Gaius' designs upon Britain seem to have inspired Cn. Cornelius Lentulus Gaetulicus, perhaps a poem *On the Britons*.[16] It may well have been in that poem that Gaetulicus ingratiatingly claimed as Gaius' birthplace Tibur, a town of Hercules, a key mythical figure of the periphery, including Germany, though not usually Britain.[17] And Gaetulicus the poet was also Gaetulicus the legate of Upper Germany, a further indication of how Gaius' German and British campaigns were intertwined. However, though Gaetulicus doubtless played a leading role in the extensive preparations for the crossing of the Rhine, he did not live to see it, killed by Gaius on a charge of treason.

After a brief foray across the Rhine late in AD 39 and a winter at Lyons, Gaius turned to Britain in AD 40. He did not get far. His triremes which had sailed on Ocean were soon transported to Rome, apparently for display in his triumph:[18] there is no sign that they had ever landed in Britain, though it is possible that a part of Gaius' forces had done that much.[19] The hostile tradition stresses that Gaius was much concerned to celebrate a triumph which was not deserved and to commemorate victories which were imaginary. His achievements, it is claimed, were a sham. Suetonius presents Gaius' British campaign accordingly: he states that Gaius drew up his battle-line on the shore of Ocean,[20] complete with artillery, and ordered his puzzled soldiers to collect sea-shells in their helmets as 'spoils from Ocean, due to the Capitol and the Palatine'. Suetonius adds that Gaius built a tall lighthouse to guide Channel shipping at night and gave to his troops a small donative, which he presented as if it was an act of huge generosity.[21]

The invasion of Britain had long been seen to require the conquest of Ocean. Evidently, the hostile tradition on Gaius' British campaign has developed from a literal interpretation of the metaphor (founded in religious belief) which was a standard feature of the discourse of conquest at the periphery, especially in Britain. No doubt Gaius did indeed present his British campaign as the conquest of Ocean. When Dio says that Gaius thought he had enslaved Ocean, so much may even be true, and, as we shall see, it was not so very different from the claims soon made for Claudius.[22] For Caesar before and Claudius later presented their British campaigns in much the same way. Indeed, Gaius had signalled his intention clearly enough in his bridge across the Bay of Naples. A lighthouse, too, would be consonant with the language of man's control of nature as exemplified by sailing on the sea.[23] We cannot hope to know what actually happened on the Channel coast in AD 40. Once again, modern attempts to rationalize the myth are not persuasive,[24] but we may be confident that the hostile tradition on Gaius has chosen to overlook the rationale which underlies its narrative, in its concern to illustrate his imperial madness.[25]

As Mandubracius had fled to Caesar, so a royal refugee came to Gaius, apparently while he was still by the Rhine.[26] The refugee was a son of King Cunobelinus: Suetonius calls him Adminius. He may well be the Amminius who issued silver and bronze coins in the Kent region, apparently before Claudius' invasion: his choice of an (unidentifiable) imperial head as an obverse type might indicate good relations with Rome prior to his flight.[27] Driven out by his father, Adminius crossed the Channel to put himself and his small escort in the hands of the emperor. Gaius, we are told, sent a bombastic letter to Rome, exaggerating his success against Britain.[28]

Probably he did, for to trumpet the arrival of such 'suppliants' was hardly innovative: Tacitus could read the speech in which Tiberius had made a mountain out of his receipt of Maroboduus, while Augustus lists such 'suppliants' – including Britons – among his achievements.[29] As usual, the tradition on Gaius is excessively hostile. Adminius may well have been displayed to the Roman public in Gaius' triumph.[30]

CLAUDIUS

Whatever Gaius' purposes and achievements on the shore of Ocean in AD 40, Claudius soon decided to launch his own invasion of Britain. The tradition on Claudius' invasion is far more positive, though it is hardly more informative about its reasons than the tradition on that of Gaius. However, if Gaius' presence across the Channel had had (or had been intended to have) some influence upon the political, and perhaps the economic, situation in southern Britain, his return to Rome and his assassination there in the following year can only have served to weaken or destroy that influence. As the Roman empire teetered on the edge of civil warfare, the rulers of Britain were likely to risk giving it offence, as they were to do again in AD 69. If Gaius' project was more than an act of random madness, as seems most probable, then Claudius' invasion is best seen as an attempt to take up the matter of Britain where Gaius had left off.

At last, a Roman emperor had decided that diplomacy, even armed diplomacy, was not enough. Cassius Dio names 'a certain Berikos' as responsible for persuading Claudius to send a force to Britain: Berikos, he says, had been driven from the island as a result of political conflict. Evidently, Berikos had taken refuge in Rome, where he may have spent several years before the invasion of AD 43: though our sources on Britain are meagre enough, we hear of a steady trickle of British exiles coming to the Roman empire. These exiles are often described as kings in our sources: in the last half-century it has become conventional to identify Dio's Berikos with the King Verica who is attested on British coins, and whose relationship with Rome seems to have been sustained and friendly.[31] Since the names Berikos and Verica are almost identical, the identification is very plausible, though Dio says nothing of Berikos' status, and distinct individuals could have had the same name.[32]

However, the identity of Berikos is a marginal issue: the key point is that Dio's evidence seems to confirm that Claudius' invasion was launched in the context of political instability in southern Britain. At the same time, Suetonius states that Britain was in a state of open hostility to Rome because 'deserters' (*transfugas*) had not been returned to the island.[33] Evidently, their political enemies had seized power in Britain and requested their return; Rome had refused, whether under Gaius, or Claudius, or both. But who were these 'deserters'? Suetonius had earlier used the word to describe Adminius and his entourage, who had fled to Gaius in Gaul: these men must be meant. However, there is also Dio's Berikos, whom Suetonius does not name: he had left the island in much the same circumstances as had Adminius, perhaps as a member of his entourage if he is not Verica the king. That Berikos was among the men whose return was denied seems to be confirmed by his role (according to Dio) in precipitating an invasion which was launched in the context of hostility that had arisen from the issue of men like Berikos (according to Suetonius).

However, we may doubt whether Berikos' persuasion of the emperor was a significant factor in the decision to invade. Just as Gaius is commonly presented as mad in our sources, so Claudius is regularly presented as prone to persuasion by others, not least by his slaves, freedmen and wives. Claudius did not need much persuading to launch his invasion of Britain: he needed a striking military success to confirm his imperial stature. Moreover, an invasion of Britain retained much of the aura of daring and exoticism that it had had in the time of Julius Caesar: Dio claims that the Roman troops were loath to cross the Channel and fight 'outside the inhabited world'.[34] Most important, perhaps, an invasion of Britain would establish a link between the new emperor and Julius Caesar:[35] by contrast with earlier emperors, Claudius was not a descendant of Caesar and Augustus, even by adoption. Claudius' accession had been far from the obvious consequence of Gaius' assassination, when there were other strong candidates among the aristocracy of Rome. Perhaps a further bonus for Claudius in the invasion of Britain was its key role in Druidism, which Caesar mentions:[36] although it was largely tolerated previously, Claudius prohibited Druidism.[37] In any event, we may be sure that the historically inclined Claudius read Caesar's *Commentaries*: he will have been alive to the epic overtones of a British invasion.[38]

Figure 25 The silver Augustus-medallion, Lexden Tumulus (Colchester), diam. 25mm.

Figure 26 An elite Late Iron Age burial, Welwyn Garden City (reconstructed).

Figure 27 Imported silver cup from the burial at Welwyn Garden City.

Careful consideration of extant British coins has provided a basis for attempts to reconstruct the troubled history of Britain from the end of the 30s AD. However, as we saw in Chapter 5, fundamental uncertainties in the chronology of these coins (both absolute and often relative, not to mention the dangers of over-imaginative infer- ences from coin-types and coin distribution) mean that any detailed reconstruction of that history can only be speculative. Archaeology has provided a general indication of the impact of Roman goods and culture upon the British elite, as illustrated by the excavation of the Lexden tumulus, which was deposited near Colchester in the last decade of the first century BC.[39] Further, we can be sure of one major factor in the upheavals of southern Britain: Cunobelinus had died.

In AD 39 or 40 Cunobelinus had driven his son Adminius out of Britain. By AD 43 Cunobelinus was dead.[40] The fact that two other sons of his, Caratacus and Togodumnus, are named as leading Brit- ish resistance to the Roman invasion suggests that he had not died as a result of conquest by an external enemy.[41] We may suppose that Cunobelinus had died either by natural causes or as a result of a dynastic struggle; the expulsion of Adminius indicates the existence of dynastic struggle, but that might itself be best explained in the context of Cunobelinus' advancing years.

There were unforeseeable risks in the invasion of Britain, as Caesar's *Commentaries* are at pains to show. Accordingly, by contrast with both Caesar and Gaius, Claudius did not lead the expedition in person. Rather, his general Aulus Plautius was entrusted with the establishment of a substantial bridgehead in Britain in AD 43. In the event of a disaster, Plautius might take the brunt of the blame. However, Plautius succeeded. The route of his invasion remains uncertain, but we are told that he left Gaul from Boulogne, and a convincing case has recently been made for Hampshire and Sussex (not Kent) as the first theatre of his operations in Britain.[42] The only extant narrative (that of Cassius Dio) names two sons of Cunobelinus, Caratacus and Togodumnus, as the first British leaders whom Plautius defeated. It has been suggested that these two rulers were the men who had issued requests for the return of 'deserters' from Rome.[43]

At this point Dio gives us the briefest glimpse of the political situation that Plautius found in Britain, a glimpse that is easily misconstrued or missed completely. First, he stresses the plurality of rulers among the Britons: 'they were not autonomous, but they variously obeyed various kings'.[44] Second, he indicates a political arrangement akin to that described by Caesar in his *Commentaries*: namely, the development of imperial structures, however Lilliputian. A people whom he calls the Bodunni – almost certainly the Dobunni – had been ruled over by Caratacus and Togodumnus, though they were Catuvellauni: the defeat of these external rulers gave the Bodunni/Dobunni the opportunity to come over to the Roman side. The narrative of Dio has often been mistranslated at this point, but it is not ambiguous:

> First, he [Plautius] defeated Caratacus, then Togodumnus, sons of Cunobelinus. When they had taken flight, he brought over a part of the Bodunni, of whom too they were the rulers, although they were Catuvellauni. And after leaving a garrison there, he proceeded to advance.
>
> (Dio 60.20.1–2)[45]

In particular, the verb which Dio uses to express Caratacus' and Togodumnus' rule over the Bodunni (ἐπῆεχον), here rendered as 'of whom too they were the rulers', would be particularly appropriate in a case wherein the rulers exercised authority over a people or area which was somehow additional to their own domains.[46] The point is more than pedantry: Dio conveys the fact that Caratacus and Togodumnus were alien to the Bodunni, not only by stating that they were Catuvellauni, but also by his choice of verb. The Bodunni were part of the 'empire' of Caratacus and Togodumnus, rather as in Caesar's day, when the Trinovantes and apparently kings of Kent were within the 'empire' of Cassivellaunus. As Cassivellaunus' empire began to fragment upon his defeat by Caesar, so the empire of Cunobelinus' sons began to disintegrate after Plautius' defeats of them.

Dio's narrative has Plautius pursue the hostile Britons to the Thames estuary, conquering Britain as much as the Britons themselves: rivers are overcome by Roman ingenuity employing Germans accustomed to swimming across substantial waterways. Togodumnus had been killed; Dio treats his death as a source of inspiration (together with marshy terrain) to British resistance, and a cause of British unification.[47] Presumably there was indeed greater unity in the sense that Caratacus was left as sole leader, but the death of Togodumnus can only have threatened further disintegration of the brothers' imperial domains. At the same time, the notion of encouragement through loss constituted a rhetorical trope which doubtless appealed to Dio's sense of artistry but which was hardly original: as we shall see, Tacitus offered a similar thought on the encouragement the Silures may have drawn from the loss of their leader, Caratacus.[48] Moreover, the allegedly stiffened resolve of the Britons in Dio's account is further suspect because it offers a rationale for Plautius' sudden fear, which, we are told, led him to halt his advance and send for the emperor Claudius. Stiffened British resolve and Plautius' fear were at least concordant with the needs of imperial image-making: it seems probable that they were manufactured to give a suitably important and decisive role to the emperor. Claudius had avoided much of the risk of a failed campaign by putting it in the hands of Plautius, but he now needed to attract to himself the prestige of a successful campaign: it was better that he should join an army whose advance had halted and whose general was in a state of fear. Claudius could have his cake and eat it too.

The emperor crossed Ocean, bringing with him even elephants, redolent of Rome's other far frontiers (and elephants had figured prominently in Caesar's Gallic triumph of 46 BC). Upon his arrival at the Thames, we are told, he assumed command. After victory in battle, he captured Camulodunum, which had been the royal residence of Cunobelinus, and which is regularly mentioned on his coins. Thereupon Claudius won over many of the Britons by diplomacy as well as force: the imperial pretensions of Cunobelinus' sons had sustained another major blow. After a mere sixteen days in Britain, Claudius left further campaigning in the capable hands of Plautius. He had achieved the prestigious victory he needed and sent ahead news of his success to Rome, where the Senate responded as the emperor will have wished. In any case it would perhaps have been unwise of the new emperor to spend much more time so far from Rome, barely two years after his turbulent accession.[49]

Meanwhile, the geographer Pomponius Mela incorporated into his survey of the world an enthusiastic allusion to the importance of Claudius' British expedition, of a sort that the emperor will have greatly enjoyed. Once again, Britain could be seen to offer a land and peoples unknown:[50]

> Britain – what sort of place it is and what sort of inhabitants it produces – will soon be described more precisely and on the basis of greater exploration. For, behold, the greatest of emperors is opening it up after it has been closed so long, the conqueror of peoples not only unconquered but unknown to boot! The truth of the actual facts – as he is pursuing it in warfare, so he is bringing it back to display in his triumph!
>
> (Mela 3.6.49)

Claudius was formally granted a triumph and the title Britannicus: he had already received multiple salutations as *imperator*. An annual festival was to be established to celebrate Claudius' British success, while two triumphal arches were to be built, one in Rome and one in Gaul at Boulogne, his place of departure for Britain. Amongst other honours bestowed upon the imperial family, Claudius' son was also to be Britannicus, by which name he became regularly known.[51] Soon, from c. AD 46, Claudius issued coins which depict the Roman arch with the legend DE BRITANNIS, recalling his father Drusus' arch in Germany, which had figured with the legend DE GERMANIS on Claudius' early coinage.[52] The arch itself has survived only in fragmentary form and at Rome, where it seems to have formed an organic part of the restored Aqua Virgo: there is no trace of the Boulogne arch. The form of the arch remains uncertain in detail, and its dedicatory inscription for Claudius requires substantial restoration, though it provides a date of dedication in AD 51–2 (the arch had appeared on Claudius' coins five years earlier). Recently, in an exemplary and cautionary treatment of the inscription, its discovery, transcription and restoration over the centuries, Barrett has demonstrated just how little of its text is secure. As commonly restored, the inscription is taken to declare Claudius' conquest of eleven kings of Britain, but Barrett has shown that it could as well declare his receipt of eleven, or even twenty-one, kings of the Britons.[53]

Claudius' victory resounded around the Roman world. Near Ravenna, Claudius celebrated his victory by sailing on the Adriatic in a palatial ship: the affair was sufficiently notable to be recorded by the Elder Pliny.[54] The mood of celebration is further illustrated by an inscription which happens to have survived at Rusellae in Etruria, where it was cut in AD 45, perhaps on the base of a statue of Victory:[55]

> In fulfilment of a vow, for the safety and the return and the British victory of Tiberius Claudius Caesar Augustus Germanicus, pontifex maximus, in his fifth year of tribunician power, imperator ten times, father of his country, consul designate for the fourth time; Aulus Vicirius Proculus, priest of Augustus, military tribune, fulfilled his vow for the British victory.

Further afield, a guild of travelling athletes sent a gold crown to the emperor in honour of his British victory: Claudius acknowledged its receipt with thanks in a letter which has survived on papyrus, dated to AD 46.[56] At Aphrodisias in Caria, a sculpted relief amply portrayed the epic image of Claudius' conquest, showing the emperor grappling with a personified Britannia.[57]

But it was at Rome that Claudius most needed to make an impact. Through his name, the young Britannicus embodied the British victory; Claudius took a delight in showing him off.[58] Claudius also re-enacted the capture and sack of Camulodunum as a great public spectacle on the Campus Martius which in turn provides some context for Gaius' spectacle on the Bay of Naples: such spectacles were the stuff of politics and imperialism at Rome, not indications of insanity. On the Campus Martius, Claudius presided in person over the theatrical surrender of British kings, dressed in his general's cloak.[59] The circumstances of the celebration are not known: perhaps the triumphal arch at the meeting-point of the Via

Figure 28 Claudius and Britannia (Aphrodisias, south-west Turkey).

Figure 29 Silver didrachm
of Claudius (obverse),
Caesarea mint: BMC 237.

Figure 30 Silver didrachm
of Claudius (reverse),
Caesarea mint: BMC 237.

Figure 31 Lead ingot from Blagdon (Som.) bearing the name
Britannicus.

Lata and Aqua Virgo formed a backdrop.[60] In AD 44 Claudius celebrated a triumph 'in the grandest style';[61] he encouraged provincial
governors to come to Rome to view the parade and even recalled
some exiles. At the climax of the triumphal parade, Claudius chose
to ascend the Capitol on his knees, supported by his sons-in-law on
either side: ascent on his knees concealed his difficulty in walking
and may have recalled Julius Caesar.[62] He also used the occasion to
shower honorific awards upon the elite: according to Dio, he
granted triumphal ornaments to the senators who had participated
in the British campaign. Suetonius states that it was on this occasion
too that he honoured Posides the eunuch, one of his favourite freedmen.[63] The problem of slavery was never far away from imperial
conquest.

Thereafter, when Plautius himself returned to Rome in AD 47,
Claudius awarded him an ovation and thereby echoed and almost
relived his own triumph. Claudius met Plautius as he entered the
city and accompanied him – albeit in the less honorific position –
on to the Capitol and back again.[64]

We can only guess how far such celebrations were replicated
around the empire, but the case of Cyzicus is at least suggestive.
There, Roman citizens and Cyzicenes together raised a triumphal
arch to celebrate the British victory, whose inscription seems to
reproduce the inscription on the arch at Rome (and probably at
Boulogne also): no doubt the arch itself was intended somehow to
reproduce its Roman counterpart, albeit less grandiosely.[65] In addition to the arch, we may assume extensive celebrations in Cyzicus
and elsewhere which have not left a material record. For example,
the travelling athletes who had sent a crown to the emperor no
doubt participated in some such festivities.

Ocean figured prominently in the celebrations. On Ocean,
Claudius had followed and excelled his father's example. As Claudius' biographer notes at the outset of his *Life*, Drusus had been the
first Roman general to sail northern Oceanus.[66] Claudius' British
victory had taken him not only on but across that Ocean: it could
later be said even that he had reached as far as the Orkneys.[67] The
British victory had been surrounded by echoes of Claudius' family
history.[68] Claudius fixed a naval crown on his house on the Palatine,
beside the civic crown which hung there, on the grounds that
'he had crossed and, as it were, defeated Ocean'.[69] Poets set
about celebrating Claudius' achievement in verse. Again, Ocean is
prominent:[70]

Distant Tiber used to bound your realms, Romulus;
This was your boundary, religious Numa.
And your power, Divine One, consecrated in your sky,
Stood this side of farthest Ocean.
But now Ocean flows between twin worlds:
What once was a limit of the empire is now part of it.

(Anth. Lat. 423)

Again,

A land never despoiled by Ausonian triumphs
Struck by your thunderbolt, Caesar, lay prostrate
And Ocean observes your altars beyond himself;
The boundary of the earth was not the boundary of the empire.

(Anth. Lat. 419)

The British victory was the running theme of Claudius' reign: in AD 49 it provided grounds for the ritual extension of the sacred boundary of Rome, the *pomerium*. Aulus Gellius, the second-century antiquarian, provides an explanation of the *pomerium* and the process of its rightful extension:

The augurs of the Roman people who wrote the books *On auspices* defined the nature of the *pomerium* as follows: 'The *pomerium* is the area inside the designated countryside, around the circuit of the whole city behind the walls, de-limited by fixed lines, which marks the boundary of city auspices.' In fact the most ancient *pomerium*, which was insti-tuted by Romulus, was delimited by the foothills of the Palatine. But that *pomerium* was extended several times as the state expanded, and it came to embrace many high hills. In fact the right of extending the *pomerium* belonged to the man who had contributed to the growth of the Roman people by the capture of land from enemies . . . in the past the Aventine was outside the *pomerium*, as I have said; subsequently, it was included by the divine Claudius and regarded as inside the *pomerium*.

(Aulus Gellius, *Attic Nights*, 13.14)[71]

Tacitus, who recounts the ritual, confirms that it was the extension of the boundaries of the empire that gave Claudius the right to extend the *pomerium*.[72] The inscribed *cippi* which marked Claudius' new *pomerium* indicate the rationale for the extension:

Tiberius Claudius Caesar Augustus Germanicus, son of Drusus, pontifex maximus, in his ninth year of tribunician power, imperator 16 times, consul four times, censor, father of his country, having expanded the boundaries of the Roman people, has extended and delimited the *pomerium*.

(*ILS* 213)

Britain is not specified, and Claudius' regime could boast successes elsewhere around the empire,[73] but it was in Britain that Claudius had played a direct and personal part in the extension of Roman power beyond the limit of the inhabited world, Ocean itself. Accordingly, when Claudius reviewed Roman history in arguing for the admission of Gauls into the Senate in AD 48, it was his advance beyond Ocean that seemed the focus and summit of his achievements:

If I were now to recount wars – whence our ancestors began, and whither we have advanced – it is my fear that I might seem to be too arrogant and to have sought to boast of the glory of having advanced the empire beyond Ocean.

(*ILS* 212)

Claudius' disingenuous expression of anxiety provided him with an opportunity to mention again his key military achievement. And the extension of the *pomerium* in full ceremony in AD 49 offered yet another opportunity for the commemoration of the successful invasion of Britain.

COGIDUBNUS

The Claudian invasion had not removed kings from southern Britain. That fact should not surprise us, for we have seen in previous chapters that the Roman empire made regular use of friendly kings: Roman rule and royal rule were not stark alternatives. Tacitus singles out one king for mention in the earlier chapters of his *Agricola*. His name is problematic. Usually known as Cogidubnus, he could as easily be Togidubnus: Tacitus' text, which is the only complete version of his name is open to question on this point,[74] while the first two letters of his name are completely (and the third partially) restored in the only other place in which it occurs, the famous inscription from Chichester.[75] However, given the weight of tradition, the name Cogidubnus is best retained.

Tacitus mentions Cogidubnus in the context of a list of the early governors of Britain: Aulus Plautius, Ostorius Scapula, Cogidubnus, Didius Gallus, Veranius and Suetonius Paulinus.[76] His dates are elusive: Tacitus' sequence indicates that Cogidubnus was king before the arrival of Didius Gallus in AD 52, while his treatment of Plautius and Scapula together leaves the possibility that the king was appointed even earlier in the process of invasion, when his influence would have been of particular value to Rome. As we shall see, his nomenclature suggests that he is unlikely to have had a kingdom before the invasion, certainly not before AD 41. Of course, king and governor had much in common, as Tacitus' list indicates. Tacitus comments with characteristic bite:

> Certain states were given to Cogidubnus the king (he remained most faithful down to our own memory), by the ancient and long-accepted habit of the Roman people, that it should have as instruments of servitude even kings.
>
> (Tac. *Agr.* 14)

As we shall see in the next chapter, Tacitus and other ancient writers regularly explore the polarity of king and slave, not least when it seems to be defeated or reconciled in the form of the 'slave king' or 'royal slave'.[77]

No coins of Cogidubnus have been identified:[78] perhaps his association with the Roman *provincia* was so close that he had neither the need nor the desire to mint. Tacitus apart, we have only the inscription from Chichester, a chance survival; the best available reading is that of Bogaers, though it remains speculative in part:[79]

> To Neptune and Minerva, for the welfare of the divine house, by authority of Tiberius Claudius Cogidubnus, great king of Britain, the college of engineers and its members gave this temple from their own resources, [. . .]ens, son of Pudentinus, presenting the site.

The inscription (which may date from the reign of Claudius or of Nero)[80] has a distinctly Roman air. Not only is it well cut in good Latin, but it also indicates the presence of a college of engineers within the realm of Cogidubnus. Moreover, that college dedicated a temple to Roman deities, Neptune and Minerva, who would be particularly deserving of the attentions of naval engineers or shipwrights, which the college-members may have been. At the same time, the dedication was made for the welfare of the imperial family: imperial cult figured prominently in other kingdoms.[81] Further, the site for the temple was presented by the son of a man with a name that seems at least Romanized, Pudentinus. It is useless to speculate on the name of Pudentinus' son, but the size and layout of the inscribed text requires a short name, such as Pudens or Valens for example. But neither father nor son is given the nomenclature that would suggest his Roman citizenship.

It is the citizenship of Cogidubnus that stands out: his nomenclature shows that he derived his citizenship from a grant of Claudius. Such a grant would accord with Tacitus' brief mention in the *Agricola*: it was also Claudius who bestowed 'certain states' upon the king. Further inferences may be drawn. Since kings friendly to Rome had standardly been awarded Roman citizenship (where they did not already have it) from the reign of Augustus, if not earlier, and since Cogidubnus' nomenclature suggests that he had not inherited his citizenship, we may be confident that Cogidubnus was not the son or grandson of one of the kings who had maintained good relations with Rome under previous emperors. Accordingly, suggestions that Cogidubnus was a son of Tincommius or Verica are not attractive, for both should have been Julii. Of course, he may have been a more distant relation.[82]

In all probability, it was the Romans who elevated Cogidubnus to the status of king. Beyond that, his antecedents are a matter of speculation, though Cogidubnus may have been among those 'deserters' whom Claudius had refused to return to Britain on the eve of his invasion in AD 43. However, the inscription seems to show Cogidubnus not only as a king, but as a 'great king'.[83] Although the title *rex* had become familiar enough on the coins of kings friendly to Rome, a *rex magnus* was something new in Britain. In a sense the title *rex magnus* was appropriate to its context, a grandiloquent dedicatory inscription for a ruler whose kingdom embraced more than a single state. The scale of its grandiloquence seems to have attracted scant attention: Cogidubnus is termed 'great king of *Britain*', or 'of *the Britons*'. The claim is, of course, preposterous, for Cogidubnus' realm was far less than that. However, it is preposterous in a familiar way: Claudius' re-enactment on the Campus Martius is said to have involved the surrender of 'kings of Britain', so too perhaps the arch at Cyzicus and its counterpart at Rome (where 'kings of the Britons' is also conceivable). We can only

wonder whether Cogidubnus' overblown title was that acknowledged by Rome, or the formulation sported by the king himself, or
simply the engineers' attempt at ingratiation, or some combination
of the three.

A large area of uncertainty surrounds the name of the people over
whom Cogidubnus reigned: they seem to have been termed the
Regni, or Regnenses.[84] It is at least a remarkable coincidence that
the subjects of this *rex magnus* should bear a name that so evokes
the Latin for kingdom, *regnum*. All the more so when we note
that Cogidubnus is the only *rex* whom Tacitus sees fit to mention in
his bare summary of Roman rule in Britain before Agricola.
In a sense, Cogidubnus was not only a great king, but also *the* king.
At the same time, the sources that preserve the name Regni or a
similar name are later than the first century AD: the earliest is the
Geography of Ptolemy.[85] Coincidence may be explained and dis-
counted, for it is surely likely enough that the realm of Cogidubnus,
steadfast over time (as Tacitus explicitly and implicitly shows),
became known to the Romans simply as 'the kingdom', *regnum*.[86]

Familiar attempts to interpret the fine building at Fishbourne as
the residence of the king have the virtue of neatness, in that they
bring together two of the key features of our knowledge of the
region in the first century AD: namely, king and building. But, as
Barrett has shown, the chronology does not work well: Tacitus'
words are only comprehensible if Cogidubnus was dead before
(probably well before) the arrival of Agricola in AD 78; while
Cunliffe dates the construction of the so-called 'palace' at Fishbourne to the period AD 75–80 and shows its so-called 'audience-
chamber' to have remained in use for some two centuries thereafter.[87] It is worth remembering that, impressive as this 'palace' was,
Fishbourne was not the only site of a grand structure in southern
Britain in this period.[88]

In a judicious study of the evidence for Cogidubnus, Barrett
tentatively concludes that he died in the reign of Nero but after the
rebellion of Boudica, i.e. in the period AD 61–8.[89] Indeed, he explains
Tacitus' reference to Cogidubnus' outstanding fidelity in terms of
Boudica's rebellion, when, he suggests, the king took the opportunity to display his allegiance to Rome. The suggestion is entirely
plausible, but three associated considerations encourage some
doubt. First, no very particular display of fidelity need be sought: it
is long-term loyalty that Tacitus stresses. Second, although Tacitus
provides a fairly full narrative of the rebellion of Boudica, he makes

no mention of Cogidubnus, for all his importance and despite the opportunities he might have provided for rhetorical points about slavery. Third, there is a possible indication – no more – that the king was dead by AD 58: Barrett rightly acknowledges that Tacitus' formulation would permit a death for the king in the 50s.[90] That indication is the absence of Cogidubnus' name from a dedication to the emperor Nero at Chichester in AD 58 (or the very end of 57), which most probably took the form of a statue.[91] An expensive dedication to the emperor might be expected to have included mention of the king, as does the dedication by the college of engineers near which it was found. However, the point should not be pressed: we know nothing about the fuller context of the dedication. Although we may be confident enough that Cogidubnus was made king early in the 40s, the date of his death cannot be fixed without more evidence. Given his closeness to Rome, he may well have bequeathed his kingdom to the emperor, as did Prasutagus of the Iceni.[92]

CARATACUS

Of the sons of Cunobelinus for whom we have names, only one seems to have survived the early stages of the Roman invasion. Togodumnus had been killed, while Adminius disappears from the historical record after his flight to Gaius. Caratacus remained, with brothers whose names are unknown and whose significance seems to have been minimal;[93] his continued resistance and subsequent treatment at Rome generated, even in antiquity, a myth. To seek an objective reality behind that myth would be a futile endeavour, but to explore the myth of Caratacus is to develop an understanding of Roman perceptions and preconceptions in thinking and writing about Britain, Britons and British kings. Cassius Dio's account (as abbreviated by the Byzantine Zonaras) highlights one facet of the myth:

> And Caratacus, a barbarian leader, having been captured and brought to Rome, and after receiving a pardon from Claudius, went about the city upon his release. When he saw the splendour and great size of it, he said, 'So, when you have this and the like, do you covet our little tents?'
>
> (Dio 60.33.3c)[94]

The idea of the barbarian impressed with the great imperial city will have appealed to the Byzantine *epitomator*, for Byzantines liked to imagine the impact of their own city upon the barbarian visitor. Not only Dio, but Tacitus too, enjoyed the culture-clash involved as barbarism and civilization met, with all their respective strengths and weaknesses.[95] But Dio's purpose is to highlight the folly of imperialism when the rich strive to conquer the poor, taking risks for minimal gain. The notion was not original: it was central to the outlook of Herodotus, who has the Spartan Pausanias make the same point when displaying the luxurious accoutrements of the tent of the Persian Mardonius.[96]

Tacitus also focusses upon Caratacus at Rome, though he has something to say about his role in Britain and doubtless said more in the lost section of the *Annals* wherein he narrated Plautius' invasion. Claudius made much of Caratacus, rather as Gaius had done with Adminius. And as the receipt of Adminius had been less than the great victory Gaius claimed, so Claudius' treatment of Caratacus was also exaggerated and distorted, on Tacitus' account. Tacitus states that the name of Caratacus had captured the imagination of the Roman west, where his reputation spread from Britain all the way to Italy and Rome itself; he had resisted the empire for eight years.

Tacitus dwells upon Claudius' attempt to milk the reputation of Caratacus for all it was worth: the emperor posed as the conqueror of the renowned Briton. Claudius had earlier re-enacted the surrender of British kings on the Campus Martius. Now, in AD 51, he put the actual Caratacus on show on another side of the city, in front of the praetorian barracks by the Porta Viminalis. The praetorians were assembled in arms, embodying the military might of the empire and its emperor. The retainers of the king were paraded by, with torcs, *phalerae* and other evocative paraphernalia. Next came the king's brothers, who had surrendered in Britain, and his wife and daughter, who had been captured. Finally, the centrepiece, Caratacus himself.[97]

Tacitus plays up the dignity of the captive king: 'while the emperor exalted his own honour, he conferred glory upon the man defeated'.[98] Caratacus provides Tacitus with an opportunity to develop the themes of the chance nature of success and failure, of nobility in the face of adversity and of royal barbarian morality in the face of, and in contrast with, imperial Roman degeneracy. Stood before the imperial tribunal on which Claudius presided, Caratacus immediately established his quality in contrast to the other Britons who had been put on show with him. Where the others had begged for pity, in terror for their lives, Caratacus did not; instead, he looked up and addressed Claudius with an elegant speech. Tacitus carefully chooses his vocabulary to make the point that Caratacus' appeal was made not at an emotional level, but in rational terms: rather than beg for pity (*misericordia*), he presented a reasoned argument for clemency (*clementia*). The distinction is important to any understanding of Tacitus' account: Caratacus retains control of himself and of the situation, showing himself to be the exceptional figure he is.[99]

Tacitus' version of Caratacus' speech is worth quoting in full, for it gives a strong flavour of the author's strategy:

> If my nobility and lot in life had been matched by an appropriate share of good fortune, I would have entered this city as a friend, not a captive, and you would not have disdained to receive in peace, under treaty, the scion of famous forebears and the ruler of numerous peoples. My present predicament is hideous for me, but splendid for you. I had horses, men, arms and wealth: is it surprising that I was unwilling to lose them? For if you desire to rule everyone, does it follow that everyone should embrace slavery? If I had surrendered immediately and been handed over, neither my lot nor your glory would have been illustrious: oblivion would have followed my punishment. But if you preserve me, unharmed, I shall be an eternal example of your clemency.
>
> (Tac. *Ann.* 12.37)

The mutability of fortune was a key moral and rhetorical concern at Rome: the plight of defeated kings was a favourite context for the exploration of that fact of life and the proper human response to it, not least by the exercise of *clementia*. A rhetorical treatise of the late Republic is quite explicit on the matter, stressing tradition, when it presents the following argument:

> Our ancestors did well when they never executed a king whom they had captured in warfare. Why so? Because when Fortune gave us the opportunity, it would have been unfair to use it to punish one whom that same Fortune had shortly before placed in a position of the highest status. What of the fact that he led an army against us? I cease to recall it. Why?

114

Because it is the duty of the brave man to consider those who fight against him for victory to be his enemies, while it is his duty to adjudge those defeated to be his fellow-men, so that bravery ends war, and humanity advances peace.

([Cic.] *Ad Her*. 4.23)[100]

At the same time, Caratacus' speech contains an implied critique of Roman imperialism in terms of enslavement, one of the main strands of Tacitus' thought, as we shall see again in the next chapter.[101] The speech is not only profoundly Roman, but also typically Tacitean: however Caratacus had behaved in AD 51, it is most unlikely that he spoke in this vein. Indeed, only shortly before in the same book, Tacitus had used Claudius' public display of King Mithridates VIII of the Bosporus in much the same way, albeit more briefly: he too, according to Tacitus, had retained his composure amidst the Roman soldiery and had spoken bluntly to the emperor: 'I have not been sent back to you, I have come back. If you doubt it, send me away and find me.'[102]

Mithridates VIII had been spared: he lived on until executed by Galba for complicity in a bid for power by the praetorian prefect, Nymphidius Sabinus, late in AD 68. Caratacus too was spared, together with his wife and brothers.[103] The next act of Caratacus and his family shows the reader the gulf between the strong king and the weak emperor: freed from their chains, they praised and thanked not only Claudius, but also Agrippina, who also presided prominently upon her own quasi-tribunal. Tacitus draws attention to the breach of traditional protocol that was involved in the prominence of a woman presiding over Roman standards. We are left to perceive the obvious contrast: Caratacus' wife is not even named and would certainly not have been allowed such licence by a proper ruler like Caratacus.[104]

The reader proceeds to view a bombastic senatorial session, wherein the capture of Caratacus is set on a par with the greatest military feats of the Roman past: Claudius, it was said, had achieved no less illustrious a success than had Scipio or Paullus or whoever else had exhibited kings in chains to the Roman people.[105] The reader already knows enough of Claudius to baulk at comparisons of him with the greatest figures of republican history. And the emptiness of such claims is also apparent from the fact that Caratacus had been betrayed more than captured,[106] while his removal had only stiffened resistance: we proceed immediately from senatorial bombast to imperial reality and defeat in Britain.[107]

Although a real historical figure, Caratacus was of more interest to our literary authorities as an opportunity for moralizing, in particular as a counterpoint to Claudius. The periphery of the empire was the immediate interface of the empire and the outside, the other: it was there, at the periphery, that the morality and identity of the empire and imperialism could best be examined. And when the other came to Rome, the political and cultural centre of the objective Roman ego, there was a stark comparison, almost a confrontation, between the norms and values of the two. For such purposes, Britain and the British were as attractive and evocative as any part of the periphery, for they constituted another world beyond Ocean.

FROM CLAUDIUS TO GAIUS

Claudius' invasion of Britain had been the recurrent and central theme of his reign, virtually from its beginning in AD 41 until its end in AD 54. The invasion of AD 43 had generated major celebrations in Italy and in the empire at large. In AD 44, Claudius had celebrated a particularly extravagant triumph, echoed in the construction and dedication of a grand arch on the road that led north from the city, and re-echoed on his coinage and in poetry. The ovation of Plautius in AD 47 was something of a second triumph for the emperor, who took a prominent part. In AD 49 conquest in Britain provided the principal justification for the emperor's ritual and spectacular enlargement of the *pomerium* of Rome. At some stage, the success at Camulodunum, and the emperor's receipt of surrendering British kings, was acted out, while in AD 51 Caratacus himself – already famous in Rome – was presented as a public spectacle (complete with his family), presided over by the emperor. Caratacus stayed in Rome, it seems, no doubt welcomed by Claudius as a living example of his military prowess and clemency.

In such an atmosphere, Gaius' interest in Britain could only be diminished and ridiculed. In any case, much of Claudius' image was that of the healer of the wounds inflicted upon Rome by his predecessor.[108] Claudius' regime could not encourage a view of his invasion, his greatest achievement, as in any sense a continuation of Gaius' undertaking.[109] Rather, in the case of Britain as in much else, it was in Claudius' interest to establish the greatest distance and contrast between himself and his assassinated predecessor: stories of the mistreatment that he too had suffered under Gaius, despite his apparent participation in Gaius' regime, were valuable grist to the mill of the new emperor. We may be sure that Gaius' reputation suffered terribly under Claudius. And with regard to Britain, Claudius was to suffer a similar fate at the hands of the Flavians, who seem to have claimed the credit of the invasion for themselves, and especially for Vespasian, as we shall see in Chapter 9.

8

BOUDICA AND CARTIMANDUA

QUEENSHIP AND SLAVERY: APPROACHES

Queens fascinated Roman men. They occupied a special place in the torrid imaginations of the male writers whose accounts we use as sources. In these accounts queens constituted a category that was also a stereotype: queens were not so much an assortment of individuals as a recognizable type, recurring from time to time and from place to place. Of course, as we have seen, kings were often treated in much the same way: they were the Elder Cato's 'flesh-eating creature'.[1] But the tendency is still more marked and still more significant in Roman male attitudes to queens – in part, no doubt, because ruling queens were much fewer in number, from among whom still fewer were made to stand out.

For our Roman sources, more was at stake in queenship than in kingship. All the problems surrounding kingship were applied also to queens: in essence, these amounted to the abuse of unfettered power (notably, disregard for the law, murder, seizure of property, and sexual impropriety). But in addition, of course, queens were women. Anxieties about power intersected with anxieties concerning gender and gender-roles. An all-powerful man was threatening enough, but an all-powerful woman was awe-inspiring. For example, Semiramis, an archetypal queen in the Roman mentality, was said to have indulged not only in luxury, but also in a sexual lifestyle alien and inimical to Roman conceptions of the proper behaviour of a decent woman. For example, she was said to have set out a pleasure-garden wherein she had sex with the most handsome of her soldiers: she chose them, had sex with them and then killed them. This archetypal queen was imagined not only as enjoying illicit sex, but also as exercising all the power in so doing: it is the queen who does the choosing and the queen who then kills. Indeed, her victims disappear completely. She did all this, we are told, because 'she was not willing to marry lawfully, taking care that she would not be deprived of her ruling power'.[2] Small wonder that Semiramis could be associated with Amazons and that her name could be thrown at a Roman governor as an insult, as by Cicero in attacking Gabinius, appropriately governor of Syria.[3]

At the same time, if kings were exotic and attractive creatures, queens were still more exotic and attractive; for queens were rarer. And queens broke the dominant rules of gender-roles within Graeco-Roman society: they were more powerful than the men of their realms, they controlled those men and they had the freedom to behave exactly as they wished.[4] Queens could choose and function in both male and female roles in society and politics, while as monarchs they also stood above and apart. Even more than kings, they combined for our male sources the sexuality of power and the power of sexuality. Whether gender is perceived as a polarity of male and female or as a sliding scale, queens encompass both poles and every location on that scale. It is probably more than coincidence that, in contemporary English usage, the term 'queen' evokes not only female rule, but also homosexuality, not least when expressed overtly and powerfully. For British society still, the queen embodies many of the problems and contradictions of sexuality and power.

Of course, gender and gender-roles had long been an issue in Greek and in Roman society by the first century AD. With the development of the Principate, that issue had become still more significant: now the most outstanding among queens in the Roman imagination was Cleopatra VII of Egypt. The Principate had been founded upon her defeat, for it was Cleopatra whom Augustus presented as the enemy he had conquered at the Battle of Actium.[5] By contrast, Antony was depicted less as an enemy in his own right than as a victim of Cleopatra's powerful wiles. In that sense Antony became not so much an opponent of Augustus' regime as an example of the fate from which the new emperor had saved the Roman state, namely enthralment to an overwhelming power that was thoroughly untraditional in Roman terms – female, foreign, and almost magical in the strangeness of her power.

Among the most overt treatments of these issues is a poem of Propertius, which expresses anxieties about queens in general and

about Cleopatra in particular while proclaiming the success of
Caesar Augustus in overcoming the problem:

Why are you surprised if a woman governs my life
    and draws a man enslaved beneath her sway?
Why do you invent base charges of a lazy head,
    since I cannot break the chains, crack the yoke?
Coming death a sailor better foresees,
    wounds teach a soldier to have fear.
I boasted like that in a youth that's gone:
    now, you, learn fear from my example.

The Colchian woman forced blazing bulls under yoke
    of adamant, and sowed the ground with armed battles,
And closed the wild maw of the serpent guardian,
    so that the golden fleece might go to Jason's halls.

Once, fierce Penthesilea dared to face the Greek
    fleet with arrows, on horseback
And she who bared her face from golden helmet
    conquered with shining beauty the conquering man.

Omphale achieved so much with her beauty,
    a Lydian girl wet with the lake of Gyges,
That he who had set pillars on a pacified world,
    draws soft wool with hands so hard.

Semiramis set Babylon as a city of the Persians,
    to raise a solid work of baked earth,
And two chariots driven head-on along the walls,
    could not clash their sides, touch their axles.
She brought Euphrates too amid the citadel she founded
    and told Bactra to bow to her power.

Yet why should I bring charges against heroes, against gods?
    Jupiter disgraces himself and his house.
What of her who just brought shame on our arms,
    a woman even humped by her own slaves?
The obscene bride-price she demanded was Roman
    walls and the Fathers enslaved to her realms.

Noxious Alexandria, land best fit for entrapment
  and so bloody with our evil, Memphis,
Where the sand drew three triumphs away from Pompey!
  No day will remove that stain from you, Rome.
Better a death for you on Phlegraean field,
  or if you'd bared your neck to your father-in-law.

The queen-tart of unchaste Canopus,
  the single blot burnt on Philip's blood,
Dared to face barking Anubis against our Jove,
  and force Tiber to bear the threats of Nile,
And to drive off the Roman trumpet with clattering rattle
  and chase Liburnian prows with barge-poles,
And stretch vile mosquito-nets on the Tarpeian Rock,
  and give laws amidst even the statues and arms of Marius!

What good that Tarquin's axes were broken,
  whom a haughty life marks with haughty name,
If a woman was to be endured? Take, Rome, the triumph
  and, safe, pray for a long life for Augustus!
You fled to the wandering waters of timid Nile:
  your hands received Roman chains.
I saw your arms, bitten by sacred snakes,
  and the secret track of slumber drew your limbs.
'I was not to be feared, Rome, when you have so great a citizen!'
  she said, her tongue buried in unremitting wine.

The lofty city on seven hills, presiding over all the world,
  scared by female Mars, feared threats?
Now where are Scipio's fleets, where the standards of Camillus,
  or you, Bosporus, just captured by Pompey's hand?
Where the spoils of Hannibal and monument of conquered
                                              Syphax,
  and Pyrrhus' glory broken at our feet?
Curtius set monuments, lakes filled,
  but Decius broke the battle, his horse spurred on;
A path witnesses the cut bridge of Cocles;
  and there's he to whom a crow gave his name –
These the gods had founded, these walls too the gods protect:
  scarcely would Rome fear Jove, while Caesar lives.

Apollo of Leucas will recall battle-lines routed:
  such a work of war did one day bear.
But you, sailor, whether you seek ports or leave them,
  recall Caesar throughout the Ionian sea.

(Prop. *Eleg.* 3.11)

Propertius the love-poet explores the connections between the power of a woman to enslave him, and the enslaving power of a familiar list of women drawn from myth and history, culminating in the person of Cleopatra. Medea, the Colchian princess, betrayed her family for her lover and used her potions to defeat forces physically stronger than both of them, both bulls and serpent. Her story was very well known: the poet could afford to be allusive. Penthesilea, the Amazon queen, for all her man-like prowess in war, was conquered by Achilles, but she too overcame physical strength by her arts, in this case her beauty revealed: in that way she conquered her conqueror. Omphale, the Lydian queen, had all-conquering Hercules as her slave by the will of Jupiter, or, in Propertius' version, by her beauty: for her he works wool, woman's work. Omphale too is a royal woman able to overcome the strongest of men with her beauty, insubstantial and irresistible. More constructively, Semiramis boasted male achievements, founding a great city, building an empire and bending even the mighty river Euphrates to her will.

Jupiter himself was prey to women: even the king of the gods could not resist female power. The thought prepares us for Cleopatra. She is so promiscuous that she has sex even with her slaves; a man might do the same.[6] She is the 'queen-tart of unchaste Canopus' (*incesti meretrix regina Canopi*), exacting a price for her favours, for her obscene marriage with Antony (himself her slave), typical of the land that had been the place of Pompey's wretched murder. Her price is the enslavement of the senators of Rome and the control of the city's defences and identity: she is an Omphale and a Semiramis, only as immoral as immoral can be. And she is foreign to Rome, with foreign gods, foreign terrain and foreign river: the manly Roman trumpet she faces with her female and alien rattle. Her nets were poised to ensnare and cover the monuments of Romanness; she seeks to establish her rule and her laws at the heart of Rome, amid the images of Roman traditions, to which she constitutes an anathema.

Dominant Graeco-Roman ideology insisted that to be enslaved by a woman was a disgrace for a male: that disgrace is a recurrent theme of Greek and Roman literature in general, not only of poetry.[7] For both women and slaves were in a sense excluded from Greek and Roman society, in that they were not permitted all the rights and privileges of the citizen male.[8] Moreover, as with the examples employed by Propertius, powerful women are regularly also foreigners, beyond the normative limits of Greek and Roman society. From Herodotus onwards, if not earlier, the exploration of gender-roles is regularly bound up with the exploration of cultural otherness.[9] To be enslaved by a queen was all too comprehensible, but hardly excusable: she embodied disgrace for the Roman male, which could only be expunged by her conquest.

As real power moved away from the traditional institutions of state, notably the Senate, and towards the emperor, so access to the emperor and influence with him became ever more the dominant criteria of social and political success and effectiveness. Accordingly, members of the emperor's household seemed to wield massive political influence for the very reason that their position within the household gave them outstanding opportunities for access to the emperor and even for the control of the access of others from outside. How far that appearance was also a reality is very difficult to estimate, but our sources show little doubt: they tend to present 'bad' emperors as under the control of their households, and 'good' emperors as exercising control over their households, like the bad governor and the good governor respectively. However, we can have little confidence in the stories, rumours and stereotypes that form the bulk of our information about the internal practices and personalities of the imperial household from reign to reign. Ancient views of these palace politics were profoundly ideological. There was an inherent contradiction at the centre of power from the perspective of the senatorial elite, which claimed a traditional right to status, influence and prestige, even if power were to be diminished and lost; and it was the senatorial elite that produced the great bulk of our literary sources. The perceived contradiction was stark: in the imperial household the emperor's slaves, freedmen and wives enjoyed a status, influence, prestige and even power that was the complete inverse of what they deserved and of what tradition demanded they should receive.

From a senatorial perspective, slaves, ex-slaves and women in the imperial household threatened to seize and direct imperial power for themselves, that is, to subvert the social and political order. From that traditionalist viewpoint, it was the proper task of the emperor to control his household and himself. The issue is a commonplace of the political analysis and historical writing produced under the emperors. It is regularly expressed in terms of the polarities of *licentia* (excessive, irresponsible freedom and self-indulgence) and *servitium* (slavery, often entailing flattery of the emperor, and the loss of prestige), between which the golden mean is *libertas* (true freedom, especially of senatorial debate, and the prestige that came with it). The stereotypical 'bad' emperor ruled with *licentia* and permitted it to his household, while imposing *servitium* upon the senatorial elite. Under the 'good' emperor, *libertas* could be achieved – or at least claimed.[10]

An understanding of this framework of political and historical analysis at Rome is vital to an appreciation of the agendas and outlooks of our sources on Britain and, indeed, on the empire at large. Britain offered a theatre for presenting and viewing the key issues that formed that framework – in particular, the power of slaves and women, and the social inversion that such power entailed. It would have been remarkable if Tacitus, for example, had not analysed Britain, that alternative world, in the same terms as he analysed Rome. But there is still more at stake than that. In writing about 'the other', Tacitus was also writing about 'the self': as his narrative moves back and forth between Rome and the provinces, there is a powerful echo. That may involve the presentation of opposites, of similarities or of evocative alternatives. In particular, where slaves and women appear in accounts of Britain, Roman readers are at once invited to consider them and their positions at Rome – indeed, they could hardly do otherwise. In approaching British queens, we must therefore maintain a permanent and vigilant awareness both of the evocations of queenship and of the agendas of our sources, for in writing Britain they are also writing Rome.

CARTIMANDUA

Strictly speaking, we know of only one queen in early Roman Britain: she is not the famous Boudica,[11] but Cartimandua. The observation derives from Tacitus' account, upon which we primarily rely: Tacitus several times terms Cartimandua a queen (*regina*) but never refers to Boudica in that way.[12] Where Boudica was no more than the wife of a king, Cartimandua seems to have ruled in her own right, albeit with consorts. Tacitus mentions her illustrious birth: she may have inherited her power and with it, perhaps, Roman citizenship.[13] If she had not inherited Roman citizenship, she would have received it from Claudius and had the right to call herself Claudia Cartimandua. She is mentioned first in the context of the year AD 51, but seems to have been in power for some years before that date.[14] Her people were the Brigantes; they formed a large tribal agglomeration in northern England, which seems to have been more a federation than a strongly unified tribe. The size of their territory is uncertain in detail, but was clearly very large in the mid-first century AD: it seems to have reached from the River Don in the south to north of Hadrian's Wall and to have stretched from coast to coast, in places at least.[15]

The sheer size and diversity of her realm may help to account for the unsteadiness of her grip on power. The Brigantes were a refractory grouping: about AD 48 substantial unrest among them, apparently incipient civil warfare, brought Ostorius Scapula back from the brink of the Irish Sea. Cartimandua is not mentioned by name, but she was almost certainly already in power, albeit unsteadily.[16] Meanwhile, at Rome, the Brigantes gained a reputation for awkwardness; hence they are cited ironically in the *Apocolocyntosis*, a satire on Claudius which was written early in the reign of Nero:

He [Claudius] ordered the Britons,
beyond the shores of the known sea,
and the Brigantes, blue with their shields,
to give their necks to Roman chains
and Ocean himself to tremble at
the new laws of the Roman axe.

(Sen. Apoc. 12.13–18)[17]

In the context of the satire, this passage must be read as something between an overstatement and a ludicrous untruth: wherever it is placed on that scale of irony, it indicates that the Brigantes were far from being under Roman control *c.* AD 54. A further point of interest is the apparent distinction drawn here between the Britons and the Brigantes: it is tempting to speculate that on at least some occasions the term 'Brigantes' was applied rather loosely to the Britons of the north and even the English Midlands, the 'Britanni' being their southern counterparts. Certainly, it is striking that two different authors are usually thought to have used the term 'Brigantes' in error:[18] perhaps the error is rather ours in taking the term always to denote a particular tribal agglomeration.

Of course, Tacitus shows little concern for analysis of the fundamental difficulties of the queen's position; rather, he offers moralizing narrative. For Tacitus, Cartimandua's difficulties arise not from the nature of her realm, but from her very queenship, and in particular from her sexual impropriety. For Tacitus the key factor is the queen's adultery. In that way, the historian is a prisoner of his historical context and outlook: Tacitus' Cartimandua is a reflection of Cleopatra, Semiramis and the like. In addition, it seems very likely that Berenice, daughter of Agrippa I, was of particular significance in the development of Tacitus' views on queens, for she had been an issue at Rome in Tacitus' own lifetime, while she features prominently in the extant portion of his *Histories* and doubtless figured still more prominently in the portion that we have lost. She and Cartimandua are the only two women described as 'queens' in Tacitus' extant narratives.[19] And Berenice had been the focus of sharp political rumour and debate under Vespasian, when her critics had presented her as a Cleopatra to the future Emperor Titus' Antony.[20] A queen, particularly a queen in difficulties, could hardly escape a moralizing treatment in a historiographical tradition which was prone to moralizing, and in a context where the power of women was a dominant concern in contemporary historical and political analysis.

The brief outline of Cartimandua's reign is uncontroversial. In AD 51 it was Cartimandua who handed over Caratacus to the Romans. She was married to one Venutius, an alliance which seems to have strengthened the allegiance of one section of the Brigantes. But that allegiance was lost when she replaced Venutius about AD 57 with Vellocatus, who is described as Venutius' armour-bearer. She lost her throne to Venutius in an armed coup in AD 69, when Roman forces saved her life; no doubt she spent her declining years under Roman protection, perhaps even in Rome, like Caratacus. Among the Brigantes, her capital has been located variously (e.g. at York and at Aldborough, Yorks.): if she had a single centre (which cannot be assumed), then archaeology suggests that Stanwick near Scotch Corner is its most likely location. It is interesting to observe the amount of Roman material, including roofing-tiles, that have been found even by incomplete excavation at the site: however, any direct connection between such items and allegiance to Rome remains hazy at best.[21] Even so, everything we know about

Cartimandua indicates her allegiance to Rome, which seems to have been a constant feature of her rule. Indeed, Tacitus' evidence tends to suggest that she depended upon Roman support for the retention of her throne, particularly *c.* AD 48 and 57, and for her salvation in AD 69.

Beyond the stark outline, there is much controversy: the central issue in dispute is the relationship of two passages in Tacitus' *Annals* and *Histories* respectively. But there is even more at stake. It is worth pausing to review Tacitus' statements on Cartimandua in full, not only to explore long-standing controversy, but also – and probably much more importantly – to illustrate the moralistic approach of the historian to her, her position and her reign.

Cartimandua enters history in the pages of Tacitus in the year AD 51, when she handed in chains to the Romans the British leader Caratacus, a thorn in their side for almost a decade.

> He [Caratacus], as adversity is largely unsafe, when he had sought the good faith of Cartimandua, queen of the Brigantes, was bound and handed over to the victors, eight years after the war in Britain had been begun.
>
> (Tac. *Ann.* 12.36)

It seems that she had been mentioned earlier in Tacitus' narrative in a lost section of the *Annals*: her consort, Venutius, seems to have been mentioned in that section.[22] That probability is more than a speculation of passing interest: any earlier account of her in the *Annals* will have done much to shape the reader's interpretation of her role in Book 12. Nevertheless, it is hard to see how her surrender of Caratacus can have been seen as anything but negative by sympathetic readers of Tacitus, however convenient it may have been for Roman interests. In the quoted passage, the queen's moral bankruptcy is highlighted by Tacitus' starkly stated polarity: Caratacus had sought her good faith (*fides*) and was handed over to the Romans for his pains. The reader is left to estimate her *fides* very low where British resistance is concerned, while excessive in regard to Rome. The point is sharpened by her use of bonds: bonds and chains were considered inappropriate for the detention of personages of high status, like Caratacus.[23] At the same time, the worth of Caratacus has been a feature of the preceding narrative, where he has been shown as a champion of prized *libertas* and an active leader of the British cause against *servitium* under Rome: the extended nature of that resistance is further indicated by Tacitus'

observation that Caratacus had been handed over eight years after
the invasion. By insulting such a man with bonds and handing him
over to the Romans, the queen has shown her own *servitium*, like
loyal Cogidubnus and the 'servile' kings who flocked to support
Vespasian in AD 69.[24] Caratacus' subsequent nobility of word and
deed serves further to show, by contrast, the subservience of the
queen. Although Cartimandua is Rome's friend, and Caratacus is
Rome's enemy, Tacitus encourages the reader to admire the *libertas*
of the latter and despise the *servitium* of the queen.

It is worth pausing to consider a rather similar incident earlier in
the same book of the *Annals*, where Tacitus puts a very different
gloss on events.[25] He recounts how Mithridates VIII, king of the
Crimean Bosporus, who had waged a war against Rome, took refuge
with another ruler, Eunones of the Aorsi. Mithridates too was
handed to the Romans by his host. And, like Caratacus, he displays
notable royal bravery when put on show by Claudius in Rome.
In their structure, the stories of Mithridates and Caratacus are strikingly similar. Tacitus' tendency to write in this fashion, presenting
different events in similar vein, has encouraged the idea of his 'self-
imitation'. In this instance, the great difference is Tacitus' treatment
of the roles of the two hosts involved, Eunones and Cartimandua.
We have seen that Cartimandua's surrender of Caratacus to Rome
is treated briefly, but with strongly censorious overtones. By contrast, Eunones' role is developed. He hears Mithridates' dignified
supplication and is 'thoroughly moved by the fame of the man, the
mutability of fortune and a supplication that was not ignoble'.[26]
Having received Mithridates warmly, Eunones writes to the
emperor urging that the suppliant-king should not be triumphed
over or executed. Claudius considers the situation and decides that
Mithridates should not suffer those indignities: the king is handed
over and put on show.

There is no such drama and no such correspondence in Tacitus'
account of Cartimandua's treatment of Caratacus, though the rest
of the story is much the same. An obvious explanation of the difference would be that nothing of that sort happened in the British case.
Perhaps Tacitus' information was not as detailed as for Mithridates'
case, though since both Caratacus and Mithridates lived on in
Rome, there is no overwhelming reason to suppose as much.
Another possibility is more a suspicion: could it be that the affair of
Caratacus gave Tacitus an opportunity to express his hostility to the
queen and to queens in general, without going into fictitious detail?

At the least, it seems not unlikely that the general Roman hostility to queens shaped Tacitus' perception and interpretation of Cartimandua's surrender of Caratacus: a queen cannot have behaved in the proper, measured manner of Eunones.

Cartimandua occurs next in the *Annals* in AD 57, when Tacitus recaps events since AD 51: here we meet Venutius for the first time in the extant books of the *Annals*, though he had evidently been treated earlier in a lost book:

> But after Caratacus had been captured, a man outstanding in his knowledge of military matters, Venutius, from the tribe of the Brigantes, as I mentioned above, and long faithful and defended by Roman arms when he held Cartimandua the queen in marriage, having soon fallen out with her and immediately gone to war, had entered hostilities even against us. But at first fighting was between themselves, and Cartimandua, with cunning arts, seized the brothers and relations of Venutius. By that her enemies were incensed, stimulated by disgrace, lest they should be subject to the rule of a woman; warriors, strong and picked for prowess, invaded her kingdom. The affair had been foreseen by us, and cohorts sent to help fought a fierce battle, which had an uncertain start but a happier ending. A similar result was fought out by the legion which was commanded by Caesius Nasica. For Didius, weighed down by old age and a great abundance of posts, used to hold it sufficient to attack and defend against the enemy through servants. These actions, though carried out by two propraetors over several years, I have brought together lest they be divided and forgotten: I return to chronological order.
> (Tac. *Ann.* 12.40)

Again, Cartimandua is shown in a close relationship with Rome, but at odds with a worthwhile Briton, Venutius. He has something in common with Caratacus: not only are both male, but they are also talented in military matters. In this case too the queen does not fight fair: she seizes Venutius' brother and relations 'with cunning arts' (*callidisque Cartimandua artibus*). Tacitus' imagining of the motivation of her enemies closely resembles his own view of queenship, as expressed in the *Germania*: they were driven, claims Tacitus, by a sense of disgrace through female rule, while Tacitus himself judges the German Sitones as having sunk even below slavery in accepting the rule of a woman.[27] For the first time in

Tacitus' extant narrative, Cartimandua's combination of female gender and royal power is made an explicit issue, central to the course of events. However, that issue is not very far below the surface in his account of her treatment of Caratacus and, particularly, in his mention of the 'cunning arts' she employed to capture Venutius' brother and relations. And, as we have seen, enslavement to a woman occupied a particular and familiar place in the classical lexicon of disgrace: Tacitus hardly needs to draw the issue to the attention of Roman readers, for whom the word 'queen' is enough to evoke it.

It is only thanks to prompt military support from Roman forces that Cartimandua retains her throne in AD 57, as apparently in the previous decade: she is not so fortunate in AD 69, when she appears for the first and last time in the extant portion of Tacitus' *Histories*:[28]

> In the context of that discord and much talk of civil war, the Britons roused their spirits, inspired by Venutius, who, in addition to his natural ferocity and hatred of the Roman name, was fired by personal animosity against Cartimandua the queen. Cartimandua was the ruler of the Brigantes, mighty in her illustrious birth. And she had increased her power after she captured King Caratacus by treachery and seemed to have decorated the triumph of Claudius. Thence came wealth and the luxury of prosperity. Venutius spurned (he had been her husband), she took his armour-bearer Vellocatus as her husband and her consort. Her house was immediately shattered by the outrage: the husband had the passion of the tribe, the adulterer had the queen's lust and cruelty. So Venutius, having gathered support and with the simultaneous defection of the Brigantes themselves, took Cartimandua to the very brink of disaster. Then help was sought from the Romans. And our cohorts and cavalry, after uncertain fighting, managed to extricate the queen from danger: the kingdom was left to Venutius, warfare to us.
>
> (Tac. *Hist.* 3.45)

Superficial similarities have encouraged the view that this passage is somehow a doublet of *Annals* 12.40.[29] However, that is to ignore the fundamental differences between the two passages: for example, the depiction of Venutius, the queen's fate and the mention of Vellocatus. More important, it is also to misconceive the manner of

Tacitus' writing: comparison of his accounts of Mithridates and of Caratacus respectively has already illustrated his style, his so-called 'self-imitation'. Such similarities as have been noted between *Histories* 3.45 and *Annals* 12.40 arise from the fact that the former passage reprises, as summarized background to the events of AD 69, the events of the 50s AD which Tacitus was later to relate in the *Annals*.

The Cartimandua of the *Histories* is painted still more darkly than the queen of the *Annals*. Her surrender of Caratacus is described as her capture of him by treachery. Venutius is driven by animosity against the queen, in addition to his own hatred of Rome (his earlier pro-Roman stance is not mentioned). That is, the queen is made to bear much of the responsibility for Venutius' onslaught. Moreover, it is the queen's alienation of her tribe that contributes significantly to Venutius' success. Although Venutius is an enemy of Rome, he is presented as morally in the right: he is her husband, whom she has spurned. Worse, she takes an adulterous lover, Vellocatus. Worse still, Vellocatus was her husband's subordinate. The adulterous pair have only the queen's lust and cruelty to support them. Finally and belatedly, Roman help is sought: the queen is saved, but Rome has gained nothing but an enemy and war to come. Throughout this passage, it is the queen's immorality that predominates – her treachery, her adultery, her lust and her cruelty. Tacitus and his readers would expect as much from a queen.

However, we should strive to see beyond the moralizing value-judgments of Tacitus. Cartimandua had done Rome a great service through the middle of the first century AD, though Tacitus would take that as typical of her *servitium* and perhaps also as a feature of her cunning. But the Brigantes were not an easy people to rule and Cartimandua's difficulties with Venutius, which Tacitus couches in personal and moralistic terms, may well have been symptomatic of a broader unrest in her extensive and heterogeneous realm.

After her escape in AD 69, Cartimandua's fate is beyond our knowledge. A fragmentary inscription from Chester, which may mention a woman, has been taken to refer to her: it has been suggested that she lived out her days there. We may be confident that Cartimandua enjoyed a privileged retirement, like other client rulers with similar histories, but there is nothing to connect her with Chester.[30] It is just as likely that she retired to Italy, even Rome, where she might have seen Caratacus again. Since she

was well established as queen by AD 51, she was probably dead by
AD 100.

BOUDICA

Where Tacitus' Cartimandua is a tool of *servitium* and proponent
of *licentia*, his Boudica is a victim both of *servitium* under Rome
and of Roman *licentia*, against which she is a champion of barbarian
and specifically British *libertas*. In that sense, the two women are
presented as opposites: while Cartimandua is shown very much as a
queen, Boudica is presented not as a queen, but as a woman. Accordingly, in Tacitus' narrative, Boudica escapes the very negative asso-
ciations of queenship and gains the accolade which Tacitus is
prepared to bestow upon women who are driven to resist oppression and to provide men with an example of how they too should
behave. We may compare his extended account of the bravery under
torture of the freedwoman Epicharis in the context of the Pisonian
conspiracy of AD 65. Tacitus concludes:

> A freedwoman offered a rather fine example under extreme
> duress in protecting those with whom she had no connection
> and whom she hardly knew, when men who were noble and
> Roman knights and senators, untouched by torture, each
> betrayed their nearest and dearest.
>
> (Tac. *Ann.* 15.57)[31]

Tacitus' Boudica has more in common with his Epicharis than with
his Cartimandua. That simple observation is fundamental, for
Tacitus' narrative constitutes the basis for the great bulk of modern
accounts of Boudica.

Like the Brigantes, the Iceni had caused Ostorius Scapula a
problem *c.* AD 48. They had been led to rise up by his attempt to
disarm suspect Britons and to establish a new and more advanced
group of camps. Hitherto, they had come willingly into alliance
with Rome, without battle and defeat: their ruler was doubtless
among the eleven whose surrender Claudius claimed to have
received at Camulodunum.[32] Now they were the first to resist
Ostorius' measures, inspiring neighbouring peoples to join them –
but to no avail, for the uprising was swiftly crushed.[33] Boudica's
name is not mentioned in Tacitus' account of these events, but that
should not surprise us: nor is that of her husband, King Prasutagus.

32   33

Figure 32 Silver coin of Prasutagus (obverse): recently discovered hoard, south-west Norfolk.

Figure 33 Silver coin of Prasutagus (reverse): recently discovered hoard, south-west Norfolk.

It is not until the eve of the revolt of AD 61 that Prasutagus and his family are first mentioned in the extant books of Tacitus. There, the king is described as 'famous for his long-standing prosperity'.[34] He was doubtless ruling the Iceni before the turbulence of AD 48, which may have been directed as much against him as against the Romans, rather as in the case of Cartimandua c. AD 57. Also like Cartimandua, Prasutagus had evidently prospered in his relationship with Rome. It is likely enough that both received subsidies to reinforce their control of their peoples: from the Roman perspective this was money well spent. His coinage displays a new Romanness: by contrast with previous coins of the Iceni, the coins of Prasutagus which survive present his Romanized head on the obverse, with an unusually full Latin legend. There can be no real doubt that Prasutagus held Roman citizenship, which provided a legal basis for his bequest to Nero. And a grant to Prasutagus will have been accompanied by a grant to his wife, Boudica, if she did not possess it already.[35]

Tacitus' account of the famous revolt begins with Prasutagus' will, by which, we are told, he made the emperor Nero joint heir with his two daughters. The nature of the division is not at all clear. Tacitus is usually taken to mean that Nero was to receive half the kingdom, and his daughters together the other half, but other interpretations are possible. For example, Nero may have been appointed as guardian of Prasutagus' daughters, or he may have been appointed as heir to the kingdom, with the king's daughters as legatees: either possibility would give a new turn to our understanding of Tacitus' narrative. At any rate, the royal practice was not

133

new: such wills had a long tradition in Rome's relations with kings, from the second century BC if not earlier. They seem to have been made when a king did not have a son to whom he wished to leave his kingdom: we may be sure that Prasutagus had only daughters.[36] At the same time, the making of a will – if we take Tacitus at his word – in itself constitutes a further illustration of Prasutagus' Romanness. Further, the rationale which Tacitus gives him is not only very Roman, but also redolent of Roman political ideology under the Principate. Prasutagus had made the will, Tacitus claims, 'thinking that by such subservience both his kingdom and his household would be far from injury'.[37] It is only under bad emperors that parents find it necessary to include the emperor in their wills.[38] In that sense, Prasutagus' rationale in the *Annals* constitutes an indirect assault in the Tacitean narrative upon Nero and perhaps upon Roman imperialism in general. It is also replete with the grim irony that Tacitus favoured.

Prasutagus' intention was not only disappointed: it was completely subverted. As often, Tacitus uses issues of social status to sharpen his emotive point: the kingdom falls into the hands of mere centurions, while the household falls to slaves: both are ravaged, as if they have been captured. Once again, surrender is treated like conquest: we may compare Claudius' reception of Caratacus. It is at this point that Boudica is first mentioned in the extant books of the *Annals*: it is unlikely that she had been mentioned in the earlier lost section. Her importance hitherto has been negligible, for it is striking that she is not named as a beneficiary under her husband's will: her daughters are to inherit, not she.

When Tacitus' readers first meet Boudica she is not a queen, but a wife (*uxor eius*) and a mother of high status: that is, by the traditional norms of Roman society, a decent woman. The fact that she is not raped and her daughters are would lead the reader to imagine her as at least mature in age: her reported speech later implies her 'old age'.[39] Of course, she is also a barbarian, but hardly less a decent woman for that. In any case, at this point Tacitus' narrative does not encourage readers to consider her as a barbarian. It is her propriety, further supported by the rather Roman behaviour of her husband in making his will, that renders her flogging and the rape of her daughters so insupportable an outrage. Their abuse is all the more intolerable because it is treatment that is completely at odds with their royal status, and because it is meted out by their social inferiors: Tacitus states that the household was ravaged by slaves.

The physical abuse of slaves by those of high status usually lay within the bounds of toleration of Roman morality, depending upon cause and context, but the reverse was revolution, the destruction of society itself, and particularly where the high-status victims have behaved with complete propriety. The issue of status is less obvious and less important to modern sensibilities, but it was fundamental to Roman conceptions of justice, wherein inequality before the law was the norm in theory and in practice, and wherein those of high status could expect to avoid corporal punishment even when they were found guilty of a major misdemeanour.[40] Only a few chapters later in Tacitus' narrative the issue is explored again in the context of Rome itself, where the city prefect, Pedanius Secundus, is murdered by his slave, and where the fear of slaves' subversion of the social order is made explicit in the expansive context of a senatorial debate. Throughout Tacitus' writing there is a persistent, artful and multi-faceted interaction between events at the centre and at the periphery respectively: the student of Britain should avoid the temptation to excerpt.[41]

Other relations of the king were made slaves, says Tacitus: again, social inversion. At the same time, the rich are expropriated, the standard centrepiece of classical conceptions of revolution. When the British resist they are, of course, taking up arms against Rome, but they are also fighting for key Roman values, which the agents of Roman imperialism and their imperial master have not only abandoned but inverted. Tacitus has them resist not through some wild irrationality, but in response to *contumelia* and the fear of still worse when they have been brought firmly under direct Roman rule: in that sense too British resistance is rational and, even in the terms of Roman morality, just. The Iceni are joined by the Trinovantes and 'those others not yet broken by *servitium*' in the resurrection of *libertas*.[42] They have suffered *licentia* on top of that of the veterans settled at Camulodunum, who had also been indulging in expropriation and had treated the Britons overtly as slaves. Tacitus invites his readers to appreciate how the temple of the divine Claudius at Camulodunum looked to the Britons to be 'a citadel of eternal despotism', while Britons were given the superficial honour of priesthoods which drained them of their wealth. Finally, the corruption and impropriety of Roman behaviour is underlined by the failure of Roman commanders to anticipate trouble by building defences for the colony, abandoning utility in favour of decoration.

It is the imperial procurator, Decianus Catus, whom Tacitus makes primarily responsible for the British uprising: 'his greed had driven the province to war'.[43] As imperial procurator, Catus had the task of managing the financial aspects of the annexation of the Iceni, and of overseeing taxation within the province: according to Tacitus, he had been at best an over-zealous agent of his imperial master. Dio adds further information: he claims that Catus demanded the return of sums which Claudius had given to the leading Britons, no doubt including Prasutagus, who, like Cartimandua, had been rich as a friend of Rome.[44] Catus' title conveys his role to a Roman audience,[45] but Tacitus' account of his actions invites no sympathy with his position. His response to Camulodunum's request for help is quite inadequate: when the colony falls through incompetence, as predicted by supernatural happenings, and the Ninth Legion is routed, its infantry slaughtered, Catus runs away in terror across the Channel to safety in Gaul. Tacitus leaves his Roman readers with scant room for doubt as to where justice lies in the outbreak of British rebellion: while the Britons have behaved in the best traditions of Roman morality, the Romans – with possible exceptions – have broken those very traditions.

It is only as the rebellion unfolds that moral judgments become less clear-cut. After the flight of the odious Catus, Tacitus brings to the fore the governor himself, Suetonius Paulinus:[46] now the Roman cause is guided rationally and with 'remarkable steadiness' (*mira constantia*), for Paulinus is stalwart under pressure from the Britons and from emotional appeals on his own side. Moreover, by contrast with Catus, the governor is untainted by the abuse of Prasutagus' will: he was far away in Anglesey, engaged in the virtuous business of warfare. His absence might be thought culpable, but Tacitus does nothing to suggest the view. Rather, in Tacitus' account, it is with the return of Suetonius Paulinus that the Romans again become Roman.[47] Now too the Britons of Tacitus' narrative show that for all the justice of their cause and the propriety of their behaviour at first, they are 'enemies' and 'barbarians', as Tacitus now terms them.[48] Now it is the Britons who set upon the old and female. It is they who loot easy pickings rather than engage in proper and necessary warfare. It is they who inflict inappropriate punishment, rejecting the norms of civilized warfare. The Romans under Suetonius Paulinus have regained the moral high ground, while the British have descended to the level of a Catus.

Throughout the narrative of the uprising to this point, Boudica has been notable by her absence: once flogged, she is not mentioned again until the crucial battle in which Suetonius puts an end to the rebellion. Tacitus' account of that final battle begins with the familiar polarity of Roman rational intelligence on the one hand, and seething barbarian emotion on the other. Suetonius chooses a favourable site for his limited but well-organized and disciplined forces; by contrast, the Britons are said to leap about in their disorganized droves, bringing (in their foolishness) their wives to witness the expected victory from carts set around the edge of the battlefield.

It is at this point that Boudica recurs in the narrative. She has not been directly implicated in the British descent into barbarism and retains her personal moral superiority. Tacitus gives her a speech which focusses the attention of his readers upon the origins of the rebellion and the issues at stake:

> Boudica, in a chariot, bearing her daughters before her, as she came to each people, stated that the Britons were accustomed to fight under the leadership of women, but that at that moment she was not a woman of great ancestry who had lost her realm and wealth, but was one among many who had lost their liberty and who was taking vengeance for her beaten body and the sullied honour of her daughters. She said that the Romans' lusts had reached the point that they did not leave bodies, not even old age or virginity, unpolluted. She said that the gods of just vengeance were with them: that a legion had fallen when it dared to fight, while the remnants skulked in camp or looked for an escape. She claimed that these would not even bear the din and battle-cries of so many thousands, let alone their onset and combat: if they were to assess the forces involved and the causes of war, they would see that this was the battle in which they must stand victorious or fall. That was a woman's decision, she said: the men might live and be slaves.
>
> (Tac. *Ann.* 14.35)

We cannot know whether Boudica did indeed course through the ranks in her chariot, displaying her violated daughters and speaking in these terms. However, the epic overtones of her action are striking: not for the first time in Britain, we may recall Homer, Homeric chariots and Homeric rallying-cries.[49] And those rallying-cries are not only distinctly Roman in content and turn of phrase, but are also closely balanced in Tacitus' narrative by the corresponding speech of Suetonius Paulinus. The latter tells his men to ignore the noises of the barbarians, to see that they include a lot of women and that numbers are not everything. Earlier in the *Annals*, Tacitus had had a conservative senator stress that it is in barbarian armies that women are to be found; their dangerous influence should be kept out of the Roman army.[50] Now Paulinus concludes with instructions for the battle, while Tacitus describes the powerful effect of his words upon the confidence of his troops, whose experience is duly stressed.

Boudica's speech encapsulates Tacitus' presentation of events and serves to presage the failure of the uprising. Her recollection of the outrages against herself and her daughters, together with her call to *libertas*, are all well and good: the reader 'knows' them to be true, having already been given the narrative of these very events. But her judgment is patently awry: the reader has seen enough of Suetonius Paulinus' careful choice of battlefield to think that his forces will offer a resistance that is much stiffer than Boudica encourages her troops to expect. Suetonius' speech and his experienced soldiers' reaction immediately confirm the reader's suspicion. Tacitus' Boudica has a just cause, but one which has perhaps already been pursued too far, beyond the moral parameters of proper vengeance. She shows great bravery, but it is a bravery without disciplined thought: such was the stereotype of barbarian courage, lacking any rational underpinning.[51]

And she is a woman, a point which Tacitus has her stress at the beginning and end of her speech. She hardly needs to tell the Britons that they are accustomed to being led to war by a woman, though the Roman reader is fascinated by the possibility: though a wife and mother, she evokes also the Amazon.[52] However, it is her concluding sentence that sharpens the point, bringing together the interrelated issues of gender and freedom: this woman, for all her shortcomings, stands for freedom or death, where men may prefer life and slavery. Again, the echoes of Roman internal politics are loud indeed: elsewhere Tacitus tends to suggest that the choice need not be so stark, that at least for a member of the Roman elite a life of dignity can be lived even under a tyrannical regime.[53] In that light, Boudica's closing sentiment may look less admirable than it has often seemed, all the more so when death to no purpose is what follows.

Roman tactics and technique cancel the overwhelming numerical superiority of the undisciplined Britons. The ultimate irony is that the Britons suffer still heavier casualties than might have been taken, because the carts that were signs of their false confidence in victory served only to impede their escape in defeat. The Romans gained a famous victory, akin to great victories of the past. Boudica ended her life with poison, we are told, like Cleopatra: no doubt, no one knew for sure, but Tacitus considered poison more appropriate to her gender than the sword which was chosen at the same time by the errant Roman camp-prefect, Poenius Postumus. We may contrast Dio's version, where she dies of illness.[54]

It is all too easy to sympathize with the predicament of Tacitus' Boudica and to admire her guts, but we are left also to consider the nature of her achievement. In short, she had achieved nothing beyond a grand gesture, which had brought death upon her and many thousands of the Britons, not to mention Romans. Her resistance to the regime of Nero was no more effective than that of Thrasea Paetus and the like, about whom Tacitus voices a particular suspicion only a few chapters later in his narrative:[55] even Catus had escaped scot-free, as far as we are told, save for the historian's condemnation of his memory. The futility of Boudica's gesture, and indeed of the more widespread resistance of which it was part, is made apparent by the narrative that follows her suicide. Nothing significant has changed:[56] Catus is replaced by another procurator, whom Tacitus presents as hardly more moral, one who placed the public good second to his personal schemes, not least against the hero of the hour, Suetonius Paulinus.[57]

The futility of Boudica's stance against *servitium* is finally hammered home to the reader by Tacitus' conclusion to his narrative of events in Britain in the year AD 61. When Catus' successor, Julius Classicianus, writes to Nero against Suetonius Paulinus, the emperor's response proclaims the scale of the problem with which Boudica had sought unwittingly to engage. Archly, Tacitus relates how Nero sent a freedman, Polyclitus, to settle the dispute between the governor and the procurator and to restore order among the Britons:

> Therefore, to examine the state of Britain was sent one of the freedmen, Polyclitus, bearing Nero's great hope that by his authority not only could concord be engendered between legate and procurator, but the rebellious attitudes of the bar-

Figure 34 Tomb-monument of C. Julius Classicianus.

barians could be calmed in peace. Nor was Polyclitus at a loss in being a burden to Italy and Gaul as he processed with his enormous entourage; when he had crossed Ocean, his progress brought terror to our soldiers too. But to the enemy he was a laughing-stock: among them the flame of liberty still burnt and the power of freedmen was not yet known. They were astonished that a general and an army which had won so great a war took orders from slaves.

(Tac. *Ann.* 14.39)

Tacitus liked to describe barbarian innocence of the power of slaves and freedmen:[58] since, in Roman eyes, barbarians functioned

140

close to nature, their innocence of the phenomenon illustrated and supported its artificiality and aberrance. For all Boudica's gesture, not only Britons, but also their conquerors, are ruled by the servile. When the Britons laugh, they show their liberty, but they also show an ignorance which, however admirable in some respects, illustrates the hopelessness of their position. Tacitus was not the first historian to indicate ignorance by laughter: Herodotus is particularly fond of the strategy.[59] Nor was Tacitus the last to explore the grim humour of freedman-power in the British arena: Cassius Dio claims that when Aulus Plautius' army would not follow him and invade Britain in AD 43, it was the arrival of the imperial freedman Narcissus, and his attempt to address them from the general's tribunal, that shamed them into obedience to Plautius, mocking Narcissus with the cry 'Io, Saturnalia!'[60]

However, Dio presents a very different Boudica. He says nothing of her flogging, or of her daughters' rape. Indeed, he omits all mention of her daughters: she is not presented as a mother, by contrast with Tacitus' account. Nor is she a wife: Prasutagus finds no place in Dio's version. Instead, Dio's Boudica is a ruling queen; to that extent, she is closer to Tacitus' Cartimandua than to his Boudica. In other words, Dio invites none of the sympathy that Tacitus evokes for Boudica. Rather, Dio's Boudica is a monstrous figure.

In Dio's account, her gender is immediately identified as a central issue:

> While this was played out in Rome, a terrible catastrophe occurred in Britain: two cities were sacked, 80,000 Romans and provincials were killed and the island was alienated from us. However, all this was inflicted upon them by a woman, a further reason for their deepest shame.
>
> (Dio 62.1.1)

The causes of the British uprising are entirely financial in Dio's account: Boudica is not a victim, driven to justified vengeance, so much as the principal agitator:

> But the one who had especially aroused them and persuaded them to go to war against the Romans, adjudged worthy of their command and of the generalship of the whole war, was Boudica, a British woman of royal stock and with a mind greater than a woman's. For she gathered a force of about 120,000 and ascended the tribunal, erected in the Roman

141

fashion. She was very tall of body, very grim to look upon and most terrifying in her gaze. In addition, she had a harsh voice, with hair down to her hips which was very thick and tawny; she wore a large torc of gold and a tunic of many colours, with a thick cloak fastened over it. Such was her standard dress. But at that time she had also taken a spear, so that she could use this too to strike universal awe.

(Dio. 62.2.2–4)

She is a woman but not a woman. Psychologically, she is like a man. Physically too she is like a man: she is the size of a man, with the voice of a man, and she inspires terror, all the more so when wielding the weapon of a man. By contrast, Tacitus had offered no description of Boudica and, in presenting her as wife and mother, had done nothing to problematize her gender. As in Tacitus' version, Dio's Boudica is given an extended speech centred upon the theme of freedom and slavery, but the nature of Roman oppression is now identified essentially in terms of taxation. Dio has her speak at the beginning of the uprising, before the sack of Camulodunum; he appends a portrait of her as a prophetess, suggesting a magical dimension to her power such as might be expected of such a queen as Dio makes her:

With these words, she loosed a hare from a fold of her robes as a form of prophecy. And when it ran on the side they consider auspicious, the whole mass of them shouted in delight, while Boudica raised her hand to the sky and said, 'I thank you, Andraste, and invoke you, woman to woman: I do not rule the burden-bearing Egyptians like Nitocris, nor the merchant Assyrians like Semiramis (for we have learnt of these from the Romans), nor indeed the Romans themselves, as did Messalina and then Agrippina and now Nero (who has the name of a man but is in fact a woman: the proof is that he sings, plays the lyre and preens himself). No, I rule British men, who do not know farming or crafts, but who know all about warfare and who hold women and children and all else in common, so that women too have the same bravery as men. Therefore, as the queen of such men and such women, I pray to you and ask for victory, salvation and freedom from men who are insolent, unjust, insatiable and impious – if it is right to call them men when they bathe in warm water, eat manufactured dainties, drink unmixed wine, anoint themselves with

142

myrrh, sleep on soft cushions with young boys and grown men and are enslaved to a lyre-player – and a bad one at that. Let Lady Domitia Nero no longer queen it over you and me! Let her do her singing as mistress of the Romans (for they deserve to be slaves to such a woman, after putting up with her tyranny so long). As for us, Mistress Andraste, may you be our leader, alone and always!'

(Dio. 62.6.4–5)

Dio's strategy is as clear as it is clumsy. His Boudica claims to be more a man than her counterpart, the Roman emperor Nero, who constitutes the climax of a list of female rulers. Evidently uncomfortable with Boudica's classical learning on the subject of Nitocris and Semiramis, key models of queenship, Dio has her explain how she and her audience have come to know about them. At the same time, Boudica's speech makes explicit the echoes which we heard in Tacitus' account between the issue of female rule in Britain on the one hand, and that of female rule in the imperial household at Rome: Dio's Boudica perceives Messalina and Agrippina as among her sister-rulers.

Dio's readers might readily concur with her judgment of Nero, but her presentation of Roman femininity and of the superior masculinity of the Britons over Romans (and Egyptians and Assyrians) is more problematic: Nero is not a typical Roman; nor does his position imply general Roman weakness. Ultimate defeat at Roman hands illustrates her mistake. As with Tacitus' Boudica, the hard and courageous barbarian has a point, but she is at fault nevertheless in her reasoning and judgment.

However, Dio presents Boudica's death in a very different way from Tacitus. Whereas Tacitus' very female and proud Boudica took poison in defeat, as becomes a woman of dignity,[61] Dio's manly Boudica is ready to fight on after defeat, while the Britons regroup. Dio's Boudica is only stopped by chance illness, from which she dies.[62] Significantly, it is her death that puts a stop to the uprising. Dio, far more than Tacitus, makes the British uprising very much the revolt of Boudica: he identifies her as the principal instigator, he gives much space to her description and her speeches, and he has the Britons feel themselves properly defeated only when Boudica has died and been accorded a splendid burial.

It is orthodox to dismiss Dio's account as largely worthless, though the vividness of his description of the appearance of Boudica

has led some to exempt her portrait from the general stricture and
to accept it as in some sense accurate. We may speculate about the
source(s) used by Dio: Cluvius Rufus could well have been among
them.[63] However that may be, the reason for the neglect of Dio's
version is, of course, Tacitus: his account in the *Annals* is preferred
at the expense of Dio's. No doubt Dio's description of Boudica's
appearance would also have been cast aside if Tacitus had offered a
description of her that might have taken its place. Indeed, it is significant that Tacitus does not give a garish picture of Boudica: as we
have seen, he stresses her more Roman image, as wife and mother.
By and large, students of Roman Britain feel themselves at home
with Tacitus, not least with the fact that his text is in Latin. By
contrast, Dio not only wrote in Greek but also constitutes a less
familiar figure for many. More substantially, Tacitus was closer in
time to the events he purports to describe: in the case of Boudica,
Tacitus wrote some fifty years after her death, while Dio wrote
some 150 years after it. In addition, few indeed would question the
fact that Tacitus has produced an account which is far more sophisticated and intelligent than that of Dio. But, as we have seen, it
would be facile in the extreme to treat artful Tacitus as no more
than a reporter of events: for Tacitus, as for Dio, Boudica provides
an opportunity to make points, to construct and to illustrate a
social, political and historical analysis. In particular, Dio's account
has the virtue of demonstrating how differently Tacitus might have
depicted Boudica – as another Cartimandua, perhaps.

Moreover, we have the opportunity to compare two accounts of
Boudica by Tacitus himself, for she also figures significantly in the
Agricola, composed some twenty years before the *Annals*. It is salu-
tary to observe that the Boudica of the *Agricola* bears scant resem-
blance to the Boudica of the *Annals*; indeed, she seems to have more
in common with Dio's Boudica. In the *Agricola* Tacitus has the
Britons grumble about their loss of liberty and their sufferings at
the hands of the Romans, but neither the Iceni in general nor
Boudica in particular are identified as the seat of the revolt as in the
Annals. Rather, British resentment is depicted as widespread:
Boudica is mentioned not in the role of a victim, as later in the
Annals, but in the role of a female and royal leader:

> Driven by the exchange of these arguments and the like, they
> all took up arms, with Boudica, a woman of royal stock, as
> their leader, for they make no distinction on grounds of

gender in matters of command.

(Tac. *Agr.* 16.1)

There is no hint of the wronged wife and mother of the *Annals*, no mention of her flogging, the rape of her daughters, or Prasutagus' will. Significantly, Tacitus here draws attention instead to her royalty, though he stops short of describing her as a queen. The grumbles of the Britons receive no special validation from Tacitus: they are commonplaces, such as Tacitus elsewhere describes as 'the accusations usually made against great empires'.[64] Later in the *Agricola*, in the famous speech of Calgacus, her forces are character-ized as Brigantes, not Iceni;[65] while her successes are said to have included the conquest of at least one Roman camp, an encounter which the Britons are said to have avoided in the version of the *Annals*. Rather than dismiss the Boudica of the *Agricola*, with Dio, as inaccurate, it is more instructive to consider the fragility and non-essentiality of the version in the *Annals*. At the same time, we must also consider the authorial strategies that form the agenda of the *Agricola*, which will be treated in the final chapter.

In both Tacitus and Dio, Boudica embodies issues of gender and power. Dio's Boudica is not Tacitus' Cartimandua, but she has much in common with her. She is different because she is not inspired by illicit sex and because she seems to have a capacity to rule beyond that of Cartimandua's unstable regime. However, she is a very masculine woman, who therefore and almost paradoxically is seen as prone to promiscuity, for such is her power and the male-ness of her potential. In the *Annals*, Tacitus' Boudica is very much a decent woman, driven to a brave gesture that is both a challenge to men and an ill-judged act of futility; even amid the outrages com-mitted by the Britons, she retains substantial sympathy as an abused wife and mother, hardly tainted by the negative images of the queen. As a loyal wife and mother, her sexuality is channelled in traditional and acceptable fashion; she is not an uncontrolled adulteress like Cartimandua or Messalina, or a man-eater like Dio's Boudica.

To seek historical reality behind or beneath these images of powerful women in Britain is largely to miss the point. The charac-terizations of Tacitus and Dio tell us little about Boudica or Carti-mandua, but they speak volumes about these authors' attitudes to women in power. The distinction is fundamental to any reading of the ancient historians of Britain and, indeed, of the frontier in general. Certainly, historians like Tacitus and Dio were concerned to present accounts of Britain and British society that were 'true', but their truths were functions of their broader world-views. Dio's account of Boudica's invocation of Andraste provides the most explicit testimony of the dominance of the centre of power over the periphery in the concerns of historians. Their analyses and constructions of British history are guided overwhelmingly by their preoccupations with the issues of Roman society and politics at the centre. Of course, there is a significant element of feedback, for historians' awareness of the issues of the periphery also impinged upon their analyses and constructions of the centre. However, the priority of the centre is overwhelming: views of Messalina and Agrippina did much more to shape treatments of the powerful women of Britain than vice versa.

At the same time, the poetry of Propertius offers one among many illustrations of the ideological baggage which Tacitus and Dio brought to their characterizations of Boudica and Cartimandua. These accounts cannot be interpreted satisfactorily only in the insular context of Britain: as Dio's Boudica again makes explicit and as Propertius would have known, the likes of Semiramis and Cleopatra constitute a traditional framework of ideas about queens within which any powerful woman – in Britain, Rome or elsewhere – was likely to be constructed.

9

AGRICOLA AND TACITUS, TRAJAN AND THE FLAVIANS

THE ALLURE OF BRITAIN

Under the Flavian emperors, from AD 69 to 96, the prestige of the conquest of Britain remained an object of imperial desire. The achievement of Claudius, the leitmotiv of his imperial propaganda during his reign, had been belittled by his successor. Indeed, the emperor Nero is said seriously to have considered withdrawing Roman forces from Britain altogether. Although we are told that he decided not to do so for shame that he might be thought to be undermining Claudius' reputation, the explanation is at best simplistic: Nero showed marked ambivalence towards Claudius' memory.[1] The Claudian conquest is duly mocked in the *Apocolocyntosis*, written under Nero by his principal adviser, Seneca: there was quite enough unrest in Britain under Nero to validate such mockery, not least the rebellion of Boudica itself, which has in turn been taken as the cause of Nero's rumination upon withdrawal.[2] However, Vespasian preferred to recall the Claudian conquest and to reinstate it as a success. To do so was in accordance with his broader tendency of rehabilitating Claudius in the face of Nero,[3] but in this case there was the additional advantage that he could himself be presented as a principal figure in Claudius' success in Britain.

Josephus, a historian close to the Flavians, made the Claudian conquest very much the achievement of Vespasian:

> The chaos of Nero's soul was revealed by his thoughts as he pondered to whom he might entrust the disturbed east, who would punish the revolt of the Jews and warn off both them and the similarly afflicted peoples around them. He could find only Vespasian to meet his needs, able to assume the mass of

147

so great a war, a man who had spent his life on campaign from boyhood, who had long since established Roman peace in the west, harried by the Germans, a man who by warfare had added to the empire Britain, hitherto unknown, whence he brought a triumph to Nero's father, Claudius, without the emperor's exertion.

(Jos. *Jewish War* 3.3–5)

The biographer Suetonius is more restrained, but he also makes much of Vespasian's role in Britain: he credits Vespasian not only with three engagements with the Britons, but also with the conquest of two very strong tribes, in addition to twenty towns and Vectis, the Isle of Wight, both under the command of Aulus Plautius and of Claudius himself.[4] We can only speculate on the nature of Fabius Rusticus' version of events in Britain; it was influential but has been lost.[5] However, Tacitus, who counted Fabius Rusticus among his sources, gives Vespasian a large place in Claudius' success at the expense of Aulus Plautius. Perhaps Tacitus was sensitive to Trajan's connections with Vespasian:[6]

The divine Claudius was the author of the great invasion task, crossing with legions and auxiliaries and taking Vespasian to share in the enterprise, which was the beginning of a destiny that was soon to come: tribes were conquered, kings were captured and Vespasian was shown to the fates.

(Tac. *Agr.* 13.3)[7]

As emperor, Vespasian is given further responsibility for Roman success in Britain: Tacitus says that once Vespasian recovered Britain, with the rest of the world, Roman generals were great, armies were outstanding and the hopes of the enemy were diminished.[8] After all, it was to be Vespasian who appointed Agricola as governor of Britain, while Tacitus himself began his career under that emperor.

Extraordinarily, Dio seems to have had Vespasian's son Titus display his daring military prowess when Vespasian was in a tight corner in Britain, though Titus was then still an infant. The mistake may illustrate the desperation of panegyrists to associate even Titus with the British adventure.[9] Alternatively, Dio or his source may have been misled by the presence in Britain of Vespasian's brother, Titus Flavius Sabinus, whom Dio mentions elsewhere as fighting beside Vespasian in Britain.[10] In any event, Titus served as a military

tribune in Britain, just possibly with Agricola.[11] When Titus celebrated the completion of the 'Flavian amphitheatre', the so-called
Colosseum, in AD 80, a Caledonian bear was sent into the arena to
rip out the entrails of a a crucified criminal.[12] By then Caledonia
was already in the news.

The Flavians sought to appropriate the glory of the conquest of
Britain, an enterprise that continued to excite the imagination
almost 150 years after Julius Caesar had shown the way. The distance between Julius Caesar and the Romans of Vespasian's reign
could be reckoned at the lifespan of a long-lived Briton:[13] it was
time perhaps to supersede Caesar and Claudius by completing the
conquest. As usual in Roman government, there was a substantial
element of reaction. As we have seen, the so-called rebellion of
Boudica had been revolt on a wide front, while the expulsion of
Cartimandua in the upheavals of AD 69 had left the mighty Brigantes
under a king markedly hostile to Rome: Vespasian inherited a substantial problem in Britain.

In AD 77 the Elder Pliny offered a view of the Roman position in
Britain on the eve of Agricola's governorship: 'in some thirty years
by now, Roman arms have not advanced knowledge of Britain
beyond the neighbourhood of the Caledonian forest' (Pliny *Hist.
Nat.* 4.102). Caledonia had become the objective, the remaining field
for excellence: while Caledonian creatures began to be displayed in
the arena, the name Caledonia began to appear in Latin literature.[14]
Soon after the publication of the *Natural History*, from a perspective in the reign of Domitian (AD 81–96), Statius imagined
Vettius Bolanus (governor of Britain, AD 68–71) as campaigning in
Caledonia, evidently in order to gratify Bolanus' son.[15] Also under
Domitian, another poet, Silius Italicus, describes Vespasian's
achievements in Britain in terms of Caledonia: he has Jupiter
prophesy:

> Thence the father will have unknown Thule conquered
> and into Caledonian groves will be first to bring armed columns:
> he will hold the Rhine at its banks and tireless will order the
> Africans,
> and palm-bearing Idumaea he will conquer in old age.
> He will not have the Stygian lakes and realms void of light,
> but the seat of the gods and honours amongst us.
>
> (Sil. Ital. *Pun.* 3.597–602)

149

Since the Jewish War is specifically described as an achievement of Vespasian's old age, the mention of Caledonia, and indeed Thule, has been taken as an exaggerated claim for the younger Vespasian's role in Britain with Claudius, though on that view the exaggeration would be substantial indeed.[16] So too the famous preface of another Flavian poet, Valerius Flaccus, here invoking Vespasian:

> and you who have greater fame of an opened
> sea, after Caledonian Ocean has borne your
> sails, having hitherto contemned the Phrygian Iuli.
>
> (Val. Flacc. *Argon.* 1.7–9)

Vespasian's fame, the poet claims, is greater than that of the subject of the poem, the Argonauts: they opened the Black Sea, while he opened up the Caledonian Ocean.[17] He also, stresses the poet, surpassed the Julii – especially Caesar – in sailing his ships upon an Ocean which had refused to tolerate them. As Silius states explicitly, Vespasian's penetration northwards is claimed as a major first.

Critics have been quick to observe that Vespasian seems to have come nowhere near Caledonia during his service with Claudius: his signal achievement seems to have been the conquest of the Isle of Wight. However, Vespasian's generals had done much more: quite apart from Statius' grand claim for Bolanus, Vespasian's appointee Agricola had not only sailed the Caledonian Ocean but also examined Thule, though his final conquest of Caledonia occurred in the early years of Domitian himself.[18] It seems that Silius Italicus presents an ongoing Vespasianic conquest which began with Claudius and proceeded into the reign of Vespasian, through the agency of others. Flavian claims of such a sort may have encouraged the rather startling later tradition that Claudius had brought the Orkneys under Roman suzerainty.[19]

Neither Silius nor Valerius Flaccus need be convicted of mindless exaggeration; rather, they accorded Vespasian the most dramatic and impressive of the Roman imperial achievements in Britain that could be claimed for him. Such embellishment was the craft of panegyrical poets. And Domitian could afford to give Vespasian credit for Britain: Silius Italicus explains the approach when he proceeds to stress that Domitian excelled even the achievements of his father Vespasian and brother Titus, not least by his own successes in the north.[20] Vespasian had a long-standing and strong role in the Roman conquest of Britain, which Flavian writers like Josephus strove to embellish further. Domitian did not seek to deny his father's achievements there, but, rather, saw them through. And Domitian did not seek to appropriate the glory of final success in Britain, as far as we know: his panegyrists are notably silent on his part in the conquest. It seems that his political strategy was rather to assert the greatness of his family's achievements and to proceed to claim the superiority of his own achievements even over them, as Silius has it. Accordingly, Domitian's campaign against the Chatti was claimed as more important than the conquest of Britain. As we shall see, that imperial stance not only helps an interpretation of the *Agricola* of Tacitus but also serves to account for the publication of both his *Agricola* and his *Germania* together in the aftermath of Domitian's assassination.

CALGACUS AND THE *AGRICOLA*

Tacitus' *Agricola* dominates any consideration of Flavian involvement in Britain. The centrepiece of the work is the battle at Mons Graupius and the exchange of speeches that precedes it between Calgacus the Caledonian and Agricola. The site of the battle need not detain us.[21] The figure of Calgacus may be no more than an invention, like, it seems, Juvenal's Arviragus, his 'contemporary', who is accorded the usual British chariot.[22] However, any adequate understanding of Tacitus' presentation of Calgacus and Agricola requires an analysis of the work as a whole. We cannot sensibly ask why Tacitus wrote the work, for we have no access to his psychology, but we may certainly identify its principal themes, structure and argument.

The *Agricola* has a well-defined frame, consisting of a three-chapter preface and a three-chapter conclusion.[23] As both preface and conclusion demonstrate, the work is certainly a biography,[24] but it is also much more than that label might suggest. The *Agricola* is intimately and explicitly engaged with the political issues of the late 90s AD, centred upon the transition of imperial power from Domitian through Nerva to Trajan. That transition is presented by Tacitus and others (notably his friend the Younger Pliny in his *Panegyricus* of AD 100) as the transition from slavery (*servitium*) under Domitian to freedom (*libertas*) under Nerva and Trajan.

Tacitus opens his preface with an assertion of the traditional place of exemplary biography in Roman society. So much is stressed from the first sentence on: 'To convey illustrious men's deeds and ways to later generations was the regular practice in the past'

(Tac. *Agr.* 1.1). The writing of biography is then associated with the doing of fine actions. Even autobiography was an accepted part of an upright life, claims Tacitus, and was not regarded as arrogance. However, current views require that he apologize for the narration of the virtues even of a dead man, he complains, when he might have launched an attack upon him without need for excuse. In this way Tacitus both announces that this is to be a laudatory biography and stresses the traditional propriety of such a work: it is a return to morality.

Tacitus proceeds with the politics of biography and starts to name names: he asserts that Rusticus' biography of Thrasea Paetus, and Senecio's biography of Helvidius Priscus, brought execution both to those authors and to their books, which were publicly burnt. The burning, he argues, was an attempt to destroy the voice of the Roman people, the *libertas* of the Senate and the moral conscience of humankind.[25] And that attempt was bolstered, he continues, by the expulsion of the profession of wisdom, and the exile of moral practice. Whereas the past saw the ultimate in *libertas*, we have seen the ultimate in *servitium*: silence was enforced, so that we were free neither to speak nor to hear. Memory has survived silence, but only because to be silent was possible and to forget was not.[26]

The missing name is also the principal figure in this section of the preface, the emperor Domitian. It was Domitian who executed Rusticus and Senecio and had their books burnt. It was Domitian who had recently sought to banish champions of moral thought and action. And it was Domitian, Tacitus suggests, who sought to impose silence. For the very essence of *libertas* was freedom of speech, not least in the Senate: silence was slavery. In presenting the suppression of laudatory biographies of good men as a practice of Domitian, Tacitus seeks further to validate his own laudatory biography of a good man. He associates himself with the cause of freedom, while he invites a comparison of his subject (as yet unannounced) with Paetus and Priscus. By writing he has spoken, albeit rather late.

He has been empowered by the accession of Nerva, he proclaims: spirit has returned and endurance is no longer required. Nerva has blended two things which were long alien to each other, the Principate and *libertas*, while Trajan is each day increasing the good fortune of the times. The body politic is undergoing a slow but steady cure after fifteen years of silence. In that context, Tacitus announces that he will speak, albeit in a voice unpractised and unsophisticated, in memory of former slavery and in testimony of present goods. He concludes the preface by naming his present subject: 'Meanwhile, this book is written in honour of Agricola, my father-in-law: with my declaration of filial duty it will either be praised or excused' (Tac. *Agr.* 3.3). Through the preface Tacitus has offered an artful justification of his work in terms of the traditional morality of the biographical genre. It is to be a work for the new regime against the old regime of Domitian, expressing and embodying the new regime's ideals and spirit: there is scope now for talent and morality and for writing about them. The *Agricola* testifies that silence has been replaced by speech, or so its author claims – no doubt to the satisfaction of Nerva and Trajan, however deserved.

The conclusion takes up the themes of the preface. Tacitus expatiates on Agricola's physical appearance, which accords with his inner goodness. Indeed, ancient thinkers had long accorded much significance to the function of a fine appearance as a tool of leadership, not least on the part of the good king.[27] Tacitus ponders the positive side of Agricola's early death: he had glory appropriate to a long life, he had had his fill of the key achievements that reside in the virtues, he died with his dignity untarnished, his reputation glowing and his relations and friends alive. In particular, by a premature death he had escaped the final bloody years of Domitian. His principal loss by an early death is identified as his missing this blessed age when he could have rejoiced in the sight of Trajan as *princeps*. Tacitus even claims that Agricola used to foretell this happy event in his hearing when engaged in auguries and prayer.[28]

In this way Tacitus leads his readers from Agricola to the comparison of the tyrannical Domitian and his beneficent successors. In a rousing and designedly emotional peroration, Tacitus proceeds to enumerate Domitian's victims and denounce their executions. He proclaims himself a participant in the slaughter and at the same time a victim of it who lived to tell the tale, one who had outlived his faculties in Domitian's fifteen years, as the preface has it.[29] Tacitus had lived, but under the malevolent and unreadable gaze of the tyrant Domitian, who could read his and his fellows' expressions.[30]

Agricola's good fortune resided, observes Tacitus, not only in the illustriousness of his life, but also in the timeliness of his death. Even in death, Tacitus suggests, Agricola had shown his moral superiority, as it were bestowing innocence upon the emperor by accepting his fate. Tacitus bemoans his absence from the death-bed, but suggests that the contemplation of Agricola's virtues is more appropriate than mourning: the proper tribute to Agricola, the proper act of filial duty, is to admire, praise and aspire to emulate those virtues. It is not the body of the man or his images that matter, but the shape of his mind. Tacitus concludes, finally:

> Whatever we have loved in Agricola, whatever admired, abides and will abide in the spirits of men, in the eternity of time, by the fame of his achievements. For oblivion has enveloped many men of the past, as if they had no glory or nobility. Agricola, recounted and conveyed to posterity, will live on.
>
> (Tac. *Agr.* 46.4)

Tacitus completes the work on the note with which he began it: Agricola's death is redeemed by his biography. Tacitus claims to have given him life beyond death and doubtless would be gratified indeed by the importance of his father-in-law and his *Agricola* to modern students of Roman Britain and Roman history in general.

Within this political and justificatory framework, Tacitus presents the life of his subject. However, it is a notably selective life. Of course, selection is fundamental to all writing, but Tacitus has chosen to say very little about Agricola's life before Britain and to give a similarly slight account of his life upon his return to Rome.[31] Tacitus has taken the authorial decision to make Britain the focus of his *Life*. His decision is so familiar to those who have spent time with the *Agricola* that it can easily be overlooked, taken as somehow natural, but it is no less striking for that – particularly so, when a principal distinction between biographical writing and historiography was the biographer's taste for the apparently trivial: wars and campaigns were more the stuff of full-blown history.[32] Small wonder that the *Agricola* has often been thought peculiar as a biography.

Space is a better guide than imagined intention. We cannot be confident in the author's intentions in writing a work, but we can measure the proportions of space that he sees fit to accord to particular subjects, topics and themes. And in the *Agricola* it is Britain that dominates the work, and more particularly Agricola's activities there. To ask why is not only reasonable but obligatory: what principles can be discerned in a process of selection that produced such a result?

Selection has been most severe in the few chapters given to Agricola's years before Britain. The few details of those many years that have escaped omission may offer a clue to the process of choice. At least a brief outline of his subject's family background was a firm requirement, but it could be sketched variously. Tacitus has chosen to focus upon Agricola's father as a man of virtue, known for his love of eloquence and wisdom. His virtues, says Tacitus, caused his death at the hands of the tyrannical Gaius, who had him executed when he refused to prosecute M. Silanus.[33] Agricola's mother is identified as a woman of special chastity: it was she who fostered Agricola's virtues and who, by his own account, warned him of the dangers of extremism in his concern with philosophy. His reason came to prevail and he achieved a balanced wisdom.[34] The outline conveys Agricola's innate virtue and the upright education of that virtue: it also sets him in a tradition of principled − but not flashy − resistance to imperial tyranny. The scene is set for Agricola's display of his own virtue against his own tyrant. A further detail is picked out for comment, consonant with Tacitus' broader outlook: it was in the refined yet simple atmosphere of Massilia that Agricola grew up. That is, the youth of Agricola was not corrupted by the evils of the capital.

After these scant details, Tacitus whisks his readers immediately to Agricola's activities in the provinces, and first in Britain. There, says Tacitus, he was singled out by Suetonius Paulinus, whom Tacitus treats positively elsewhere.[35] He avoided the standard pitfalls:

> Agricola did not loosely (as young men tend to do, turning military service into impropriety) or idly derive pleasures and furloughs from the rank of tribune and inexperience. Rather, he strove to know the province, to be known to the army, to learn from the experienced, to follow the best, to attempt nothing for the sake of boasting, to refuse nothing through fear, at the same time both anxious and eager to act.
>
> (Tac. *Agr.* 5.1)

The rebellion of Boudica brought glory to Suetonius Paulinus, but gave Agricola technique, experience and stimulus. It was at this point, says Tacitus, that Agricola conceived a desire for military glory against the spirit of the times, when eminence meant danger for those of good and bad repute alike. The reader is left to infer that Agricola's virtues were not cowed by the age of Nero, any more than the virtues of his father had been cowed by Gaius or than his would be at the hands of 'the bald Nero', Domitian.[36]

Britain, then, occupies a central place even in the few chapters that Tacitus accords Agricola's life before his governorship there: it is in Britain that his story begins. And, after a few words upon his marriage in Rome, Tacitus returns swiftly to the provinces. Now it is Asia, where Agricola is quaestor. His office was financial, while the province of Asia had a reputation for the corruption that it could inspire, as Cicero reminds his brother.[37] Tacitus reassures: Agricola was corrupted neither by the plum province nor by his greedy proconsul, keen to conspire in extortion.[38]

In Rome again, Agricola was inactive, even as tribune and then praetor. Tacitus credits him with the understanding that inactivity was wise under Nero: this was not simple idleness, but deliberate silence. Required to put on games, Agricola maintained a balance; he was no less proper when appointed by Galba to inquire into the misappropriation of gifts to temples. He showed no less propriety upon the murder of his mother. But he was soon abroad again, and again in Britain. Mucianus, for Vespasian, gave him command of the Twentieth Legion in Britain: it had been recalcitrant, but soon succumbed to Agricola's diplomatic regime.[39]

Tacitus stresses Agricola's respect for authority: he had the sense of hierarchy that traditional Roman morality required of the virtuous. Accordingly, when Agricola wished to adopt an aggressive stance in Britain, but Vettius Bolanus, his governor, preferred a more cautious strategy, Agricola conformed with the style of his superior, even though, as Tacitus has it, Agricola was right. When Bolanus' successor, Petilius Cerialis, arrived with a more active approach, Agricola's 'virtues had space for distinction'.[40] Even so, says Tacitus, Agricola always gave his governor the credit for his successes, avoiding envy and gaining glory.

Agricola's return to Rome is only mentioned as the moment of his adlection among the patricians by Vespasian. With scarcely a pause, Tacitus whisks the reader again to the provinces: Vespasian made Agricola governor of Aquitania, implying future consulship. Details are omitted; instead, and more important, Tacitus offers a broad characterization of the tenor of Agricola's first governorship. In so doing, he bestows the praise that the reader by now anticipates, and in a fashion determined by previous writing on governorship:

> Many believe that soldiers' characters lack subtlety, because rule in the camp carries no consequences and is blunter and

more summary, not requiring the skill of the forum. Agricola, with his natural foresight, behaved affably and justly though his subjects were civilians. He maintained a sharp distinction between business and leisure. When the responsibilities of the assize-courts demanded, he was serious, attentive and strict, yet more often merciful. When he had done his duty, he did not maintain the image of power: he had eschewed gloom, arrogance and greed. And in his case – a quality rare indeed – his affability did not diminish his authority, nor did his strictness diminish the affection that he evoked. To dwell upon the integrity and self-restraint of so great a man would be a slur on his virtues. As for fame, which even good men often court, he did not seek it by a display of virtue or by artifice: far from competing with colleagues, far from wrangling with procurators, in such matters he considered victory inglorious and defeat ignominious.

(Tac. *Agr.* 9)

Tacitus has rumour of Agricola's appointment in Britain overshadow his return from Aquitania. His consulship is hardly mentioned, save for his betrothal of his daughter to the author. Agricola is sent immediately after to Britain, having also been given a priesthood.[41]

These chapters on Agricola's life before his governorship of Britain contain a variety of details, but they are substantially devoted to the same theme. That theme, appropriate to the biographical genre, is the exercise of virtue, particularly in the variously demanding contexts of the provinces, and not least in Britain itself. Agricola excels outside Rome, away from imperial tyranny and engaged with the traditional concerns of the active Roman male, warfare and government, in which he has scope to display his virtues. Tacitus' account of Agricola's governorship in Britain is a lengthy demonstration of the enactment of those virtues at the pinnacle of power in a difficult and testing province.

Throughout, as in Aquitania, Agricola exemplifies the ideals of governorship which had been theorized by the end of the Republic. Their intellectual origins lay not only in traditional Roman morality, but also in Greek ideas about monarchy, as we saw in Chapter 2. Tacitus' Agricola embodies the 'good ruler'. The early chapters of the *Agricola* prepare readers for his presentation as such, briefly in peaceful Aquitania and then at length in troublesome

Britain. The *Agricola* is not simply a biography, but the biography of a sort of ruler: that fundamental point has been quietly acknowledged by those who have, quite rightly, seen Tacitus' *Agricola* as the heir of Isocrates' *Evagoras* and Xenophon's *Agesilaus*, not to mention the latter's *Cyropaedia*, a work beloved of Roman writers on rulership.[42] It is the issue of rulership that gives the biography much of its point, for the reader is invited to compare Agricola and Domitian as rulers, and perhaps to consider Nerva and Trajan in the light of that comparison.

Britain furnishes the realm over which Agricola can display his talents as a ruler. His regime there may be compared with Domitian's behaviour as ruler of the empire at large, of which Britain is both a counterpart and a microcosm. Britain remained, after all, another world, the other side of Ocean: in its case something of the ignorance of Caesar's day abided, or so the interested might claim. Tacitus stresses that it was only with Agricola's complete conquest of the island that a writer could offer a thoroughly reliable account of it; in that sense, Tacitus' disquisition on Britain is a claim to achievement by the author and his subject alike.[43] It is idle to object that Agricola's conquest was not complete: here and elsewhere, Tacitus conceives of his conquest as complete but immediately left aside,[44] for, as we shall see, his victory over the Britons at Mons Graupius is presented on both sides as the final act of British resistance to Rome, the last stand. It was Agricola, stresses Tacitus, who first had a fleet circumnavigate Britain and established that it was indeed an island: the Orkneys were discovered and conquered. Thule itself was viewed, 'farthest Thule', the stuff of fantasy.[45] By virtue of Agricola's conquest and Tacitus' writing, the terrain is given a geographical reality and its peoples are given some history for the first time, having neglected their origins in barbarous fashion.[46] Britain proves a testing realm for Agricola, but, as Tacitus stresses, he passes the test with flying colours.

The Britons are presented as the perfect subjects for the display of the effectiveness as well as the propriety of Agricola's virtuous regime:

> The Britons themselves discharge the levy and taxes and the demands of the empire with energy, provided that there are no abuses. They take abuses badly, having been subjugated to the point of obedience but not yet to slavery.

> (Tac. *Agr.* 13.1)

Among the Britons, Agricola's virtue is seen to be both moral and practical. The contrast with Domitian need not be stressed, but Tacitus had also to compare his subject with other governors of Britain: Agricola was a far better ruler not only than Domitian, but also than other governors of Britain. A brief survey makes the point. Plautius and Scapula are declared outstanding in war, but their peace-time qualities are omitted. Didius did as much as was necessary to win himself glory. Veranius is distinguished only by a swift death in office, while Suetonius Paulinus performed well (with Agricola as his lieutenant, we should recall) but left his rear open to rebellion. After a sketch of Boudica's uprising, Tacitus completes the survey: Petronius Turpilianus steadied the province, but ventured nothing, while his successors, Trebellius Maximus and Vettius Bolanus, were both lax in the extreme.

Vespasian's governors were a great improvement, in Tacitus' view: Petilius Cerialis won hard-fought victories and had an impressive successor in Frontinus, who did likewise. This was the immediate context of Agricola's governorship:

> This was the state of Britain, these the vicissitudes of war that Agricola found when he crossed in midsummer, our soldiers being disposed to relaxation, as if a campaign were ruled out, and the enemy being disposed to seize their chance. Shortly before his arrival, the tribe of the Ordovices had destroyed a cavalry unit in its territory almost to a man: that had put the province on its mettle. Those who wanted war chose to applaud the example yet to await the temper of the new governor.
>
> (Tac. *Agr.* 18.1)

Tacitus achieves much here: he praises Vespasian's governors as good in war, while leaving their peace-time talents a mystery (as with Plautius and Scapula), and still manages to present as critical the British situation to which Agricola succeeds. All depends, we are told, on the temper (*animus*) of the new governor: we are confident in the outcome, for by now we know enough about Agricola's character and his abilities both in peace and in war.

Immediately, Agricola demonstrates his energy and his awareness of the psychology of power, though circumstances suggested inaction to his soldiers at least: he begins as he wishes to continue, by punishing the Ordovices and taking Anglesey, which Paulinus had had to leave, by his fine tactics, 'the reason and steadiness of the general' (*ratio et constantia ducis*). Now, says Tacitus, Agricola was held to be outstanding and great (*clarus ac magnus*). Tacitus develops two points: first, Agricola chose labour and danger, when others would have chosen personal display and the soliciting of attention; second, he made light of his success, calling it containment, not conquest: he eschewed even laurelled despatches. By deprecating his renown, he increased it. The thought, like much else in this account, was familiar.[47]

Key to Agricola's quality is his knowledge: he knows what to do and how to do it, whether dealing with rebellious Britons, dozing soldiers or the judgments of the Roman public. Tacitus describes the enactment of that knowledge in detail in a passage which encapsulates and explains the success of Agricola's regime:

> But aware of the feelings of the province, and at the same time convinced by the experiences of others that victory is worth little if followed by abuses, he decided to root out the causes of wars. Commencing with himself and his own, he first put his own house in order, which for most is as hard as governing their province. He transacted no public business through freedmen or slaves; he did not take upon his staff a centurion or soldiers through private considerations or through commendations or entreaties, but considered the best most loyal. He knew everything but did not always pursue it: he pardoned minor peccadilloes but was severe with major crimes, more often satisfied with repentance than with invariable punishment; he preferred to appoint to duties and responsibilities men who would not misbehave, rather than condemn them when they did. He mitigated the exaction of grain and taxes by equalizing the burdens, cutting off schemes, invented for plunder, which caused more resentment than the taxes themselves.
>
> (Tac. *Agr.* 19)

Tacitus concludes by making explicit the comparison that has long been implicit between Agricola's regime and that of previous governors. Since Agricola found abusive practices in Britain, we are invited to observe that even his fine immediate predecessors had permitted them, not to mention earlier inadequate governors of the province:

> By suppressing such maladministration immediately in his first year, he wreathed peace in excellent renown, peace which

through either the carelessness or the harshness of his predecessors used to be feared as much as war.

(Tac. *Agr.* 20)

The thought is fundamental to the treatment of peace in the *Agricola*. Tacitus has had nothing positive to say about peace in Britain under even the best of Agricola's predecessors: exceptionally, under Agricola peace is good for the provincials. Here at least, Tacitus does not invite the identification of peace with servitude, as in the *Histories* and later in the *Agricola*.[48]

As summer comes again Agricola has scope for a full campaign: Tacitus dilates upon his qualities as a general, which are both standard and outstanding. He marches with his men, encourages and forces them along, personally chooses camp-sites, personally tests dangerous estuaries and forests, keeps the enemy occupied and, when he has inspired them with fear, offers clemency and displays the attractions of peace. By the exercise of these practical virtues, supremely rational, Agricola induced many states to abandon hostilities and come under Roman protection, which he deployed with great reason and care (*tanta ratione curaque*).

Winter offers Agricola the opportunity not for leisure, but for the energetic and well-reasoned encouragement of peaceful lifestyles amounting to Romanization among the Britons:

The following winter was taken up with very salutary plans. For, in order that men scattered and uncultured and therefore prone to war might become accustomed through pleasures to quiet and leisure, he exhorted individuals and gave assistance to communities to construct temples, fora and houses, by praising the enthusiastic and chiding the slow. Accordingly, rivalry for prestige took the place of coercion. And now he educated the sons of the leading men in the liberal arts and placed the natural talents of the Britons ahead of the diligence of the Gauls. In consequence, those who used to reject the Roman tongue aspired to eloquence. Then came the prestige of our dress, and the toga was commonplace. Gradually there was a straying into the diversions of vices, porticoes and baths and the elegance of banquets. That, among the ignorant, was called civilization (*humanitas*), although it was a facet of slavery.

(Tac. *Agr.* 21)

This passage has caused not a little excitement among modern scholars: Tacitus would have been surprised at the fuss. The first sentence sets the tone for the reader: Agricola's plans are 'very salutary' (*saluberrimis consiliis*). Likewise his tactics are copy-book.[49] Further, his promotion of a Roman identity, though much better attested in Rome than in a provincial context, was nothing new or objectionable in principle.[50] In AD 77 the Elder Pliny offered a wide-ranging assertion of Romanization as key to the Roman imperial mission:

> And I am aware that it might reasonably be considered the work of a churlish and idle mind if treatment in passing and of this cursory nature is accorded to the land that is both the foster-child and the parent of all lands, chosen by the power of the gods to make the very heavens more bright, to bring together scattered realms, to soften customs, to bring to talk together the discordant and wild tongues of so many peoples by the exchange of conversation, and to give civilization to mankind (*humanitatem homini daret*), in sum to make one country of all the peoples in the whole world.
>
> (Pliny *Hist. Nat.* 3.39)[51]

Like Tacitus in the *Agricola*, the Elder Pliny writes of *humanitas*: the Roman mission is to spread it, not least through softening peace and the fostering of the Latin language. On offer to the barbarian was *humanitas*, no less than full membership of the human race. The Elder Pliny would have approved of the 'civilizing' endeavours of Tacitus' Agricola. Meanwhile, evidence from the eastern empire suggests that it was the need of the local elites to engage with Roman law and legal procedures that inspired them to have their sons trained in studies which no doubt gave a principal place to the satisfaction of those needs.[52] Membership of the Roman imperial elite, indeed of the human race, was a goal that was desirable and attainable: by chance, the epigrammatist Martial celebrates the Romanness of a woman of British stock, a Claudia Rufina.[53] It is not until the closing sentences of the section that Tacitus sounds a more negative note. Even here he establishes a clear distance between Agricola's activities, which are accorded nothing but praise, and the gradual corruption that set in thereafter.[54] Nothing in this section implies that Agricola could or should be held responsible for the ensuing corruption that followed his measures; indeed, any such censure would be completely at odds both with the opening sentence of the section and with the consistently, almost overwhelmingly, positive presentation of Agricola throughout the work.

The target of Tacitus' closing remarks is not Agricola, but the Britons: his salutary planning is contrasted with their misidentification of the nature of civilization. Inappropriate naming, a sure sign of warped thinking, is a familiar concern of the historian concerned with setting forth his version of truth and claiming to expose the untruth of others, not least of those who figure in his text.[55] Agricola has the Britons construct temples, fora and houses, while the Britons, victims of their own ignorance without his guiding wisdom, subsequently and gradually go astray and indulge in porticoes, baths and fine banquets. Of course, although the latter indulgences may seem unexceptionable to modern sensibilities, in antiquity they constitute standard features of the life of idle vice.[56] Agricola's virtuous projects are corrupted into luxury. The Britons have embraced the rudiments of civilization under Agricola, only to pervert them. They have done so because they have acted in ignorance throughout: they have no adequate understanding of the nature and issues of freedom and slavery. It was Agricola who steered them towards civilization and advanced the education of their elite, but without him they veer into vice.[57] Tacitus' readers may recall his passing sneer at the regime of Trebellius Maximus in Britain, when the Britons learnt to pardon attractive vices under a governor whose principal characteristic is sloth, *segnitia*.[58] Tacitus makes no particular claim for the originality of Agricola's brand of Romanization, but, rather, stresses its virtues and the energy with which Agricola proceeded in this as in all else, by contrast with the likes of Trebellius Maximus.[59]

At the same time, however, the perversion of civilization in Britain proceeds in harmony with the perversion that is Roman society itself, where porticoes, baths and fine banquets proliferate. The Britons adopted more Romanization and a different Romanization from that which Agricola had offered. In that sense, Tacitus' closing remarks in this section also exemplify his much-repeated criticisms of Roman society at large: we should recall that he takes care to tell his readers that Agricola had grown up at Massilia, not Rome. Nor are such criticisms of Roman society peculiar to Tacitus: his acquaintance the satirist Juvenal, whose works also indicate an awareness of the philosophy of rulership and governorship, gives a similarly critical portrayal of Romanization:

Arms we have advanced beyond
the shores of Hibernia and the recently captured
Orcades and the Britons, at home with the shortest night,
but the deeds done now in the city of the conquering people
are not the acts of those whom we conquered.
Armenian Zalaces is said, softer than all the ephebes,
to have bestowed himself upon an amorous tribune.
See what exchanges do: he had come as a hostage;
here men are made. For if a longer stay gives the city
to boys, they will always find a lover.
Gone will be trousers, daggers, reins and crop:
praetextate ways they take back to Artaxata.

(Juv. 2.159–70)

In this satire Rome is the centre of the disease of corruption:
Romanization is the process by which that disease is spread
throughout the empire. The young Armenian 'hostage' has come to
Rome to acquire Roman culture, to be made a man: instead of traditional Roman virtues to complement his Armenian heritage, he
acquires the current vices of the capital and takes them with him
home to Artaxata, his Armenian strengths abandoned.[60] Stark
images are to be expected of the satirist, but they are not so far from
the tone struck in the works of the historian. As we have seen, the
treatment of the periphery is also the treatment of the centre, not
least in satirical vein, as in much of Tacitus' *Germania*, where corruption of German simplicity by Roman culture is a sustained
theme. Indeed, Tacitus himself characterizes the effect of time in
Rome upon an Armenian 'hostage':

> Tigranes, who was chosen by Nero to take power [in
> Armenia], from the Cappadocian nobility, the grandson of
> King Archelaus, but, because he had long been a hostage in
> Rome, sunk into servile obedience.

(Tac. *Ann.* 14.26; cf. 15.1)

The perception of barbarians as noble in their simplicity, however
flawed they may be, requires that the advance of Roman culture
among them be viewed in terms that are at best ambivalent and at
worst critical. For such a perception can only view Romanization,
at least in part, as a loss: it is a loss of simplicity and a loss of freedom. And where it is thought that Roman culture has been debased
and perverted before it has reached the barbarians, its advance must

be seen not only in terms of loss, but also as the gain of something poisonous. In short, we should not be surprised to find writers expressing ambivalence or outright criticism of the spread of Roman culture among barbarians when they also express both substantial admiration for barbarian society and fundamental criticism of contemporary Roman society and culture. On the contrary, such writers are being no more than consistent. For them, it is a given that Roman imperialism requires the imposition of slavery when Rome itself is enslaved to an emperor at odds with freedom.

Too much has probably been made of Tacitus' remarks on British misidentification of civilization. This section of the *Agricola* has often been excerpted from the context of the work, which indicates the limitations of its significance. In context it can be seen to be largely a further assertion by Tacitus of Agricola's intelligent and virtuous regime in Britain. The notion that Rome's empire was all the stronger when its subjects were convinced of the benefits of peace was in essence a commonplace of Roman imperialist rhetoric and practice.[61] Be that as it may, Agricola has made telling use of the winter and with the arrival of summer he redeploys his energy and reason on campaign; the knowledgeable, claims Tacitus, observed that no general placed his forts more wisely than Agricola. The claim was something of a commonplace, made also for Hannibal and Philopoemen.[62]

At last potential criticism of Agricola starts to emerge, only to be quashed and turned to praise. He was generous in acknowledging the achievements of his subordinates but there were those who thought him rather too harsh in reproof. The distant criticism has an element of familiarity: Cicero had warned his brother against the fault. But Agricola's anger was expressed and then ended: he did not harbour secret hatred, and there was no cause for fear in his silence. The reader may recall the malign silence of Domitian and, by extension, of such emperors as Tiberius, Gaius and Nero; later in the *Agricola* Tacitus makes much of Domitian's silence.[63]

Tacitus does little more than sketch the progress of Agricola's campaigning. Evidently such details were much less important to him than were broad observations: only the major stages of military progress matter, and even then it is the manner of that progress that really counts. A whole chapter is given to Ireland, particularly because it affords a further example of Agricola's excellence, wisdom and foresight, despite the fact that Agricola's stated belief in the ease of its conquest does not impress the modern reader.

Leading from the front, Agricola establishes strongpoints facing Ireland 'in hope, not in fear', in case the island might be added to the empire. He has troubled to receive a refugee Irish kinglet under the guise of friendship in case he might be needed. Tacitus claims often to have heard Agricola express the view that Ireland could be conquered and held with one legion and a few auxiliaries and that a conquered Ireland would help Roman control of Britain 'if Roman arms were all around and liberty were removed, as it were, from sight'.[64] There is no sign that Tacitus or Agricola had reservations about the removal of liberty in this instance: as we have seen, Roman imperialism demanded as much. The essential difficulty for both Tacitus and his readers is that the removal of liberty can appear variously as good or as bad in his works. Of course, at Rome its removal from Romans is largely viewed as negative, while outside Rome its removal by Romans is more often treated as positive; but in neither situation does Tacitus offer a completely unalloyed moral judgment.[65] For provincials, Tacitus seems to argue, Roman rule and peace may not amount to *libertas*, but under the best Roman government they constitute the next best thing and the only practical option.[66]

Agricola is the first again, claims Tacitus, to advance by sea as well as by land, exploiting the psychological advantages of such a procedure: his forces are encouraged, while the Britons are dumbstruck. Agricola's military skill and speed combine with his steadfastness in the face of panicky advice to inspire his army against Caledonia, 'the end of Britain'.[67] Meanwhile, the Britons persist in their arrogance. After a diverting section on the circumnavigation of Britain by deserters,[68] Tacitus takes his readers to the climax of Agricola's campaigning in Britain, the victory at Mons Graupius, to which he was driven in part, says Tacitus, by the death of his infant son.

Tacitus sets the scene briefly: at last the Britons have come together, full of fight, to resist enslavement. At last, this is a British army to be reckoned with. And outstanding among its many commanders, in virtue and birth, is Calgacus, says Tacitus. He is outstanding also in Tacitus' narrative, for he is the first and only Briton to speak in the *Agricola*. The set piece required the traditional pair of balanced speeches, one by each of the commanders, Calgacus and Agricola, the latter responding to the arguments raised by the former. In all, the climax at Mons Graupius is accorded ten chapters, more than one-fifth of the whole work. Tacitus' portrayal of the virtue of Agricola required not only a substantial climax, but also a worthwhile enemy. Battles had been won before in Britain by previous Roman commanders: these had to be surpassed if Agricola was to attain significant pre-eminence.

As usual in ancient historiography, the pre-battle speeches explore the perspectives and issues at stake at Mons Graupius. At the same time, these speeches enable Tacitus vividly to characterize this battle as climactic not only in the life and governorship of Agricola, but also in the history of the Roman conquest of Britain. In a sense, such speeches as those of Calgacus and Agricola are invention, required by the genre and exploited by the author. Indeed, Tacitus claims nothing else on the Caledonian side, for he writes that Calgacus 'is said to have spoken in this vein': he claims accuracy in spirit, not in detail, and could scarcely claim more.[69] Even Agricola 'spoke in this manner': the introduction is designedly all-embracing.[70] However, invention is not the whole story: an able and appropriate address to the troops in such circumstances was reckoned a necessary talent of the general, Greek as well as Roman, as Caesar himself has it.[71] In other words, the quality of Agricola's speech is in itself an instance of his worth as a commander: art and life coalesce.

Commentators have produced admirable discussions of the more technical aspects of the rhetoric employed by Calgacus and by Agricola:[72] the Roman form and content of Calgacus' speech have been established beyond question and should not surprise us. In particular, Calgacus' denunciation of Roman imperialism contains nothing new: similar sentiments can be found attributed to such enemies of Rome as Mithridates and are instanced in the works of Sallust and of Caesar, and elsewhere in the writings of Tacitus himself.[73] As Brunt acutely observes, 'Roman writers, who had learned in the rhetorical schools to state both sides of a question, were capable of expounding views of Rome's policy which her enemies had, or might have, voiced.'[74] Indeed, Romans too were well able to denounce in their own voices the wrongs done to provincials by fellow-Romans: Cicero's speeches against Verres and Piso, like Tacitus' portrayal of Decianus Catus, are replete with such denunciations.[75] Such denunciations by Tacitus also echo central themes of the political thought and satire of the Principate, as instanced by Seneca, Pliny and Juvenal – notably corruption, rapacity, misrepresentation and, above all, lack of self-control by those in power, who set private advantage before public duty. Accordingly, Calgacus' speech demands a nuanced assessment, for it is at once banal and challenging, misplaced and to the point.[76]

Calgacus' arguments may be summarized briefly. His army, he argues, stands at the very end of Britain, where freedom survives and enslavement has yet to be experienced. Again, Tacitus' favourite polarity of *libertas* and *servitium* dominates the thought. His army, he continues, is encircled by the sea and the Romans, whose greed is insatiable:

> Alone of all men they lust after wealth and want with equal passion. To pillage, butchery and extortion they give the false name of 'empire' and where they make a desert they call it 'peace'.

> (Tac. *Agr.* 30)

Persons and property, continues Calgacus, are prey to gross Roman abuse: the British are treated like the cheapest slaves or worse, while their distance and virtue make them suspect. Since a woman had led the enslaved of Britain to burn a colony and more, what more could the free men of Caledonia achieve? Again, the politics of gender intersect with the language of freedom and slavery. By contrast, he claims, the Romans do not have the same talents for virtue in war as they have for abuse in peace, while their army is a shaky alliance of Britons, Gauls and Germans as well as Romans. This army, he concludes, lacks the motivation to fight and, when this battle has been won, all Britain will lie open.

In assessing Calgacus' speech, a fundamental point is regularly overlooked: Calgacus' denunciation of Roman maladministration is completely out of place when deployed against Agricola. As earlier in the work, the Britons have misjudged their situation; for that reason, their defeat is predictable and comprehensible. For throughout the *Agricola* Tacitus has set out the virtues of Agricola, particularly his prevention of the abuses that stimulate revolt among the Britons:[77] so far from creating a desert and calling it peace, Agricola has made peace attractive. Calgacus' speech is misjudged, inadequately reasoned. That lack of reason is further indicated by Tacitus' note that Calgacus' audience received it in barbarian fashion, with chants, noise and discordant yells. Tacitus' Britons, not for the only time, show courage of a sort, but it is the animal courage of passion and ignorance.

However, at the same time, Calgacus' speech might have been appropriate against another Roman governor or against the emperor himself, whether Domitian or another 'tyrant'. Accordingly, the speech serves not only to remind the watchful reader of the virtues of Agricola and to presage the reward of those virtues in victory, but also to amplify Tacitus' criticisms in the *Agricola* of the provincial malpractice that stimulates resistance and revolt, in Britain and elsewhere. It takes the virtuous Agricola to deal with a resistance that has been fired and strengthened by the malpractice of corrupt predecessors and emperors. At the same time, Tacitus leaves readers to make their own judgment of Calgacus' motives, upon which he makes no overt comment. The reader may take his words as spoken from the heart: most readers have done so. Yet there is enough dissimulation in Tacitus' works to make a more cynical assessment possible. Indeed, in the *Histories* Tacitus provides a narrative which demonstrates his ability to portray characters espousing freedom but intending personal domination.[78] Calgacus' motives can be left to the reader's imagination, not least because beyond his speech he does not matter and may not even have existed.

Tacitus takes his readers direct from the disorganized barbarian hubbub to the controlled energy of the Roman side, where the battle-line is being deployed and the soldiers are eager to fight but just kept in order. Agricola takes a reasoned decision (*ratus*, 'thinking') to fire them further with a speech, which responds to Calgacus' fiery tirade with sound argument. More often than not modern readers have much preferred the passion of Calgacus' speech to the sobriety of Agricola's reply,[79] but in doing so they have shown scant sympathy with the Roman perspective of Tacitus. As Tacitus shows in the *Germania*, much may be said for barbarian passion, which may embody virtue of a sort, close to nature. But in the thought-world of Tacitus, uncontrolled passion was also dangerous and no match at all for reasoned control, to which it was largely opposed and inimical. Where the modern reader may find Calgacus exciting and Agricola dull, the moralistic Roman reader would more probably consider Calgacus rash and Agricola sound. Accordingly, we need not be detained by the familiar puzzle as to why Tacitus makes his subject come off second-best in his indirect duel of words with Calgacus, for the puzzle is a mirage: in Tacitean terms, if not in our own, it is Agricola who wins that duel, presaging his further victory in the battle to come.

Immediately the reader is shown that Calgacus' judgment is wrong: so far from lacking incentive to fight, Agricola's soldiers are described by the narrator as straining at the leash: while Agricola is still speaking, their ardour is evident, and the end of his speech is followed by 'enormous eagerness'. Calgacus' force had been 'eager', but no more than that.[80] It is the Romans who are the more eager for battle. And, whereas the Britons are disordered and disorderly in their eagerness, the Romans remain organized and under their general's control.

In this way Agricola's speech is shown as effective. Its principal arguments may be summarized briefly: general and soldiers are very experienced and have achieved a very great deal; they have scoured forbidding terrain in search of the enemy, who have at last been drawn from their hiding-places. Withdrawal now would be extremely dangerous, says Agricola: both safety and renown are to be gained only by fighting. The enemy is familiar and its best men have already fallen; the remainder are easy meat. His conclusion picks up his opening claim to have conquered Britain during the previous six years through the soldiers' virtue, the imperial auspices, and his own good faith and hard work:

> Have done with campaigning, set upon fifty years a great day,
> prove to the state that neither the delays of war nor the causes
> of rebellion could ever have been blamed upon the army.
>
> (Tac. *Agr.* 34.3)

This conclusion sets Agricola's achievement in a wider context, an important purpose of the speech as a whole. His victory at Mons Graupius is to be the conclusion of a process that began with the Claudian invasion of AD 43: what Claudius started Agricola would complete. In the intervening fifty years fighting has not been sustained and time-consuming rebellion has been engendered. The fault has not been the army's: it has been the fault of previous governors of Britain and possibly their emperors too. At last, Agricola is made indirectly to assert his own virtues.

Tacitus narrates the battle in some detail, but Agricola remains the focus. His dispositions are seen to be effective, and when problems arise in the course of battle it is Agricola's swift and practical thinking that saves the day: first when he sends in the Batavians and Tungrians, and again when he launches a timely charge by cavalry which he has kept wisely in reserve. British tactics are turned against themselves by Agricola's tactical awareness. Even in defeat, the British sometimes find a desperate courage and might rally but for the energetic and appropriate counter-measures of Agricola.

The scale of victory is indicated by the casualties claimed: 10,000 British dead against 360 on the Roman side.[81]

The victory at Mons Graupius is very much Agricola's. The general has played a key role at every turn before and during the battle; this in addition to the broader impact of his energy and virtue throughout his governorship in Britain, of which Mons Graupius is the culmination and climax. The extent of that victory is further illustrated by the random and disordered behaviour of the shattered Britons, which serves also to recall their lack of reason and self-control. The final expression of the total conquest that Agricola has carried through in Britain is the circumnavigation of the island that is his last act there in Tacitus' account. That circumnavigation is not a desperate venture, but a triumphal procession of studied leisure, displaying the completeness of Roman imperial control, thanks to Agricola.[82]

Tacitus, after some thirty chapters on Britain, now takes his readers to Rome and the receipt of Agricola's reports by Domitian. Both governor and emperor are characterized in the process: Agricola did not magnify his achievements in his reports, while Domitian received the news with joyful face and troubled heart. Tacitus proceeds to make more explicit the contrast between those good and bad rulers that has been implicit from the first. Whereas Agricola had achieved a real and great victory, Domitian had manufactured a false triumph over the Germans, buying and arraying people to pose as captives. The emperor feared for his position, says Tacitus, when another excelled him in military prowess, the ultimate imperial virtue: his enforcing of silence in other matters would be rendered pointless. Domitian decided to keep back his hatred until Agricola had left Britain, and his reputation and the army's favour had died down. Tacitus hints at Domitian's fear that Agricola might fight him.

The deceitful Domitian proffered honours, but Agricola showed himself to be no direct threat: he was not the stuff of civil warfare. Having handed over to his successor in Britain a province that was 'peaceful and safe',[83] Agricola followed Domitian's instructions and crept into Rome by night to the Palatine; with a formal kiss and not a word, Agricola was received and slipped into the crowd. Aware of the dangers of a military reputation, he sought a name now for tranquillity and leisure; he was modest and approachable, with no display. The majority failed to see his greatness.[84] Yet Domitian was an emperor hostile to virtues (*infensus virtutibus princeps*), like the tyrants who saw excellent subjects as a threat not a resource. And military difficulties, caused by the rashness or slowness of Rome's generals, kept Agricola's name to the fore. Throughout, Tacitus has shown us that Agricola was indeed the man for such jobs, reasoned and energetic. The mob called for Agricola, comparing his vigour, steadfastness and experience to the inertia and fear of others: Tacitus claims general agreement that Domitian heard the call, while Agricola was propelled to prominence by his virtues and by the failings of others.[85]

But Agricola preferred another course: Tacitus states that on the advice of Domitian's henchmen, Agricola asked the emperor to excuse him from further provincial duties and, when granted the request, thanked him.[86] It has often been recognized that Tacitus' admiration for Agricola's approach to tyranny contrasts with his more nuanced and not uncritical treatment of Thrasea Paetus' blunter and outspoken opposition. Agricola and Thrasea had much in common: at the beginning of the *Agricola*, Tacitus signals as much, comparing his biography of Agricola with biographies of Thrasea and his like-minded son-in-law, Helvidius.[87] However, according to Tacitus, Agricola exercised more self-control and more modesty than did Thrasea, whose ambitions and effectiveness were both open to question in Tacitus' view.[88] And in so doing, Tacitus' Agricola offered a model and an excuse for those who followed a similar path of quiet resistance, not least Tacitus himself. In the light of Agricola's life, it could be claimed as legitimate not only to have survived but actually to have prospered under a tyrannical emperor. The *Agricola* offered an opportunity for generous understanding, which was especially apposite as power passed from Domitian through Nerva to Trajan.

In the aftermath of Domitian's assassination and his replacement by Nerva and Trajan, Tacitus did well to stress distance and hostility between Agricola and the murdered tyrant. But in so doing Tacitus presents only part of the case. The simple fact, which Tacitus seeks to obscure and implicitly to deny, is that Agricola could not have pursued his expansionism in northern Britain without at least the acquiescence of the emperor. The precise chronology of Agricola's campaigns remains a matter of dispute, but he had certainly begun under Vespasian (in AD 77 or 78), continued through the reign of Titus (AD 79–81) and did not leave Britain before AD 83 at the earliest.[89] Tacitus mentions Agricola's despatches to Rome only in the context of his final victory, but these were surely regular, annual at least. The emperor laboured under a great burden of responsibilities and administration, as Fergus Millar has amply demonstrated, and cannot regularly have issued detailed instructions to his commanders far off in the field. However, an active governor, long in office like Agricola and having a new emperor, must at the very least have sought contact with the centre of power.[90] It suits Tacitus and the atmosphere of AD 98 to concentrate upon Agricola's success as a problem for Domitian and even a threat to his position. And Tacitus' depiction has convinced most.[91] But, although Domitian may very well have felt concern at the success of Agricola, he could also count that success as an asset.

Domitian could reasonably claim that Agricola was *his* general, acting on his instructions and proceeding under his imperial auspices. Later, in the mid-second century AD, Fronto claimed as much for the emperor Antoninus Pius when his general launched a Scottish campaign.[92] Indeed, if Domitian did likewise, he had a particular precedent in Claudius' arrogation to himself of the success of Aulus Plautius in Britain. Despite Tacitus, readers of the *Agricola* would do well to remember that at any point in Agricola's governorship Domitian could have recalled him to Rome or at least ordered him to desist from further conquest: Tacitus himself describes Claudius ordering back Corbulo when his success seemed to threaten the emperor's standing.[93] By contrast, the accession of Domitian seems rather to have boosted Agricola's expansionism after a lull under Titus.[94] Beyond dispute is the fact that, whatever Domitian's attitude to Agricola may have been upon his return to Rome *c.* AD 83, the emperor allowed him to live on for another ten years until his death in AD 93. And, although Tacitus strives to suggest that Domitian had Agricola killed in AD 93, he does not venture to say so directly even in the safety of AD 98.[95] Meanwhile, Tacitus himself advanced his career under Domitian: evidently his father-in-law had not been a handicap.[96]

No doubt Domitian presented the conquest of Britain in terms akin to those in which Tacitus' Agricola addressed his army before Mons Graupius. The Flavian regime had already claimed much of the Claudian invasion for Vespasian: it would have been easy and appropriate for Domitian to claim that he had finally completed the job that his father had started in AD 43. That, no doubt, was the informing ideology behind the construction of a magnificent arch at Richborough *c.* AD 87–8, apparently over 100 feet high.[97] Even Tacitus allows that Domitian greeted Agricola's conquest with delight, though he claims that his pleasure was false.[98] Tacitus also lists the honours which Agricola received from the emperor – awarded grudgingly, of course, on Tacitus' account.[99] Silius Italicus offers explanation: Domitian accepted Agricola's success as the completion of a conquest of Britain that his regime pronounced as Flavian, but he also claimed that he himself had superseded the successes of his family by his personal leadership in Germany. It was in Germany, not Britain, that Domitian's regime located the emperor's military reputation; it was on the war in Germany that Statius wrote an epic poem.[100]

There can be no serious doubt about Domitian's involvement in the British enterprise. A chance sidelight is provided by Plutarch's account of the mission, apparently in AD 83, of Demetrius, who claims to have been ordered by the emperor Domitian to explore islands close to Britain. These islands had long been the subject of geographical debate and interest:

> Demetrius said that of the islands around Britain there were many that were scattered and barren, some of which bear the names of heroes and deities. He said that he had sailed for the purpose of investigation and out of curiosity, commissioned by the emperor, to the barren island that lay nearest, which had inhabitants who were few but who were all reckoned sacred and inviolable by the Britons.
>
> (Plut. *De def. or.* 18)[101]

As Dio's brief account makes clear, Agricola's campaigns were later remembered at least as much for their explorations as for their conquests.[102] And Plutarch's brief notice supports the proposition that Domitian took an active and leading role in those campaigns.

The context of the publication of Tacitus' *Agricola* required the construction of hostility between Agricola and Domitian. Of course, in AD 98 Agricola could not be praised as Domitian's agent. Perhaps still more important, by giving all credit for success in Britain to Agricola and by suggesting that Agricola had achieved that success despite Domitian, not because of him, the *Agricola* served the valuable political purpose of denying Domitian military success in Britain. It is salutary to compare Tacitus' presentation in the *Agricola* of Domitian's campaign in Germany. Commentators have noticed that Domitian's German campaign was a far more substantial affair than Tacitus would have his readers believe. There is no reason to accept Tacitus' assertion that Domitian's triumph was a sham, a parade of made-up captives: the charge was an old one, as we saw with Cicero and Piso.[103] It is doubtless more than coincidence that the *Germania* and the *Agricola* appeared at the same time: the former purported to demonstrate the emptiness of Domitian's claims to victory in Germany, while the latter transferred victory in Britain from Domitian to Agricola. As with Julius Caesar and later with Gaius, there was a tendency in Roman imperial thought to perceive Britain and Germany together, after the manner of Silius Italicus. In the aftermath of Domitian's assassination, in the brave new world of Nerva and Trajan, the discredited emperor could not be allowed a military reputation.[104]

In that political context, Tacitus offers early ventures into issues which were to form the substance of much of his historical outlook and writing in later years: *libertas* and *servitium* at home and abroad, imperialism, morality, dissimulation, truth and its identification, and much more besides. Tacitus provides a brief but all-embracing assessment of Flavian involvement in Britain at the beginning of his *Histories*, which he completed more than a decade after the *Agricola*, in *c*. AD 110:

> I am entering upon a work full of disasters, ferocious in its battles, mutinous in its rebellions, even in peace itself savage. Four emperors killed by the sword; three civil wars, more foreign, and the majority both; positive in the East, negative in the West; Illyricum in uproar, the Gauls teetering, Britain completely conquered and immediately left aside; there rose against us Sarmatian and Suebian peoples, the Dacian ennobled by disasters exchanged, and even the arms of the Parthians were nearly stirred by the travesty of a false Nero.
>
> (Tac. *Hist.* 1.2)

Here Tacitus sets out almost poetically the contents of his *Histories*, covering the years AD 69–96. Of particular concern for the present discussion is the phrase 'Britain completely conquered and immediately left aside' (*perdomita Britannia et statim omissa*; often mistranslated: *omissa* does not mean 'abandoned', but 'left aside' or 'neglected'). Tacitus can only mean the conquest of Britain by the Flavians, culminating in the victory of Agricola at Mons Graupius, after which, as he has it, Domitian was responsible for its neglect.[105] Tacitus denies Domitian any credit for the Roman conquest of Britain but, from the same perspective, gives him full responsibility

for the partial withdrawal that followed. No doubt it was convenient for Trajan to blame Domitian for that withdrawal: Domitian
had started the process by removing Roman forces from northern
Scotland by the middle of AD 88,[106] but it was Trajan, it seems, who
brought Roman forces south to the line of the so-called Stanegate,
between Corbridge and Carlisle and beyond.[107] In any event, as
Hind observes, Caledonia had little to offer the conqueror, beyond
the conquest itself.[108] The poet Martial offers a Roman view of
Caledonia under Trajan. Seeking to curry favour with the new
emperors after too good a poetic life under Domitian, Martial's
later epigrams present Britain as a far-off place, best not visited,[109]
peopled by a baggy-trousered poor,[110] and a source of nothing
greater than a basket.[111]

It is in this very broad matrix of anti-Domitianic judgments that
the *Agricola* should be read. We have seen that what purports to be
– and indeed is – a biography also encompasses a range of large
issues. Particular sections of the work are regularly excerpted and
built into modern arguments, as is usual in the pursuit of the history
of antiquity: most often cited are chapters of Calgacus' speech (but
not Agricola's response), on Agricola's encouragement of 'civilization' and on Domitian's regime at Rome itself. However, the use of
such passages requires a wide-ranging appreciation of the scope and
ideology of the *Agricola* as a whole. As we have seen, upon close
reading the biography soon shows its other face as political polemic.

EPILOGUE

Britain occupied a special place in Roman imperialist thought and practice. Whereas the northern and eastern frontiers were conceptualized around rivers, it was the river of Ocean that set Britain apart, literally and metaphorically. For Ocean was not only the father of the other rivers, but also the boundary of the world. Accordingly, the conquest of Britain was readily imagined in antiquity as the passage from the familiar world, the 'inhabited world' (the *oikoumene*), into a strange other world. The passage was an achievement in itself: even the heroes of mythology had not dared to attempt the crossing to Britain. For an invasion of Britain meant a conquest of Ocean, which was in turn an assault upon the limits of human experience and existence. Any such undertaking was epic in every sense, as we have seen: a campaign in Britain was well suited to treatment in epic poetry, with all its evocations of the Greek crossing to Troy, which was further evoked by the British use of chariots, which so drew the attention of classical writers steeped in Homer.

The invasion of Britain was seen to be fraught with special risks, not least the tides of Ocean and the murky, unfamiliar landscape of the island itself. Although the invader might hope for booty in Britain, Caesar's invasions had suggested that great riches were not to be gained there. Rather, it was the specialness of Britain that constituted its particular attraction to Roman imperialists: in Britain there was unusual scope for achievement and glorious pre-eminence, because success there was victory in a world apart and beyond the normal limits of mankind. At Rome, such prizes were to be fought for and fought over: as often on the Roman frontiers, controversy and competition shaped Roman dealings with Britain from Caesar to Trajan. In particular we have seen how emperors sought to excel their predecessors with regard to Britain. Augustus' regime threatened major invasion greater than the expeditions of Caesar, but ultimately Augustus preferred diplomacy; under Tiberius, diplomacy remained the preferred course, while the achievement of Caesar could now be played down as a rather futile adventure. A marked change came with Gaius, at least partly in response to events in Britain. The emperor Gaius chose to resurrect the campaigns of Caesar and in so doing to excel them, as his bridge at Baiae announced. His successor, Claudius, both carried out the invasion that Gaius had threatened and, it seems, encouraged the denigration of Gaius' plans as the folly of a madman. Thereafter, in response to Claudius' persistent trumpeting of his British achievements until his death in AD 54, his successor Nero considered, we are told, abandoning the island. However, Vespasian and his sons sought rather to associate themselves with Claudius' success in Britain and, by so doing, to appropriate it for themselves. Under the Flavians it was especially Caledonia that provided fresh opportunities for glory in Britain: Domitian in particular could claim that glory. However, when, after the assassination of Domitian in AD 96, Nerva and Trajan built a regime upon the subversion and negation of Domitian's acts, the success of the Flavians was problematic. Indeed, the success of Domitian in Britain became insufferable. Tacitus, writing in that post-Domitianic milieu, provides an account in the *Agricola* which constructs the conquest of Britain as completed not by Domitian, but despite him. Rather, Tacitus claimed that glory for Agricola, an ideal governor-monarch in the alternative world of Britain. Meanwhile, Domitian could be blamed for neglecting the conquest that Agricola had completed, as Tacitus related in his *Histories*.

Throughout this period, from Caesar to Trajan, we have followed the three interwoven strands of geography, imperialism and monarchy. In the alternative world that was Britain there was particular scope for the exploration, in profoundly moralistic terms, of the use and abuse of power. Further, the notion of Britain as another world facilitated the comparison of monarchical regimes in the interplay of centre and periphery, a comparison developed notably in the *Agricola*. More broadly, we have seen how ancient accounts of Britain are dominated by concerns at the centre of power in Rome. In particular, slavery has recurred as a central concern in our texts as the counterpoint of freedom, both in Britain and at Rome. In particular, Chapter 8 has sought to explain how ancient consideration of powerful women (in Rome as well as Britain) entailed the consideration of slavery. And by examining slavery and queenship, it was noted, as often in this book, that our sources chose to present their narratives in accordance with their broader analyses. We have seen, for example, how Tacitus' account of Boudica in the *Annals* is not only fuller, but designedly more sympathetic, than his earlier treatment of her in the *Agricola*, while its approach is fundamentally at odds with the later account of Cassius Dio.

The literary sources which contain treatments of Britain are too often used as mines from which particular passages are hacked out for consideration by students of Roman Britain. Indeed, the very word 'sources', though hallowed and respected, is dangerous in that it can encourage such mining: the texts which we use as sources were often written with an eye to posterity, but they were not written to be hacked about and excerpted. Throughout this book, I have attempted to show the value of a reading that does less violence to the texts upon which we rely and which is both closer and broader. We have seen how the different and competing narratives of Roman Britain that happen to have survived from antiquity each embody particular concerns, and each employ particular literary strategies. In every case, we must seek first to understand the assumptions and objectives of those who wrote these accounts in so far as we can divine them without direct access to their authorial intentions, for only then can we hope to understand their treatments of Britain. Each account is different, but by no means completely different. Throughout, I have drawn attention not only to the particular concerns of each source, but also to the concerns which they have in common, with regard in particular to issues of geography, imperialism and monarchy.

A new book on Roman Britain has been no small undertaking. The history of Roman Britain has often been written, and written well. However, for the most part scholarship on Roman Britain has been no less an island than its subject. By and large, the island has been the preserve of a quite sharply defined group, though it is one that is quite extensive and impressive. Many budding historians of antiquity (as once the present writer) have been kindly advised by their sage seniors not to make the academic crossing to this island: in part through awareness of the demands of the crossing itself, in part through fear of the natives, and in part through anxiety that the young will be lost there, engulfed by a mass of regional detail, never to return.

The dominant discipline and method on the island has been archaeology. The remains of material culture offer valuable results and insight in return for intensive study, while, as usual outside Rome itself, the literary sources seem patchy and inadequate. Accordingly, the history of Roman Britain has become largely the preserve of archaeologists. Yet archaeology embraces a range of approaches, not least to history itself: while some archaeologists seek to construct history, others prefer to eschew it. For the latter, Roman Britain is better approached as proto-history, if not pre-history; literary sources are to be marginalized, where they cannot be ignored completely. For the former, there abides the pressing question of the relationship between the material record and the literary evidence, where, as very often, these do not seem readily to coincide or even to permit the same sorts of analysis.

This book has offered an approach to Roman Britain that largely eschews archaeology in order to maintain a sharp focus upon the literary evidence and to subject it to the rigorous method that has more often been applied to the material record alone. At the same time, the issues that form the principal concerns of this book seemed best addressed by a close and in many ways rather traditional reading of literary texts. The subsidiary claim that underlies the approach of this book is that the dominance of archaeology and archaeological questions in research on Roman Britain has permitted, even encouraged, the relative neglect of the classical texts, particularly of texts, such as poetry, which may not seem overtly 'historical'. By close reading of these texts, new issues can be identified and discussed in the context of Roman Britain, while questions familiar in the study of Roman Britain may be approached from a rather different angle.

A valuable survey of scholarship on Britain over the three decades from 1960 to 1989 demonstrates both the dominance of archaeology in the field, and the scope for reconsideration of literary evidence. For example, the survey shows little concern with the reading of the *Commentaries* of Julius Caesar as it has developed in recent years, while it properly acknowledges how much we depend upon that reading, for 'despite several decades of intense archaeological activity there is still not one jot of direct archaeological evidence for the presence of Julius Caesar's armies in Britain in 55 and 54 BC'.[1] At the same time, the survey warns us of the provisional, if not fanciful, terms in which we tend to discuss key features of the history (and archaeology) of Roman Britain; it is startling to realize that the Belgae, for all their recurrent and fundamental importance in traditional historical analyses, are not recognizable in the archaeological record.[2]

How are we to understand the literary texts that have survived? What was the nature of Roman interest in Britain? What did the name of Britain evoke in Roman mentalities, and how did such evocations change over time? What were the agendas of the various writers whose texts we use to construct our historical interpretations and narratives? In the preceding chapters I have attempted to suggest answers to these questions and, by so doing, I have sought to explore and to illustrate ways in which Britain mattered in the Roman world. Students of Roman Britain often complain that Roman authors seldom write about the island; it seems to me to be more rewarding to consider how and why they write about it at all.

NOTES

1 THE CONQUEST OF OCEAN

1. For Gallus, see Anderson, Parsons and Nisbet 1979, 141. Cf. Cicero and Lucceius *Ad Fam*. 5.12.
2. Wiseman 1985.
3. Harris 1979, 25–7. The more thoughtful in Roman society came to see the problems entailed by such an ideology: see Long 1995.
4. *RIB* 662–3.
5. Plutarch, *On the obsolescence of oracles*, 419e. See further Chapter 9.
6. See Green 1986, 138–41; Bradley and Gordon 1988.
7. E.g. Florus 2.13.88; *Anth. Lat.* 419, 423.
8. Braund 1996b. On the statue at Chesters, see conveniently Birley 1960, 27. The dedications from Newcastle are *RIB* 1319 (Neptune) and 1320 (Ocean), with Bidwell and Holbrook 1989, 101. On the Bath pediment, see Cunliffe 1986, 6–8; cf. Black 1986 on Ocean/Neptune on mosaics at Frampton and Withington. On Castlecary (*RIB* 2149), see Hanson and Maxwell 1983, 182; cf. also *RIB* 2105 from Birrens. Walls across northern Britain could be seen as connecting Ocean on the west with Ocean on the east: so *RIB* 1051. Further, Hassall and Tomlin 1987, 360
9. *Iliad* 20.7, 5.78, 21 passim, 23.148 (all observed by Dio Chrys. 4.86); cf. Men. Rhet., p. 374. Father Ocean: *Iliad* 21.195.
10. Cic. *ND* 3.52; cf. Varro *LL* 5.71. Plin. *Ep.* 8.8. Rhine-cult: *CIL* 13.5255; 7790–1; 8810–11. Danube-cult: *CIL* 3.3416; 5863; 10263; 10395. Cf., on the Nile, Bonneau 1964. On river-cult in Roman religion, see in general Wissowa 1912, 217ff.; Latte 1960, 131–2. Tiber *religiosus*: Plin. *NH* 3.55, with Becher 1985.
11. E.g. *pater Padus*: *ILS* 3903; *pater Tiberinus*: Livy 2.10.11; *CIL* 14.376.
12. E.g. *LIMC s.v.* 'fluvii' and 'Okeanos'; on the formula *qui bibunt*, see Nisbet and Hubbard 1978 on Hor. *Odes* 2.20.20.
13. The *locus classicus* is Aelian *VH* 2.33.
14. Paus. 4.34.2, lists the Indus, Nile, Rhine, Danube, Euphrates and Phasis; cf. Purcell 1995.
15. Tac. *Ann.* 1.79.

16. Diod. Sic. 4.35.3–4; Tac. *Ann.* 15.42, on Nero, *ut incredibilium cupitor*, a *spes inrita*; cf. Millar 1993, 86–90, on Vespasian.

17. Virg. *Aen.* 8.726–8, with Becher 1985, and Hardie 1986, 207–9; cf. Val. Flacc. 1.8–9. On Xerxes' bridging of the Hellespont, Aesch. *Pers.* 746 stresses that this was to treat a god as a slave by chaining him; cf. Hdt. 7.35–6, 8.109. On crossing, even Xerxes performed proper rituals: Hdt. 7.54.

18. Varro *LL* 5.83; Dion. Hal. 2.73; Serv. on Virg. *Aen.* 2.166; cf. Plut. *Numa* 9.2–3 (critical of the etymology), with, e.g., Hallett 1970.

19. Plin. *Ep.* 8.20.5; Arr. *Periplus* 10; cf. Arr. *Anab.* 6.3.1 (Alexander in India).

20. E.g. Hesiod *Works* 737–9 (in general); Hdt. 6.76 (Cleomenes at the Erasinus), 7.113 (Xerxes at the Strymon); Arr. *Anab.* 4.4.3, 5.3.6, 5.28.4, 5.29.5 (Alexander on campaign).

21. Cic. *ND* 2.9; *De Div.* 2.77. Servius states (on Virg. *Aen.* 9.24): 'Augurum fuerat consuetudo, ut si post acceptum augurium ad aquam venissent, inclinati aqua haurirent exinde et manibus et fusis precibus vota permitterent, ut visum perseveraret augurium, quod aquae intercessu disrumpitur.'

22. Virg. *Aen.* 8.473; cf. Dion. Hal. 1.9.2 on rivers as boundaries in Roman proto-history; cf. Strabo 5.2.1, pp. 218–19.

23. Brelich 1969, 376–7.

24. Lucullus: Plut. *Luc.* 24.7. Crassus: Dio 40.18.5. Caesar: Suet. *Jul.* 81.2. Danube on Trajan's Column: Lepper and Frere 1988, 50 and pl. 6. Coinage: *BMCRE* III, 168–9, no. 793. Pliny has Rhine and Danube rejoice (*gaudebant*) at Roman disgrace under Domitian: *Paneg.* 82.4. Rhine and Euphrates admire Trajan: Plin. *Paneg.* 14.1.

      Cleomenes at the Erasinus: Hdt. 6.76; cf. Thuc. 5.54 on Spartan reverence for rivers. For Roman conceptions of rivers as protecting their peoples against Rome, see Isaac 1991, 410–13, on the *De rebus bellicis*, after Homer. Trajan's wish: Amm. Marc. 24.3.9; cf. Tac. *Ann.* 1.9.

25. Nicolet 1991. For a review of issues and bibliography on environmental psychology, see Spencer and Blades 1986.

26. Nicolas of Damascus *Life of Augustus* 95; cf. Plut. *Caesar* 58.

27. Cf. Nicolet 1991; Wiseman 1992.

28. Livy 36.17.15; [Tibullus] 148–52; Virg. *Aen.* 7.100–1; Ovid *Met.* 15.829–31; cf. *Res Gestae* 26.2.

29. Cf. Cic. *Cat.* 3.26, 4.21 on empire terminated at the sky.

30. Diod. Sic. 17.104.

31. Bosworth 1988, 130–2.

32. Curtius Rufus 9.6.20ff.; Romm 1992, 22, and Roseman 1994, 121, on thickness and the other qualities of Ocean; see Chapter 9 on Agricola's opening of Ocean.

33. Tac. *Ann.* 1.60.2.

34. Tac. *Ann.* 2.23–4 and 73, with Courtney 1993, 316–17.

35. For text and commentary, see Courtney 1993, 315–19, with Romm 1992, 140–9.

36. Tac. *Germ*. 34.
37. Buccheit 1971, esp. 313–15, collects examples.
38. See further Romm 1992, 26.
39. Caesar fg. 5.4, p. 194, Klotz, with brief discussion of the text to which the speaker refers.
40. Hor. *Epode* 7.7, cf. Vell. Pat. 2.46.1, with Woodman 1983, 71; Fantham 1985.
41. On the religiosity of boundaries, see Kong 1990.
42. Buccheit 1971.
43. For rivers in triumphal procession, see Prop. 2.1.32; further examples in Nisbet and Hubbard 1978, on Hor. *Odes* 2.9.20; cf. Virg. *Aen*. 8.711ff. Apparently, Caesar's triumphs featured the Rhine, the Rhone and an Ocean of gold: Florus 2.13.88. Cf. Suet. *Claud*. 17.3; *Anth. Lat*. 419, 423.

2 KINGS, GOVERNORS AND EMPERORS

1. See Chapters 3 and 8, respectively.
2. Cicero mentions possible Greek prototypes: *Ad Att*. 12.40, 13.28.
3. See, for example, [Aesch.] *Prometheus Bound* (wherein note also a wise Ocean); Soph. *Oedipus Rex*; Eur. *Supplices*.
4. The 'monarchy' of Pericles was a favourite target: well documented by Schwarze 1971, 11 and passim.
5. E.g. Thuc. 2.65.
6. Hdt. 3.80–2.
7. See Asmis 1990, 238–9 on Philodemus' rationalization of his position in the patronage of Piso; Dorandi 1982, 22–32.
8. See, for example, Dio's narrative on the freedman Narcissus and the Claudian invasion; also Tacitus on the freedman Polyclitus' mission for Nero in the aftermath of the Boudican revolt (below, pp. 139–41).
9. Cic. *Ad Att*. 13.6.4, with Braund 1996a.
10. Erskine 1990, 180–204, offers a useful introduction to that controversy and the views of Cicero and Posidonius which bear upon it. There is much of relevance in Gruen 1984, esp. vol. 1, chs 5, 8 and 10.
11. Dion. Hal. 1.5.2–3.
12. Rich 1985, and the literature he cites; Cic. *Div. in Caec*. 65, with Braund 1985.
13. See Dunkle 1967.
14. See Buccheit 1975; cf. Hurlet 1993.
15. Chapter 8.
16. See, for example, Braund 1984, 75–90.
17. Dio 59.24.1.
18. See Braund 1985 on Cicero and Kings Deiotarus and Ariobarzanes III.
19. Cic. *In Verr*. 2.4.67.
20. Cic. *In Pis*. 84 and 87–8.
21. Cf. Cic. *Pro Mur*. 60ff., on Cato and Stoicism.
22. Cic. *In Pis*. 37.

23. E.g. Cic. *In Pis.* 42, where Piso has misconceived Epicurean philosophy as crude hedonism; and, further, ibid. 68ff., on Piso's hedonistic interpretation.
24. See the fine edition, translation and commentary of Dorandi 1982; cf. also Murray 1965, which contains much valuable material and discussion. Obbink 1995 provides a fine introduction to the world of scholarship on Philodemus.
25. Philodemus *Good King* 1, Dorandi.
26. Ibid. 3; cf. D'Arms 1995.
27. Ibid. 4.
28. Ibid. 5.
29. Ibid. 6.
30. Ibid. 7.
31. Ibid. 8.
32. Ibid. 9.
33. Wiseman 1985; cf. Murray 1965, 175–6, on Homer as a source of precepts on kingship. Philodemus' *On flattery* seems to have constituted the seventh book of his *On virtues and vices*: see Dorandi 1990, 2365, for bibliography.
34. See Chapter 3.
35. Murray 1965, 180, urges the case for completion in 58, finding the concerns of the work too general to have a bearing more specific than the life of a Roman *princeps*; but see below on the very general significance of provincial governorship.
36. Braund 1996a.
37. Cf. Cic. *In Pis.* 96.
38. For a neglected instance, see Nicolas of Damascus *Life of Augustus* 108; cf. Abbott 1907; Edwards 1993.
39. Zehnacker 1983, 42–3; cf. ibid. 44 on Balbus, albeit at Gades.
40. On philosophical metaphors for life, see Rutherford 1989, 231–44.
41. Rawson 1975, 35, expresses reservation.
42. Cf. Cic. *In Pis.* 56–7.
43. Tac. *Agr.* 39.
44. Cic. *In Pis.* 60, where Cicero imagines 'Epicurean' Piso denigrating such objectives.

3   CAESAR: THE EXCITEMENT OF INVASION

1. Dio 39.50.3; Romm 1992, 140–1.
2. See the valuable text and commentary of Roseman 1994.
3. This is the translation of De Lacy and De Lacy 1941, 35, which should perhaps be modified but not in any way relevant to the current discussion; see Sedley 1982, esp. 257–8 on the passage and its translation. The original Greek states 'living creatures', not 'men', though they may be included, as Mansfeld 1990, 3190, notes. The passage may be echoed by Cicero: see below, note 41.

4. Diels 1958, 443–4, with Mansfeld 1990 for the context of the quotation; Asclepiades died in 91 BC: Rawson 1985, 171.
5. Vell. Pat. 2.46.1; Florus 1.45.16.
6. Diod. Sic. 5.21.2 notices their absence, while Rawson 1985, 263, observes the lack of mythical figures in Caesar's own account.
7. Diod. Sic. 3.38.3; cf. Rawson 1985, 112, on Caesar's interest in astronomy, not least in Britain.
8. Cic. *De prov. cons.* 33.
9. Romm 1992, 136, on [Tibullus] 3.7.148–50.
10. Plut. *Caes.* 22.4; Wiseman 1985.
11. Pelling 1979; cf. Braund 1993.
12. Compare Cat. 11.10–11 and 45.21–2, both setting Britain on the exotic periphery; note also Dio 39.53.2.
13. Wiseman 1987, 39, captures the mood.
14. See Woodman 1988, 91, on the 'writing-project'.
15. Cic. *Ad Q. fr.* 3.1.13, though Cicero's quip at 3.9.6 mentions only its travelling from Gaul. This Erigone seems to have been the daughter of Aegisthus and Clytemnestra, not the daughter of Icarius, but certainty is impossible. Courtney 1993, 181, observes that we do not know whether Quintus' play was a tragedy, though that seems probable.
16. Cic. *Ad Q. fr.* 3.5 and 6.
17. Ibid. 3.6.3.
18. Ibid. 3.1.3, 2.14.2.
19. Ibid. 2.16.5.
20. Suet. *Jul.* 56.7, with Courtney 1993, 187–8, on Caesar as a poet.
21. Cic. *Brutus* 252–5 with Rawson 1991, 385–7; cf. Cic. *Orator* 155–60; Suet. *Jul.* 56.5.
22. Braund 1993a.
23. Cic. *Ad Q. fr.* 3.7.6; Courtney 1993, 149, thinks it may never have been published.
24. For Cotta's work, see Athenaeus 6.273b. He occurs in Caesar's commentaries at *BG* 2.11, 4.22, 4.38, 5.24–37 (his death) and 52, 6.32, 6.37.
25. Suet. *Jul.* 46; cf. ibid. 48 on his banquets in the provinces. The recently discovered texts from Vindolanda have provided intriguing insight into the active social life of the elite among the Roman forces in northern Britain early in the second century AD: Bowman 1994, esp. 127–8.
26. Cic. *Ad Q. fr.* 3.1.22.
27. Cic. *Ad Fam.* 12.24.3.
28. Ibid. 7.5; Cic. *Ad Q. fr.* 2.14.3, apparently a recommendation which won favour not only with Trebatius, but also with Caesar: cf. ibid. 3.1.9.
29. Cic. *Ad Att.* 4.16.7.
30. Cic. *Ad Q. fr.* 2.16; see Shackleton Bailey on the chronology of *Ad Fam.* 7.8.1.
31. Cic. *Ad Att.* 4.18.5.
32. Cf. Caes. *BG* 5.23.2, and see below on the information available to him even before the first invasion.

33. Cic. *Ad Att.* 4.16.7; cf. Diod. Sic. 5.21.6, who finds moral nobility in British savagery.
34. Cic. *Ad Att.* 7.10.1; cf. Drinkwater 1983, 10, on the predisposition of Caesar's account of the Gauls.
35. Cic. *Ad Fam.* 7.6.2. In the event, Trebatius stayed in Gaul, for which Cicero teases him: *Ad Fam.* 7.17.3, 7.16.1, 7.10.1–2, where again Cicero mentions chariots. On the place of chariots in the discourse and practice of the late Republic, see Rawson 1991, 389–407.
36. Caes. *BG* 4.33.
37. Wiseman 1985.
38. Diod. Sic. 5.21.5.
39. Cic. *Ad Q. fr.* 3.1.10.
40. Were British slaves among those that Quintus promised to provide Cicero at *Ad Q. fr.* 3.9.4?
41. Cic. *Ad Fam.* 15.16.2; perhaps echoing the use of Britain by Philodemus in *De Signis* 5.29–36, quoted above.
42. Plut. *Caes.* 17.4; Plin. *NH* 7.92; cf. Suet. *Jul.* 56.
43. Plut. *Caes.* 17.3.
44. Cic. *Ad Q. fr.* 3.1.25.
45. Suet. *Jul.* 56.6, with Bowman 1994, esp. 114–16.
46. Cicero wrote *commentarii* to be worked up by the historian Lucceius: Cic. *Ad Att.* 4.6.4, 4.11.2; *Ad Fam.* 5.12.10; cf. *Ad Att.* 1.19.10. Note also his attempt to interest Posidonius in a Greek version: *Ad Att.* 2.1.2; cf. ibid. 1.19.10. See, in general, Misch 1907, I, 99–100; cf. Hurlet 1993, 111–12, on the substantial *commentarii* of Sulla.
47. Wiseman and Wiseman 1980, 9, stressing the political advantage of regular book-by-book publication; cf. Wiseman 1994, 401.
48. Cic. *Brutus* 262, quoted on p. 53.
49. Cic. *Ad Fam.* 5.12, with the discussion of Woodman 1988.
50. Caes. *BG* 2.35.
51. Suet. *Jul.* 24.3, on this and the Senate's decree of a commission of inquiry into the state of Gaul under Caesar; cf. Plut. *Caes.* 22.1–3, citing Tanusius as his authority. For the senatorial debate and Caesar's attack upon Cato, see Plut. *Cato Minor* 51.1–3.
52. Cic. *Brutus* 218–19; cf. ibid. 248–62 for praise of Caesar, perhaps wise in 46, when the work was published.
53. Plut. *Cato Minor* 36.3; cf. ibid. 51–2; financial value: ibid. 45.1–2, countering Clodius.
54. Caes. *BG* 4.38.
55. Strabo 4.5.3, p. 200, quoted and discussed in Chapter 5.
56. Suet. *Jul.* 47; cf. ibid. 50.2, on his gift of a valuable pearl to Servilia. On pearls and luxury, see Purcell 1995.
57. E.g. Suet. *Jul.* 54; cf. Catullus 29. Cicero was only one of those who benefited from Caesar's financial power: Cic. *Ad Att.* 7.3.11.
58. Dio 40.1.2.
59. Ibid. 40.4.2.

60. Diodorus Siculus was not deterred, though his account of Caesar's campaigning (now lost) was in Greek: cf. Rawson 1985, 254–5.
61. Ibid. 163.
62. Cic. *Ad Att.* 2.1.2; cf. ibid. 1.19.10, with Griffin 1994, 712–13.
63. Suet. *Jul.* 37.1; Florus 2.13.88.
64. Suet. *Jul.* 37.2.

4   ARTFUL COMMENTARIES: CAESAR ON HIMSELF

1. Suet. *Jul.* 1; Plut. *Caes.* 1.2. On trophies for defeat of Cimbri and Teutones (and of Jugurtha), see Suet. *Jul.* 11.
2. Sall. *Bell. Jug.* 114, with Paul 1984, 257–8.
3. Caes. *BG* 1.11.
4. Ibid. 1.12.
5. Appian *Celt.* 3, and Plut. *Caes.* 18 have Labienus, not Caesar, defeat the Tigurini, spoiling the point about L. Piso. Livy seems to have held that it was not the Tigurini, but the Nitiobriges, who inflicted the defeat upon Cassius: Livy *Per.* 65; cf. Oros. 5.15.23–4. If so, the Tigurini had no particular debt to pay.
6. Caes. *BG* 1.13–14.
7. Ibid. 1.27–8.
8. Ibid. 1.31–2.
9. Braund 1980.
10. Caes. *BG* 1.33.
11. Ibid. 1.35.
12. Ibid. 1.36. Ariovistus is made to misrepresent Rome's earlier response to the difficulties of the Aedui: Drinkwater 1983, 13–14.
13. As, for example, is Drinkwater 1983, 16, though very aware of the 'studied blandness' of Caesar's account.
14. Caes. *BG* 1.37.
15. Ibid. 1.39.
16. Ibid. 1.40–1.
17. Ibid. 1.43.
18. Ibid. 1.44.
19. Ibid. 1.45–6.
20. Ibid. 1.47.
21. Ibid. 1.53.
22. Cf. Lintott 1993, 105.
23. Cf. Wiseman 1994, 386, on P. Considius. For the ethics of war at Rome, civil vs. foreign, see Jal 1964; cf. Wiseman 1982.
24. On the Veneti, see Caes. BG 3.9.10; Strabo 4.4.1, p. 194, thinks that the Veneti had attacked Caesar to obstruct his designs on Britain and safeguard their trading interests there.
25. Caes. BG 4.20.
26. Ibid. 6.13.
27. Ibid. 2.4.

28. Ibid. 4.21; Commius took with him an entourage of some thirty cavalry: ibid. 4.35.
29. Ibid. 4.21.
30. Ibid. 5.20.
31. Ibid. 4.23–6.
32. Ibid. 4.27.
33. Ibid. 4.27.
34. Ibid. 4.29–31.
35. Ibid. 4.32–5.
36. Ibid. 4.36.
37. Ibid. 4.38.
38. Dio 40.1.2; Mandubracius offered another possible justification, but there is no sign that his case was used in that way: see below.
39. *BG* 5.6–7.
40. Ibid. 5.9.
41. See Chapter 1.
42. See Dio 39.61; cf. Becher 1985, though largely on the imperial period.
43. Caes. *BG* 5.9.
44. Ibid. 5.10–11.
45. As Rawson 1985, 261, observes.
46. Curtius 9.9.9ff., doubtless aware of Caesar.
47. Caes. *BG* 5.11.
48. Dio 40.2.3; Plut. *Caes.* 23.3.
49. Caes. *BG* 5.11; cf. ibid. 5.18.
50. Ibid. 5.20.
51. Ibid. 1.31.
52. See Chapter 9.
53. See Cic. *Ad Quint. fr.* 3.6.2.
54. Caes. *BG* 5.20.
55. Note Plut. *Caes.* 23.3: apparently, Caesar did not enrich his men in Britain. However, given the atmosphere of polemical claim and counter-claim surrounding Caesar's governorship (see Chapter 3), any such statement requires qualification and doubt.
56. Caes. *BG* 5.21.
57. Ibid. 5.22: *maxime etiam permotus defectione civitatum.*
58. Ibid. 5.22; Diod. Sic. 5.21.2; Suet. *Jul.* 25.2.
59. Cic. *Ad Att.* 4.18.5; cf. Braund 1984, 63–6.
60. On Gallus, see above, p. 10.
61. Rawson 1985, 263, notes Parthenius in this connection.

5 COINS AND DYNASTIES

1. Barrett 1989, 127.
2. Note the concluding caution of Allen 1944, a pioneering study. On the dangers of stylistic arguments for sequence, see Allen 1975, 3; compare Van Arsdell 1989, which combines an admirable knowledge of coinage with an excess of speculation, often presented as fact. On variation

among tribes and Roman unconcern for uniformity, Reynolds 1966, 71–2, remains valuable.

3. Barrett 1989, 127.

4. On what archaeological evidence *can* do, see, for example, the militant survey of Jones 1991a, rightly complaining about the abuse of classical texts.

5. Van Arsdell 1994 exemplifies the detailed work that is needed: note his properly cautious remarks on the possibility of deriving political boundaries from coin findspots (Van Arsdell 1994, 23–4).

6. But note, for example, the consistently Celtic style of the coinage of the Dobunni in the western parts of southern England around Gloucestershire: Van Arsdell 1989, 266–86.

7. For much insight into problems of dating, see Haselgrove 1987, 75–101.

8. Compare, for example, Van Arsdell 1989, 404, no. 1969-1 (Celticized) and ibid. 414, 2045-1 (Romanized); note also the heads on coins of Tasciovanus: ibid. 367, 1698-1 (Celticized) and ibid. 381, 1814-1 (Romanized).

9. Van Arsdell 1989, 388, 1868-1 (Celticized head); ibid. 389, 1871-1 (Romanized head).

10. Ibid. 212, no. 780-1.

11. Ibid. 170, no. 533-1, and 172, no. 551-1 (Verica); ibid. 421, no. 2089-1 (Cunobelinus).

12. Crawford 1985, 273–5.

13. Haselgrove 1987, 26 and 201–2, with the general discussion of Evans 1987, and Woolf 1994.

14. Van Arsdell 1989, passim; cf. ibid. 253 for a further possibility.

15. E.g. Van Arsdell 1989, 404, no. 1971-1.

16. Ibid. 405, no. 1977-1, CAMULODUNO. But Haselgrove 1987, 29, is right to note the large inference involved: we cannot be sure that the name indicates the location of the mint, as often suggested.

17. See Mossop 1979: this type has now been complemented by the discovery of a similar coin in the so-called S. W. Norfolk hoard, under excavation by the Castle Museum, Norwich. The new coin is illustrated on p. 133.

18. Van Arsdell 1989, 144, 162ff., 173, 177–8, 422.

19. Ibid. 100, 276, with 201–3 on an Anted among the Iceni, 376.

20. For doubts, see Haselgrove 1987, 31.

21. Caes. *BG* 5.22.

22. Tac. *Ann.* 12.33; Dio 60.20.2 describes Caratacus as Catuvellaunian. Note also the case of Commius, refugee from Gaul, who seems to have established himself as a ruler in Britain, on whom more below.

23. See further, for the problems of 'tribes', Haselgrove 1987, 52–4. There is much sensible discussion of these problems in the opening chapters of Millett 1990.

24. Note also the coinage of Epaticcus, which Van Arsdell 1989, 179, sees as both Atrebatic and Trinovantian.

25. For example, Van Arsdell 1989, 319, identifies the two tribes, while Todd 1981, 52, is both critical and cautious. And whatever circumstances

caused Eppillus to reign both among the Atrebates and among the Cantii (as he seems to have done: Van Arsdell 1989, 97), warfare is not the only possible cause.

26. He is conventionally known as Tincommius, but only the first six letters are attested on his coins, while only the first three letters can be read in the *Res Gestae*, as we shall see in the next chapter – if it is indeed his name.

27. Apparently he ruled also in Kent: see Van Arsdell 1989, 97.

28. Caes. *BG* 5.22.

29. Frontin. *Strat*. 2.13.11.

30. Allen 1944, 5, the seminal discussion.

31. Cingetorix of Kent (Caes. *BG* 5.22) and his homonym of the Treviri (ibid. 5.3–4 etc.); Diviciacus of the Aedui (ibid. 1.3 etc.) and his homonym of the Suessiones (ibid. 2.4; cf. also Divico, ibid. 1.13–14). On the name Dubnovellaunus, see below, n. 35.

32. So Van Arsdell 1989, 279.

33. Note also that the identification of Verica *c*. AD 40 is also in some doubt, as we shall see in Chapter 7.

34. Van Arsdell 1989, 354, nos. 1635-1 and 1638-1; the name is usually Latinized as Addedomarus.

35. Ibid. 356–61. A ruler of the same name in Kent is usually given similar dates, though sharply distinguished in his coinage: ibid. 97.

36. Ibid. 107.

37. Ibid. 361–84, on the usual view minting at Verulamium, in part at least, but see above, n. 16.

38. Van Arsdell 1989, 179, no. 575-1, provides the fullest extant form of his name, EPATICU, conceivably with a further *S*.

39. Ibid.; though Van Arsdell there seems in doubt as to whether Epaticcus was related to Cunobelinus, he was evidently his brother.

40. E.g. Van Arsdell 1989, no. 2089-1.

41. A fourth ruler, as it seems, RUES, does not mention Tasciovanus on his very limited extant coinage: ibid. 391–2.

42. See below, p. 95–6.

43. Van Arsdell 1989, 201–12, on the sequence: the partial coincidence between the letters ECEN and the tribal name has encouraged the view that Ecen was not a ruler, but an abbreviation of the latter.

44. Ibid. 272–83, on the sequence.

45. Ibid. 301–2.

46. Ibid. 247–65.

47. Though VEP CORF cannot definitely be identified as filiation: ibid. 253.

6   FROM COMMIUS TO CUNOBELINUS

1. Wiseman 1985.

2. Hor. *Odes* 1.21.13–16.

3. Ibid. 3.4.33.

4. Ibid. 1.35.30, 4.14.48; cf. Cat. 11.11–12, 29.4; note also Virg. *Ecl.* 1.66, and Martial *Epigr.* 10.44.

5. Prop. 2.27.4–5.

6. Ibid. 2.1.75–6, 4.3.8–9.

7. Ovid *Met.* 15.752.

8. Dio 49.38.2.

9. Ibid. 53.22.5.

10. Ibid. 53.25.2.

11. So Syme 1978, 50–1.

12. See ibid. 51, on date and interpretation.

13. Cf. Dio 49.38.2.

14. Haselgrove 1987, 196.

15. Braund 1984, 62–3; cf. below on Cartimandua and Prasutagus.

16. Van Arsdell 1994, 40–2, who seems to date the coinage around the early years of Augustus' reign.

17. Virg. *Aen.* 6.853.

18. Cf. the similar second-century judgment of Appian *Preface* 7, with valuable comment by Breeze 1988, 12–13.

19. Jacob 1991, 160, offers an intellectual context for the passage.

20. Tac. *Ann.* 1.11.

21. *RG* 32.

22. Kings and coins are discussed in the previous chapter.

23. Reusser 1993; Rich 1985; Braund 1984, esp. 24–5.

24. See Braund 1993b.

25. Allen and Haselgrove 1979, 2, no. 128; see Figures 18–19.

26. By contrast, Diod. Sic. 5.21.6 mentions both dynasts and kings in Britain; Roseman 1994, 2–3, suspects the influence of Pytheas.

27. *Rex et socius atque amicus*: Braund 1984, esp. 23–4; cf. ibid. 124–5.

28. See Cunliffe 1981.

29. E.g. by Todd 1981, 32.

30. Failure to allow for such fluctuations has generated much confusion: see, for example, Braund 1991.

31. E.g. Van Arsdell 1989, 407, no. 1983-1.

32. E.g. ibid. 416, no. 2057-1.

33. Ibid. 421, no. 2089-1.

34. Ibid. 422, no. 2095-1.

35. Ibid. 402, 2091-1.

36. So Barrett 1989, 127.

37. E.g. Sorabji 1993, 122–33, and the literature he cites on οἰκεῖος, οἰκείωσις and ancient notions of the relationship between man and animals; for further bibliography, see Long and Sedley 1987, II, 506–7. On οἰκεῖος in inter-state relations, see the evidence collected in Braund 1980; cf. Elwyn 1993, who seems to me to overestimate Greek influence.

38. *Membra partesque imperii*: Suet. *Aug.* 48; cf. Cic. *De Rep.* 3.37; Sen. *De Clem.* 1.1. Cf. Strabo on Parthia: Syme 1995, 332.

39. Braund 1984, 63–6 and 184. The 'number of troops needed' was something of a topos: cf. Quint. 7.4.2; Tac. *Agr*. 24.
40. *Reguli*: Tac. *Ann*. 2.24.

7 CALIGULA, CLAUDIUS AND CARATACUS

1. Suet. *Gaius* 60.
2. See above, p. 79.
3. Barrett 1989, 211–12, at p. 212.
4. Balsdon 1934, 50–4, at p. 52.
5. Suet. *Gaius* 19.3, though the lame explanation of his grandfather is described by Balsdon 1934, 52, as servants' chatter – courtiers' chatter anyway.
6. Dio 59.16.11.
7. Ibid. 59.17.
8. Suet. *Gaius* 19.2.
9. See Chapter 1.
10. Cf. Sextus Pompey: Dio 48.19.2, with Hadas 1930, 78. On the relevance of Neptune/Ocean to Britain, see Chapter 1; note also *RIB* 91.
11. Jos. *AJ* 18.101–5.
12. Suet. *Gaius* 43.1; cf. Pliny (*Ep*. 8.8), who was very impressed by the cult-centre, though never accused of madness.
13. Suet. *Gaius* 50.3: *pelagi . . . speciem*.
14. Balsdon 1934, 89, suggests that the German and the British campaigns were alternatives for Gaius, though the sources present them together.
15. Catull. 11.10.
16. Probus, on Virg. *Georg*. 1.227, with Courtney 1993, 345–6; it remains uncertain that Probus refers to a whole poem so entitled, as Barrett 1989, 102, asserts.
17. Suet. *Gaius* 8.1; on Hercules, see Tac. *Germ*. 3. See Chapter 3 on the absence of mythical figures from Britain.
18. Suet. *Gaius* 47.
19. Dio 59. 21.3, ambiguous because it runs together the German and British campaigns, may mean that some of Gaius' officers had gained some real success in Britain.
20. Levick 1990, 152, locates the scene at a mouth of the Rhine or even the Ems.
21. Suet. *Gaius* 46; Dio 59.25.1–5 gives a similar account but does not mention the lighthouse and suggests that Gaius was indeed generous to his troops: ibid. 59.25.3.
22. Ibid. 59.25.3. E.g. Ocean could be said to have lost his freedom to Claudius: [Sen.] *Octavia* 38–40.
23. On man and the sea, see Purcell 1995.
24. Barrett 1989, 135–8, collects attempts, his own the most attractive: that Gaius' intention was to exercise diplomatic influence in Britain.
25. Cf. Tac. *Agr*. 13.

26. Barrett 1989, 137–8, imagines his picturesque reception by Gaius in mid-Channel.
27. For the coins, see Van Arsdell 1989, 109–10; cf. Nash 1982: his name was not Amminus, as often stated. As usual, dating must be less precise than is regularly claimed.
28. Suet. *Gaius* 44.2.
29. Tac. *Ann.* 2.63; *RG* 32; note also in this chapter Caratacus and Mithridates VIII of the Bosporan kingdom.
30. Suet. *Gaius* 47.1: *transfugas barbaros*; cf. ibid. 44.2: *transfugerat*.
31. On Verica and Tiberius, see above, Chapter 5. For the identification, Allen 1944, 10, is the turning-point: it had previously been a minority view, it seems.
32. Dio 60.19.1; on homonyms, see above, p. 191 n. 31.
33. *Britanniam . . . tumultuantem ob non redditos transfugas*: *Claud.* 17.1, a passage which Graves's Penguin translation embroiders almost beyond recognition.
34. Dio 60.19.2.
35. Cf. Suet. *Claud.* 17.1.
36. Caes. *BG* 6.13–16.
37. Suet. *Claud.* 25.5.
38. Ibid. 41–2; cf. *ILS* 212, where Claudius offers general comment on Caesar and the Gauls, mentioning his own dealings with Britain and Ocean. On Claudius and Caesar, see Levick 1990, 90.
39. See p. 68, with Foster 1986; much of this came from Roman Gaul, as Haselgrove 1989, 12–16, observes in his valuable survey of evidence and problems. Fulford 1991, 36, notes the acceleration of exchange between southern Britain and the continent in the middle of Augustus' reign.
40. Dio 60.20.1; coins confirm the Latin-looking form of his name, CUNOBELINUS: Van Arsdell 1989, 417, no. 2063-1. See further Chapter 5.
41. Dio, 60.20.1. There may have been further sons: coins show AGE (Van Arsdell 1989, 427) and SOLIDU(S?) (ibid. 419, no. 2073-1).
42. Hind 1989.
43. So Hind 1989, 4; direct evidence is lacking.
44. Dio 60.20.1.
45. The most accurate translation known to me is that of Hind 1989, 7, with which my own translation largely agrees.
46. *LSJ*, *s.v.* ἐπάρχω.
47. Dio 60.21.1.
48. Tac. *Ann.* 12.38.
49. Levick 1990, 142, also notes the galaxy of distinguished Romans who were in Britain with Claudius, given a share of glory and kept under surveillance.
50. Cf. [Sen.] *Octavia* 28–30, which echoes Mela.
51. Dio 60.21.5–22. 2.
52. Barrett 1991, 1–2.
53. Ibid., esp. 12–15; for his restoration of the arch, see ibid. 18.

54. Plin. *NH* 3. 119, with Barrett 1989, 33. Levick 1990, 143, has Claudius make a leisurely return to Rome which incorporated this celebration; he had been out of Rome for six months in total: Dio 60.23.1.
55. For the text, see Saladino 1980.
56. *P. Lond.* 1178, 8–16. Had it been sent for his triumph of 44, or was it perhaps a response to word of that triumph?
57. Erim 1982.
58. Suet. *Claud.* 27.
59. Ibid. 21.6: since the capture of only one *oppidum* is mentioned, that can only be Camulodunum, though the place is not expressly named. The relationship of that spectacle to other celebrations of the British victory in Rome, if any, remains unclear.
60. See Barrett 1991, 2–3, on the location of the arch.
61. Suet. *Claud.* 17: *maximo apparatu.*
62. Levick 1990, 144.
63. Dio 60.23; Suet. *Claud.* 28.1.
64. Suet. *Claud.* 24.3.
65. *ILS* 217, with the important discussion of Barrett 1991. The date is a matter of speculation, but it may post-date the dedication of the Roman arch in AD 51–2, and pre-dates the death of Claudius in AD 54.
66. Suet. *Claud.* 1.2, also on his channelling of the Rhine.
67. Eutropius 7.13, only possible in a diplomatic sense; cf. Barrett 1991, 11, on Ocean and the Orkneys in older restorations of the inscription on Claudius' arch at Rome. As we shall see in Chapter 9, the notion of Claudian contact with the Orkneys may have been generated under the Flavians.
68. Levick 1990, 144.
69. *Traiecti et quasi domiti Oceani insigne*: Suet. *Claud.* 17.3.
70. Cf. [Sen.] *Octavia* 38–40.
71. See Levick 1990, 107.
72. Tac. *Ann.* 12.23–4.
73. See Levick 1990, 149–61.
74. Murgia 1977, 330.
75. *RIB* 91, with Bogaers 1979. There can be no real doubt that Tacitus and the inscription mention the same ruler.
76. Tac. *Agr.* 14.
77. Cf. Tac. *Hist.* 2.81.
78. See Barrett 1979, 233.
79. Bogaers 1979.
80. Its mention of a divine house would be impossible under Vespasian. Cogidubnus was dead by AD 78, as we shall see.
81. Braund 1984, 109–15.
82. See Barrett 1979, 229–30, for various suggestions on Cogidubnus' antecedents: this valuable article collects and illustrates the range of speculations that have spiralled from our two pieces of evidence and a very little archaeology.

83. *Rex magnus*: the stone is damaged at this point, but Bogaers 1979 has made a powerful case for the reading, in place of the peculiarly abbreviated *rex et legatus* hitherto imagined. Birley 1981, 208–10, is right to observe that we cannot be sure of the reading without further evidence.

84. Barrett 1979, 232, for the sources, and modern discussions thereof.

85. Ptol. *Geogr.* 2.3.28.

86. Cunliffe 1973, 24, summarizes sources and solutions.

87. Barrett 1979, 239–41. Whether Cogidubnus had any direct connection with the so-called 'proto-palace' remains a matter for speculation. Birley 1981, 208–10, allows the possibility that the palace may have been erected for Cogidubnus just as he died; nothing more can be done to link king and building.

88. See further Hanson 1987, 76–8; Blagg 1990.

89. Barrett 1979, esp. 241–2.

90. Ibid. 241, though the 40s seem impossible: Tacitus' phrase would lack all point if the king did not out-last Didius Gallus at least.

91. *RIB* 92, with Barrett 1979, 239, who assumes that Cogidubnus was the dedicator, though he is not named.

92. Tac.*Ann*. 14.31.

93. See ibid. 12.35–6 on Caratacus' brothers.

94. Cf. the version of Petrus Patricius, conveniently printed in the Loeb edition of Dio, which adds that Caratacus lived on in Italy with his wife and children – not an unparalleled outcome: see Braund 1984, 171.

95. Cf. Tac.*Ann*. 13.54; on Romanization, see Chapter 9.

96. Hdt. 9.82, with Braund 1996. The coincidence of the tent is worth noting.

97. Tac.*Ann*. 12.36.

98. Ibid.

99. Ibid. 12.36–7; the distinction between *misericordia* and *clementia* is explored in these terms in Seneca, *De Clementia*, on which see the survey of Mortureux 1989.

100. Cf. [Cic.] *Ad Her.* 2.50; Cic. *De Inv.* 1.106–9. Note also the rather different argument from tradition at *RG* 27. There is evidence that some captured kings were indeed treated well: Braund 1984, 165–74, collects examples. More specifically, Levick 1990, 89, may be right to suggest that Claudius sought to outdo Caesar's execution of Vercingetorix by exercising the superior quality of *clementia*.

101. Cf. Tac. *Ann*. 12.34 for Tacitus' imagining of Caratacus' address to his forces in similar terms of slavery and freedom.

102. Ibid. 12.21.

103. And no doubt his daughter, who is not mentioned further: ibid. 12.37.

104. Ibid.

105. Ibid. 12.38.

106. On Tacitus' account, at least: see the next chapter for possible doubts.

107. Tac.*Ann*. 12.38.

108. Levick 1990, 88–90.
109. Tacitus was more perceptive: *Agr.* 13.

8   BOUDICA AND CARTIMANDUA

1. Plut. *Cato Maior* 8.8.
2. Diod. Sic. 1.13.4.
3. Suet. *Jul.* 22.2; Cicero *De prov. cons.* 9; cf. Ovid *Amores* 1.5.11.
4. Cf. Ginsburg 1993, on Tacitus and the issue of controlling Roman women in the provinces, which should be considered in this context.
5. Hamer 1993 makes the case powerfully.
6. See Bradley 1994, 49–50.
7. Griffin 1985, esp. 43 n. 79 collects examples.
8. Vidal Naquet 1981, 188 makes the point, discussing utopian treatments of slaves and women in power; cf. Pembroke 1967.
9. Rosellini and Saïd 1978; Dewald 1981.
10. Tac. *Agr.* 3 – but what else could he say? See the next chapter.
11. Boudica seems to be the best spelling of her name: see Jackson 1979.
12. Tac. *Ann.* 12.36, and *Hist.* 3.45.
13. Tac. *Hist.* 3.45; cf. Prasutagus' bequest to his daughters, below.
14. Tac. *Ann.* 12.36; her omission from the narrative at *Ann.* 12.32 suggests not that she became queen thereafter, but that she was already queen, for her accession is not mentioned in the extant books of Tacitus.
15. Hartley and Fitts 1988, 4–6.
16. Tac. *Ann.* 12.32. See Millett 1990, 54–5, on the fragmented nature of the Brigantian confederacy.
17. Cf. Sen. *Apoc.* 3.3, 8.3.
18. Tac. *Agr.* 31, Calgacus' speech; Paus. 8.43.4.
19. On Berenice as a seductive queen, see Tac. *Hist.* 2.2, 2.81.
20. Braund 1983a.
21. On archaeology at Stanwick, see Hanson and Campbell 1986, esp. 76–7; Haselgrove and Turnbull 1987.
22. Tac. *Ann.* 12.40: see below.
23. Accordingly, when chains were used they might be of precious metal, or imagined as such: Vell. Pat. 2.82 and Dio 49.39 (King Artavasdes of Armenia: different metals); Silius Ital. 17.629–30 (Syphax of Numidia; but cf. Diod. 27.6); SHA, *Tyr. Trig.* 30.26; *Aur.* 34.3 (Zenobia); in general, Prop. 2.1.33.
24. Cf. Tac. *Agr.* 14, and *Hist.* 2.81.
25. Tac. *Ann.* 12.15–21.
26. Ibid. 12.19.
27. Tac. *Germ.* 45; cf. *Hist.* 5.25, where Tacitus has ordinary Batavians prefer the rule of Rome to that of a woman.
28. Of course, the *Histories* (*c.* AD 110) were produced some six years before the *Annals* (*c.* AD 116).

29. See Hanson and Campbell 1986.
30. For sceptical remarks on the inscription, see Braund 1984a, 5–6.
31. See the important discussion by Woodman 1993, 109–15.
32. On the number of kings, see p. 103.
33. Tac. *Ann.* 12.31.
34. *Longa opulentia clarus*: Tac. *Ann.* 14.31.
35. For his coins, see p. 70. Tac. *Agr.* 16.1 claims that Boudica was of royal stock.
36. Braund 1983.
37. Tac. *Ann.* 14.31.
38. Champlin 1991, esp. 66, with literature on Tacitus, Nero and wills.
39. *Senectam*: Tac. *Ann.* 14.35.
40. Garnsey 1970; Bradley 1994; cf. the appropriate treatment of Zenobia, wife of Radamistus at Tac. *Ann.* 12.51.
41. Tac. *Ann.* 14.42–5. On freedom and slavery in Tacitus' narrative, see Roberts 1988.
42. Tac. *Ann.* 14.21; Tacitus described the spread of revolt in AD 48 in similar terms.
43. Ibid. 14.32.
44. Dio 62.2.1. On Seneca's profiteering, see Griffin 1976, 44.
45. *Dig.* 1.19.1–2 (Ulpian), with Brunt 1990, 163–87.
46. Tac. *Ann.* 14.33.
47. On Tacitus' view of Suetonius, see also Griffin 1984, 230. I find more praise than criticism of Suetonius in Tac. *Agr.* 14–16.
48. Tac. *Ann.* 14.33.
49. See Chapter 3.
50. Tac. *Ann.* 3.33; Bowman 1994, 56–7, with Chapter 9 below on officers' wives.
51. See now Eckstein 1995, 119–24.
52. On which, see now Blok 1995.
53. Tac. *Agr.* 42.
54. Dio 62.12.6.
55. Tac. *Ann.* 14.49; cf. Tac. *Agr.* 42.
56. I see no grounds for the claim of Todd 1981, 93, that the revolt of Boudica had a substantial role in improving Roman provincial administration, in Britain or elsewhere; certainly Tacitus does not suggest as much.
57. Despite modern orthodoxy, it should be noted that Tacitus does not describe Classicianus as being just in his critique of Suetonius, but unjust and improperly concerned with his own personal interests. Frere 1978, 108, curiously characterizes Classicianus as taking 'a statesman's view of the situation', after Collingwood; cf. also Todd 1981, 92.
58. Cf. Tac. *Germ.* 25.
59. Lateiner 1989, 28.
60. Dio 60.19.3.
61. Cf. Hor. *Odes* 1.37, on Cleopatra.
62. Dio 62.12.6.

63. E.g. Dudley and Webster 1962, 54. On the *Histories* of Cluvius Rufus, see Wiseman 1991, 111–18. I am indebted to the latter author for the suggestion that Cluvius' account may have contributed to that of Dio.

64. Tac. *Hist.* 4.14, with the acute observations of Ogilvie and Richmond 1967, 194.

65. Tac. *Agr.* 31.4. On the possibility of an extended use of 'Brigantes', see p. 125.

9   AGRICOLA AND TACITUS, TRAJAN AND THE FLAVIANS

1. Suet. *Nero* 18.1; Griffin 1984, 96–9; Wiseman 1982.
2. See above, p. 125.
3. On which, see Levick 1990, 190.
4. See Suet. *Vesp.* 4.1–2, on his receipt of triumphal ornaments, with Levick 1990, 144, on Vespasian in Britain.
5. Tac. *Agr.* 10.3, with Syme 1958, 289–94.
6. Through his father: see Millar 1993, 73.
7. See Ogilvie and Richmond 1967, 187, on Tacitus' reduction of Plautius' role in favour of Vespasian.
8. Tac. *Agr.* 17.1.
9. Dio 60.30.1. More mundanely, the mistake may be that of Dio's excerptor, Xiphilinus, but the origin of such an error remains obscure.
10. Dio 60.20.3.
11. Suet. *Titus* 4.1, with Birley 1975, 140, but Hanson 1991, 1750, stresses the lack of evidence for their service together and the difficulties entailed in the proposition.
12. Martial *On the spectacles* 7.
13. Tac. *Dial.* 17, set in AD 75, where Aper claims once to have met a Briton who had fought against Caesar; cf. p. 42 on long-lived Britons.
14. The word is attested first in Latin at Lucan 6.68, written under Nero. I am grateful to Matthew Leigh for discussion of the passage.
15. Stat. *Silvae* 5.2.132–51; cf. Coleman 1988, xxxi–xxxii on problems of dating poems in the fifth book of the *Silvae*.
16. The problem is not new: see Momigliano 1950, 42; Lefèvre 1971, 51–2.
17. Cf. Mela 3.6.49, quoted in Chapter 7, where it is Claudius who opens a closed Britain.
18. Tac. *Agr.* 10; cf. ibid. 25 on the 'opened' sea. The dates of Agricola's governorship are much disputed: the present argument suggests the earlier chronology, on which see below.
19. Eutropius 7.13: see above, p. 106.
20. Sil. Ital. *Pun.* 3.606–15.
21. For a glimpse of disputes on its location, see Jones 1992, 225 n. 44.
22. Juv. *Sat.* 4.124–7, for Veiento's absurd interpretation for Domitian of a giant turbot as an omen of foreign victory: 'You will capture a king, or Arviragus will drop off his British chariot-pole.'

23. Tac. *Agr.* 1–3, 44–6.
24. As Ogilvie and Richmond 1967 rightly observe.
25. Cf. Tac. *Ann.* 4.35.5, with Martin and Woodman 1989, 184: Tiberius is said to have used cruelty akin to that of foreign kings in burning books.
26. Silence is a key issue in Tacitus: see the brief discussion in Strocchio 1992.
27. E.g. Philodemus *On the good king according to Homer* 8, with Dorandi's commentary, on the proper and improper concern with and use of physical beauty by the ruler.
28. Tac. *Agr.* 44.
29. Ibid. 3.2.
30. Ibid. 45.2: Domitian's blush-like complexion, contrasted with his inner shamelessness, is a favourite theme: cf. Tac. *Hist.* 4.40. Here his ruddy face contrasts with the pallor of his closely observed subjects.
31. Tac. *Agr.* 4–9 and 40–4, respectively.
32. Cf. Plut. *Alex.* 1, with the exemplary discussion of Pelling 1988, 8–25.
33. Tac. *Agr.* 4.
34. Cf. Rutherford 1989, 66–80, on the dangers of philosophy. Tacitus seems carefully to distinguish in the *Agricola* between *sapientia* (wisdom), which is positive, and *philosophia* (philosophy), which is not wholly positive. Translations tend to blur his distinction.
35. See p. 198; modern scholars have been too quick to find Tacitus critical of Paulinus.
36. For the phrase, see Juv. *Sat.* 4.38; cf. Tac. *Agr.* 45 for the comparison of Nero and Domitian.
37. Cic. *Ad Quint. fr.* 1.1.37–9.
38. Tac. *Agr.* 6, indicating the presence of his wife with him in the province, where Tacitus' future wife was born: Agricola's case may help to explain Tacitus' interest in governor's wives (on which Ginsburg 1993), an issue which he too had to face; Bowman 1994, 56–7, acutely contrasts expressions of hostility to wives in the provinces with the evidence of the Vindolanda tablets that officers' wives and families were often there in Tacitus' day.
39. Tac. *Agr.* 7.
40. Ibid. 8.2; cf. Tac. *Ann.* 13.8, on Corbulo.
41. Tac. *Agr.* 9.
42. Ogilvie and Richmond 1967, 12.
43. Tac. *Agr.* 10.
44. Tac. *Hist.* 1.2.1.
45. Tac. *Agr.* 10. Literary antecedents to Tacitus' discussion are noted in Romm 1992, 148. On the Orkneys, see above, n. 19.
46. Tac. *Agr.* 11; cf. Tac. *Germ.* 2.2, with O'Gorman 1993.
47. Tac. *Agr.* 18, with Ogilvie and Richmond 1967, ad loc.
48. Tac. *Hist.* 4.17 and 4.67, where I do not perceive the conflict of ideas that seems obvious to Keitel 1993, 46; see below on Tac. *Agr.* 21.

49. Cf. Livy 3.63.3–4, on the general's praising and chiding; Ulpian *Dig.* 1.18.7, on private exhortation and public assistance.
50. Braund 1984, 9–21; note especially the school on the Rhine at Suet. *Gaius* 45.
51. On this passage, see further Woolf 1994, 119.
52. Millar 1993, 528.
53. Mart. *Epigr.* 11.53: possibly not first-generation, as Kay 1985, 185–6, observes.
54. This is not the enervation of peace mentioned at Tac. *Germ.* 23.2 and *Hist.* 4.64.
55. Cf. Tac. *Agr.* 30 and 31, and *Hist.* 4.14 and 4.17, with passages gathered by Plass 1988, 42; Thuc. 3.82–3.
56. For ancient critiques of banquets, baths and luxury in general, see, for example, Rutherford 1989, 109–10; Long and Sedley 1987, II, 423.
57. Mellor 1993, 108, should distinguish between the very different place of, for example, schools and banquets in this passage.
58. Tac. *Agr.* 16.
59. On Romanization as a pursuit not peculiar to Agricola, see Hanson 1987, 73-4; cf. Woolf 1994. Recently, in welcome reaction to older approaches, scholars have tended to show caution in assessing Agricola's promotion of Romanization: for example, Jones 1991, 54, rails against glosses on Tacitus' account 'verging on the fanciful'. Millett 1990, 69–74, concludes a balanced discussion with the plausible suggestion that while the initiative may have been that of the Britons, any available credit will have been claimed for the governor.
60. The Latin *obses* does not translate: see Braund 1984, 5–21, with Parthenius 14, a story which further illustrates that the relationship between 'hostage' and host was principally one of social and moral interaction and exchange, not threat of reprisal.
61. Brunt 1990, 319.
62. Livy 35.14.9, 35.28.1–9; cf. Tac. *Hist.* 2.5.
63. Tac. *Agr.* 39.3; cf. Tac. *Ann.* 1.69, 16.5.
64. Tac. *Agr.* 24.
65. Cf. Ginsburg 1993, for interesting remarks on Tacitus' avoidance of the absolute.
66. Cf. Cerialis at Tac. *Hist.* 4.74, and the Batavians at Tac. *Hist.* 5.25, with Keitel 1993, 55–8.
67. *Britanniae terminus*: Tac. *Agr.* 27.
68. Ibid. 28.
69. Ibid. 29.
70. Ibid. 33.
71. Caes. *BC* 3.90, with Pritchett 1994, 27–109.
72. E.g. Ogilvie and Richmond 1967, and the works they cite.
73. Esp. Tac. *Hist.* 4.32, on Civilis; cf. Tac. *Ann.* 12.34, on Caratacus.
74. Brunt 1990, 439 n. 9.
75. Cf. Caes. *BC* 3.31–3, with Brunt 1990, 319.

76. Pelling 1993 rightly protests at scholars' preference for a monochrome Tacitus.
77. Cf. Tac. *Ann.* 2.15, 14.31, and *Hist.* 4.14 and 4.74.
78. Tac. *Hist.* 4.17, with Keitel 1993.
79. See Weinbrot 1993.
80. Contrast *ingens alacritas* (Tac. *Agr.* 35.1) and *alacres* (ibid. 33.1).
81. Ibid. 37.
82. Ibid. 38.
83. *Quietam tutamque*: ibid. 40.
84. Ibid. 40.
85. Ibid. 41.
86. As Tacitus observes elsewhere, such thanks were 'the end of all conversations with the tyrannous': *Ann.* 14.56.
87. Tac. *Agr.* 2.
88. Tac. *Ann.* 14.12, 49; cf. 16.34–5.
89. Hanson 1991, 1751–3, offers an excellent summary of the question and wisely avoids an answer; the association of Vespasian with Caledonia supports the earlier chronology.
90. Cf. Breeze 1988, 15–18, *contra* Millar 1982, 8–9. Note also Lee 1993, which contains much of relevance, though principally concerned with a later period.
91. An honourable if idiosyncratic exception is Dorey 1960. Birley 1975 builds much on the hypothesis that Agricola was especially close to Titus, but that remains a matter of speculation, as Hanson 1991, 1750, points out.
92. Fronto *Paneg.* 8.14.2.
93. Tac. *Ann.* 11.19; Breeze 1988, 16, notes also SHA *Pius* 5.4.
94. Hanson 1991, 1753.
95. Tac. *Agr.* 43.
96. As Dorey 1960, 70, long since noted, while imagining that Agricola died of overwork.
97. Jones 1992, 133.
98. *Fronte laetus, pectore anxius*: Tac. *Agr.* 39.
99. Ibid. 40.
100. Coleman 1988, xvi.
101. Cf. Strabo 1.4.3, p. 63, on islands, with Roseman 1994, 88–90, on Pliny the Elder's view.
102. Dio 66.20.
103. Ogilvie and Richmond 1967, on Tac. *Agr.* 39. For made-up captives, cf. Suet. *Gaius* 47; on Cicero and Piso, see Chapter 2.
104. See Jones 1992, esp. 126–31.
105. The chronological limit of the *Histories* in AD 96, and the political requirements of a writer under Trajan, are more than enough to dispel the notion that Tacitus refers to the neglect of the emperor Trajan in this phrase, *pace*, e.g., Jones 1992, 133.
106. Hobley 1989.

107. Daniels 1989, 34–5; note also Jones 1992, 133–5, who collects epigraphic evidence of a 'British War' apparently of the late first century AD.
108. Hind 1983.
109. Mart. *Epigr.* 10.44, with Sullivan 1991, 44; cf. Mart. *Epigr.* 11.3.
110. Mart. *Epigr.* 11.21, with Kay 1985, 116, for the image.
111. Mart. *Epigr.* 14.99.

EPILOGUE

1. Maxfield 1989, 19.
2. Haselgrove 1989, 13.

BIBLIOGRAPHY

Abbott, F. F. 1907, 'The theatre as a factor in Roman politics', *TAPA* 38: 49–56.

Allason-Jones, L. 1989, *Women in Roman Britain* (London).

Allen, D. F. 1944, 'The Belgic dynasties of Britain and their coins', *Archaeologia* 90: 1–46.

—— 1970, 'The coins of the Iceni', *Britannia* 1: 1–33.

—— 1975, 'Cunobelin's gold', *Britannia* 6: 1–19.

Allen, D. F., and Haselgrove, C. 1979, 'The gold coinage of Verica', *Britannia* 10: 1–18.

Anderson, R. D., Parsons, P. J., and Nisbet, R. G. M. 1979, 'Elegiacs by Gallus from Qasr Ibrim', *JRS* 69: 125–55.

Asmis, E. 1990, 'Philodemus' Epicureanism', *ANRW* II.36.4 (Berlin), 2369–406.

Balsdon, J. P. V. D. 1934, *The emperor Gaius* (Oxford).

Barrett, A. A. 1979, 'The career of Cogidubnus', *Britannia* 10: 227–42.

—— 1989 *Caligula: the corruption of power* (London).

—— 1991, 'Claudius' British victory arch in Rome', *Britannia* 22: 1–19.

Becher, I. 1985, 'Tiberüberschwemmungen: die Interpretation von Prodigien in augusteischer Zeit', *Klio* 67: 471–9.

Bidwell, P. T., and Holbrook, N. 1989, *Hadrian's Wall bridges* (HBMCE; London).

Birley, A. R. 1975, 'Agricola, the Flavian dynasty and Tacitus', in B. Levick (ed.), *The ancient historian and his materials: essays in honour of C. E. Stevens* (Farnborough), 139–54.

—— 1981, *The Fasti of Roman Britain* (Oxford).

Birley, E. 1960, *Chesters Roman fort* (HBMCE; London).

Black, E. W. 1986, 'Christian and pagan hopes of salvation in Romano-British mosaics', in M. Henig and A. King (eds), *Pagan gods and shrines of the Roman empire* (OUCA; Oxford), 147–57.

Blagg, T. F. C. 1990, 'First-century Roman houses in Gaul and Britain', in T. Blagg and M. Millett (eds), *The early Roman empire in the west* (Oxford), 194–209.

204

Blok, J. H. 1995, *The early Amazons: modern and ancient perspectives on a persistent myth* (Leiden).

Bogaers, J. E. 1979, 'King Cogidubnus in Chichester: another reading of *RIB* 91', *Britannia* 10: 243–54.

Bonneau, D. 1964, *La crue du Nil* (Paris).

Bosworth, A. B. 1988, *From Arrian to Alexander: studies in historical interpretation* (Oxford).

Bowman, A. K. 1994, *Life and letters on the Roman frontier: Vindolanda and its people* (London).

—— 1994a, 'The Roman imperial army: letters and literacy on the northern frontier', in A. K. Bowman and G. Woolf (eds), *Literacy and power in the ancient world* (Cambridge), 109–25.

Bradley, K. 1994, *Slavery and society at Rome* (Cambridge).

Bradley, R., and Gordon, K. 1988, 'Human skulls from the River Thames: their dating and significance', *Antiquity* 62: 503–9.

Braund, D. 1980, 'The Aedui, Troy and the *Apocolocyntosis*', *CQ* 30: 420–5.

—— 1983, 'Royal wills and Rome', *PBSR* 51: 16–57.

—— 1983a, 'Berenice in Rome', *Historia* 23: 120–3.

—— 1984, *Rome and the friendly king: the character of client kingship* (London).

—— 1984a, 'Observations on Cartimandua', *Britannia* 15: 1–6.

—— 1985, 'Function and dysfunction: personal patronage in Roman imperialism', in A. F. Wallace-Hadrill (ed.), *Patronage in ancient society* (London), 137–52.

—— 1991, 'Hadrian and Pharasmanes', *Klio* 73: 208–19.

—— 1993, 'Dionysiac tragedy in Plutarch, *Crassus*', *CQ* 43: 468–74.

—— 1993a, 'Writing a Roman Argonautica', *Hermathena* 154: 11–17.

—— 1993b, 'Fronto and the Iberians: language and diplomacy at the Antonine court', *Ostraka* 2: 53–5.

—— 1994, *Georgia in antiquity: a history of Colchis and Transcaucasian Iberia, 550 B.C. to A.D. 562* (Oxford).

—— 1996, 'Herodotus on the problematics of reciprocity', in C. Gill, N. Postlethwaite and R. Seaford (eds), *Reciprocity in ancient Greece* (Oxford).

—— 1996a, 'The politics of Catullus 10: Caesar, Memmius and the Bithynians', *Hermathena*.

—— 1996b, 'River frontiers in the environmental psychology of the Roman world', in D. L. Kennedy (ed.), *The Roman army in the east* (JRA suppl. 18; Ann Arbor).

Breeze, D. 1988, 'Why did the Romans fail to conquer Scotland?', *PSAS* 118: 3–22.

Brelich, A. 1969, *Paides e parthenoi* (Rome).

Brunt, P. A. 1990, *Roman imperial themes* (Oxford).

Buccheit, V. 1971, 'Epikurs Triumph des Geistes (Lucr. 1. 62–79)', *Hermes* 99: 303–23.

—— 1975, 'Chrysogonus als Tyrann in Ciceros Rede für Roscius aus Ameria', *Chiron* 5: 193–211.

Champlin, E. 1991, *Final judgments: duty and emotion in Roman wills, 200 B.C.–A.D. 250* (Berkeley).

Coleman, K. M. (ed.) 1988, *Statius: Silvae, IV* (Oxford).

Courtney, E. (ed.) 1993, *The fragmentary Latin poets* (Oxford).

Crawford, M. 1985, *Coinage and money under the Roman republic* (London).

Cresci Marrone, G. 1993, *Ecumene Augustea* (Rome).

Cunliffe, B. 1973, *The Regni* (London).

—— 1981, 'Money and society in pre-Roman Britain', in B. Cunliffe (ed.), *Coinage and society in Britain and Gaul* (CBA; London), 29–39.

—— 1986, 'The sanctuary of Sulis Minerva at Bath: a brief review', in M. Henig and A. King (eds), *Pagan gods and shrines of the Roman empire* (OUCA; Oxford), 1–14.

Daniels, C. 1989, 'The Flavian and Trajanic northern frontier', in M. Todd (ed.), *Research on Roman Britain, 1960–89* (Britannia monograph 11; London), 31–5.

D'Arms, J. H. 1995, 'Heavy drinking and drunkenness in the Roman world: four questions for historians', in O. Murray and M. Tecusan (eds), *In vino veritas* (Rome), 304–17.

De Lacy, P. H. and E. A. (eds) 1941, *Philodemus: On methods of inference* (Philadelphia).

Dewald, C. 1981, 'Women and culture in Herodotus' *Histories*', in H. P. Foley (ed.), *Reflections of women in antiquity* (New York), 91–125.

Diels, H. 1958, *Doxographi graeci* (repr.; Berlin)

Dorandi, T. 1982, *Filodemo: Il buon re secondo Omero* (Naples).

—— 1990, 'Filodemo: orientamenti della ricerca attuale', *ANRW* II.36.4 (Berlin), 2328–68.

Dorey, T. A. 1960, 'Agricola and Domitian', *Greece and Rome* 7: 66–71.

Drinkwater, J. F. 1983, *Roman Gaul* (London).

Dudley, D., and Webster, G. 1962 *The rebellion of Boudicca* (London).

Dunkle, J. R. 1967, 'The Greek tyrant and Roman political invective of the late Republic', *TAPA* 98: 151–71.

—— 1971, 'The rhetorical tyrant in Roman historiography: Sallust, Livy and Tacitus', *CW* 65: 12–20.

Eckstein, A. M. 1995, *Moral vision in the Histories of Polybius* (Berkeley).

Edwards, C. 1993, *The politics of immorality in ancient Rome* (Cambridge).

Elwyn, S. 1993, 'Interstate kinship and Roman foreign policy', *TAPA* 123: 261–86.

Erim, K. T. 1982, 'A relief showing Claudius and Britannia from Aphrodisias', *Britannia* 13: 277–85.

Erskine, A. 1990, *The Hellenistic stoa: political thought and action* (London).

Evans, J. 1987, 'Graffiti and the evidence of literacy and pottery use in Roman Britain', *Archaeological Journal* 44: 191–204.

Fantham, E. 1985, 'Caesar and the mutiny', *CPh* 80: 119–31.

Foster, J. 1986, *The Lexden tumulus* (BAR; Oxford).

Frere, S. S. 1978, *Britannia* (rev. 3rd edn, London).

Fulford, M. 1991, 'Britain and the Roman empire: the evidence for regional and long-distance trade', in R. F. J. Jones (ed.), *Roman Britain: recent trends* (Sheffield), 35–47.

Garnsey, P. D. A. 1970, *Social status and legal privilege in the Roman empire* (Oxford).

Ginsburg, J. 1993, '*In maiores certamina*: past and present in the *Annals*', in T. J. Luce and A. J. Woodman (eds), *Tacitus and the Tacitean tradition* (Princeton), 86–103.

Goldberg, S. M. 1995, *Epic in republican Rome* (Oxford).

Green, M. 1986, *The gods of the Celts* (Gloucester).

Griffin, J. 1985, *Latin poets and Roman life* (London).

Griffin, M. T. 1976, *Seneca: a philosopher in politics* (Oxford).

—— 1984, *Nero: the end of a dynasty* (London).

—— 1994, 'The intellectual developments of the Ciceronian age', *Cambridge Ancient History*, 2nd edn (Cambridge), 689–728.

Gruen, E. S. 1984, *The Hellenistic world and the coming of Rome* (Berkeley).

Hadas, M. 1930, *Sextus Pompey* (New York).

Hallett, J. P. 1970, 'Over troubled waters: the meaning of the title *pontifex*', *TAPA* 101: 219–27.

Hamer, M. 1993, *Signs of Cleopatra* (London).

Hanson, W. S. 1987, *Agricola and the conquest of the north* (London).

—— 1991, 'Tacitus' "Agricola": an archaeological and historical study', *ANRW* II.33.3 (Berlin), 1742–84.

Hanson, W. S., and Campbell, D. B. 1986, 'The Brigantes: from clientage to conquest', *Britannia* 17: 73–89.

Hanson, W. S., and Maxwell, G. S. 1983, *Rome's north-west frontier: the Antonine wall* (Edinburgh).

Hardie, P. R. 1986, *Virgil's Aeneid: cosmos and imperium*.

Harris, W. V. 1979, *War and imperialism in republican Rome, 327–70 B.C.* (Oxford).

Hartley, B., and Fitts, L. (eds) 1988, *The Brigantes* (Gloucester).

Haselgrove, C. 1987, *Iron Age coinage in south-east England: the archaeological context* (BAR; Oxford).

—— 1988, 'Coinage and complexity: archaeological analysis of socio-political change in Britain and non-Mediterranean Gaul during the later Iron Age', in D. B. Gibson and M. N. Geselowitz (eds), *Tribe and polity in late prehistoric Europe* (New York), 69–96.

—— 1989, 'The later Iron Age in southern Britain and beyond', in M. Todd (ed.), *Research on Roman Britain, 1960–89* (Britannia monograph 11; London), 1–18

Haselgrove, C., and Turnbull, P. 1987, *Stanwick: excavations and research interim report, 1985–6* (Durham).

Haselgrove C., Turnbull, P., and Pitts, L. F. 1990, 'Stanwick, North Yorkshire, parts 1–3', *Archaeological Journal* 147: 1–90.

Hassall, M. W. C., and Tomlin, R. S. O. 1987, 'Roman Britain in 1986, II. Inscriptions', *Britannia* 18: 360–77.

Hind, J. G. F. 1983, 'Caledonia and its occupation under the Flavians', *PSAS* 113: 373–8.

—— 1989, 'The invasion of Britain in A.D. 43 – an alternative strategy for Aulus Plautius', *Britannia* 20: 1–22.

Hingley, R. 1992, 'Society in Scotland from 700 B.C. to A.D. 200', *PSAS* 122: 7–53.

Hobley, A. S. 1989, 'The numismatic evidence for the post-Agricolan abandonment of the Roman frontier in northern Scotland', *Britannia* 20: 69–74.

Hurlet, F. 1993, *La dictature de Sylla: monarchie ou magistrature republicaine?* (Brussels).

Isaac, B. H. 1991, *The limits of empire: the Roman army in the east* (rev. edn; Oxford).

Jackson, K. 1979, 'Queen Boudicca?', *Britannia* 10: 255.

Jacob, Ch. 1991, *Géographie et ethnographie en Grèce ancienne* (Paris).

Jal, P. 1964, *La guerre civile à Rome* (Paris).

Jones, B. W. 1992, *The emperor Domitian* (London).

Jones, R. F. J. 1991, 'The urbanization of Roman Britain', in R. F. J. Jones (ed.), *Roman Britain: recent trends* (Sheffield), 53–65.

—— 1991a, 'Cultural change in Roman Britain', in R. F. J. Jones (ed.), *Roman Britain: recent trends* (Sheffield), 115–20.

Kay, N. M. 1985, *Martial, Book XI: a commentary* (London).

Keitel, E. 1993, 'Speech and narrative in *Histories* 4', in T. J. Luce and A. J. Woodman (eds), *Tacitus and the Tacitean tradition* (Princeton), 39–58.

Kienast, D. 1965, 'Alexander und der Ganges', *Historia* 14: 180–8.

Kong, L. 1990, 'Geography and religion: trends and prospects', *Progress in Human Geography* 14: 355–71.

Kroymann, J. 1973, 'Caesar und das corpus Caesarianum in der neueren Forschung: Gesamtbibliographie, 1945–1970', *ANRW* 1.3 (Berlin and New York), 457–87.

Lateiner, D. 1989, *The historical method of Herodotus* (Toronto).

Latte, K. 1960, *Römische Religionsgeschichte* (Munich).

Lee, A. D. 1993, *Information and frontiers: Roman foreign relations in late antiquity* (Cambridge).

Lefèvre, E. 1971, *Das Prooemium der Argonautica des Valerius Flaccus* (Mainz).

Lepper, F., and Frere, S. 1988, *Trajan's Column* (Gloucester).

Levick, B. 1990, *Claudius* (London).

Lintott, A. 1993, *Imperium Romanum: politics and administration* (London).

Long, A. A. 1995, 'Cicero's politics in *De Officiis*', in A. Laks and M. Schofield (eds), *Justice and generosity: studies in hellenistic social and political philosophy. Proceedings of the Sixth Symposium Hellenisticum* (Cambridge), 213–40.

Long, A. A., and Sedley, D. N. (eds) 1987, *The hellenistic philosophers*, 2 vols (Cambridge).

Mann, J. C. 1985, 'Two "topoi" in the *Agricola*', *Britannia* 16: 21–4.

Mansfeld, J. 1990, 'Doxography and dialectic: the *Sitz im Leben* of the *Placita*', *ANRW* II.36.4 (Berlin), 3056–229.

Martin, R. H., and Woodman, A. J. (eds) 1989, *Tacitus: Annals, Book IV* (Cambridge).

Maxfield, V. A. 1989, 'Conquest and aftermath', in M. Todd (ed.), *Research on Roman Britain, 1960–89* (Britannia monograph 11; London), 19–29.

Mellor, R. 1993, *Tacitus* (London).

Millar, F. 1982, 'Emperors, frontiers and foreign relations', *Britannia* 13: 1–23.

—— 1993, *The Roman Near East, 31 B.C.–A.D. 337* (Cambridge, Mass.).

Millett, M. 1990, *The Romanization of Britain: an essay in archaeological interpretation* (Cambridge).

Misch, G. 1907, *Geschichte der Autobiographie*, 2 vols (Leipzig).

Momigliano, A. 1950, '*Panegyricus Messallae* and "*Panegyricus Vespasiani*"', *JRS* 40: 39–42.

Mortureux, B. 1989, 'Les idéaux stoïciens et les premières responsabilités politiques: le *De Clementia*', *ANRW* II.36.3 (Berlin), 1639–85.

Mossop, H. R. 1979, 'An elusive Icenian legend', *Britannia* 10: 258–9.

Murgia, C. E. 1977, 'The minor works of Tacitus: a study in textual criticism', *CPh* 72: 323–43.

Murray, O. 1965, 'Philodemus on the good king according to Homer', *JRS* 55: 161–82.

Nash, D. 1982, 'Adminius did strike coins', *OJA* 1: 111–14.

Nicolet, C. 1991, *Space, geography and politics in the early Roman empire* (Ann Arbor).

Nisbet, R. G. M., and Hubbard, M. 1978, *A commentary on Horace: Odes, Book II* (Oxford).

Obbink, D. 1995, *Philodemus on poetry* (Oxford).

Ogilvie, R. M., and Richmond, I. A. (eds) 1967, *Cornelii Taciti: De vita Agricolae* (Oxford).

O'Gorman, E. 1993, 'No place like Rome: identity and difference in the *Germania* of Tacitus', *Ramus* 22: 135–54.

Paul, G. M. 1984, *A historical commentary on Sallust's Bellum Jugurthinum* (Liverpool).

Pelling, C. B. R. 1979, 'Plutarch's method of work in the Roman Lives', *JHS* 99: 74–96.

—— (ed.) 1988, *Plutarch: Life of Antony* (Cambridge).

—— 1993, 'Tacitus and Germanicus', in T. J. Luce and A. J. Woodman (eds), *Tacitus and the Tacitean tradition* (Princeton), 59–85.

Pembroke, S. 1967, 'Women in charge: the function of alternatives in early Greek tradition and the ancient idea of matriarchy', *Journal of the Warburg and Courtauld Institutes* 30: 1–35.

Plass, P. 1988, *Wit and the writing of history: the rhetoric of historiography in imperial Rome* (Madison).

Pritchett, W. K. 1994, *Essays in Greek history* (Amsterdam).

Purcell, N. 1995, 'Eating fish: the paradoxes of seafood', in J. Wilkins, F. D. Harvey and M. Dobson (eds), *Food in antiquity* (Exeter), 132–49.

Rawson E. 1975, *Cicero* (London).

—— 1985, *Intellectual life in the late Roman republic* (London).

—— 1991, *Roman culture and society: collected papers* (Oxford).

Reusser, C. 1993, *Der Fidestempel auf dem Kapitol in Rom* (Rome).

Reynolds, J. M. 1966, 'Legal and constitutional problems', in J. S. Wacher (ed.), *The civitas capitals of Roman Britain* (Leicester), 70–5.

Rich, J. 1985, 'Patronage and interstate relations in the Roman republic', in A. F. Wallace-Hadrill (ed.), *Patronage in ancient society* (London), 117–35.

Roberts, M. 1988, 'The revolt of Boudicca and the assertion of *libertas* in Neronian Rome', *AJPh* 109: 118–32.

Romm, J. S. 1992, *The edges of the earth in ancient thought: geography, exploration and fiction* (Princeton).

Rosellini, M., and Saïd, S. 1978, 'Usages de femmes et autres nomoi chez les "sauvages" d'Hérodote: essai de lecture structurale', *ASNP* ser. 3, 8: 949–1005.

Roseman, C. H. (ed.) 1994, *Pytheas of Massalia: On the Ocean* (Chicago).

Rutherford, R. B. 1989, *The Meditations of Marcus Aurelius: a study* (Oxford).

Saladino V. E. 1980, 'Iscrizioni latine de Roselle II', *ZPE* 39: 215–36.

Schwarze, J. 1971, *Die Beurteilung des Perikles durch die attische Komödie und ihre historische und historiographische Bedeutung* (Zetemeta 51; Munich).

Sedley, D. N. 1982, 'On Signs', in J. Barnes, J. Brunschwig, M. Burnyeat and M. Schofield (eds), *Science and speculation: studies in Hellenistic theory and practice* (Cambridge), 239–72.

Sorabji, R. 1993, *Animal minds and human morals* (London).

Spencer, C., and Blades, M. 1986, 'Pattern and process', *Progress in Human Geography* 10: 230–48.

Strocchio, R. 1992, *I significati del silenzio nell'opera di Tacito* (Turin).

Sullivan, J. P. 1991, *Martial: the unexpected classic* (Cambridge).

Syme, R. 1958, *Tacitus* (Oxford).

—— 1978, *History in Ovid* (Oxford).

—— 1995, *Anatolica: studies in Strabo* (Oxford).

Todd, M. 1981, *Roman Britain, 55 B.C.–A.D. 400* (London).

Van Arsdell, R. D. 1989, *Celtic coinage of Britain* (London).

—— 1994, *The coinage of the Dobunni: money supply and coin circulation in Dobunnic territory* (Studies in Celtic coinage 1, OUCA monograph 38; Oxford).

Vidal Naquet, P. 1981, 'Slavery and the rule of women in tradition, myth and utopia', in R. L. Gordon (ed.), *Myth, religion and society* (Cambridge), 187–200.

Weinbrot, H. D. 1993, 'Politics, taste, and national identity: some uses of Tacitism in eighteenth-century Britain', in T. J. Luce and A. J. Woodman (eds), *Tacitus and the Tacitean tradition* (Princeton), 168–84.

Wiseman, A. and P. (eds and trans.) 1980, *Julius Caesar: the battle for Gaul* (Boston).

Wiseman, T. P. 1982, 'Calpurnius Siculus and the Claudian civil war', *JRS* 72: 57–67.

—— 1985, 'Competition and co-operation', in T. P. Wiseman (ed.), *Roman political life, 90 B.C. to A.D. 69* (Exeter).

—— 1987, *Roman studies* (Liverpool).

—— 1991, *Death of an emperor: Flavius Josephus* (Exeter).

—— 1992, 'Julius Caesar and the *mappa mundi*', in T. P. Wiseman, *Talking to Virgil: a miscellany* (Exeter), 22–42.

—— 1994, 'Caesar, Pompey and Rome, 59–50 B.C.', *Cambridge Ancient History*, vol. 9, 2nd edn. (Cambridge), 368–423.

Wissowa, G. 1912, *Religion und Kultus der Römer* (Leipzig).

Woodman, A. J. 1983, *Velleius Paterculus: the Caesarian and Augustan narrative* (Cambridge).

—— 1988, *Rhetoric in classical historiography* (London).

—— 1993, 'Amateur dramatics at the court of Nero, *Annals* 15.48–74', in T. J. Luce and A. J. Woodman (eds), *Tacitus and the Tacitean tradition* (Princeton), 104–28.

Woolf, G. 1994, 'Becoming Roman, staying Greek: culture, identity and the civilizing process in the Roman east', *Proc. Camb. Phil. Soc.* 40: 116–43.

—— 1994a, 'Power and the spread of writing in the west', in A. K. Bowman and G. Woolf (eds), *Literacy and power in the ancient world* (Cambridge), 84–98.

Zehnacker, H. 1983, 'Tragédie prétexte et spectacle romain', in H. Zehnacker (ed.), *Théatre et spectacles dans l'antiquité: actes du colloque de Strasbourg, 1981* (Leiden), 31–48.

INDEX

Addedomarus, 74
Adminius, 65, 74, 86, 95–6, 99–100, 112, 113
Aedui, 57–8, 63
Aelius Gallus, 81
Aesu, 74
Agricola, 8–9, 22, 24, 35, 40, 151–76; in Aquitania, 156–7; in Asia, 156; and Caledonian Ocean, 150; and Claudius, 170; conquest of Britain, 171, 175; death, 153–4; Domitian's agent, 172–4; and Massilia, 155, 163; parents, 154–5; retirement, 171–3; speech, 169; and Suetonius Paulinus, 155, 159–61; Vespasian's appointee, 148, 156
Agrippa I, 30, 126
Agrippina, 115, 142–3
Albinovanus Pedo, 20–1
Alexander the Great, 20–2, 92
Amazons, 119, 122, 138
Amminius, 74, 95
Andoco, 69, 74
Anted, 71, 74
Antiochus IV of Commagene, 30
Antonine Wall, 15
Antoninus Pius, 173
Aorsi, 128
Aphrodisias, 103–4
Aqua Virgo, 102, 106
Argonauts, 150
Ariovistus, 44–5, 55–9, 64–5, 80
Aristotle, 26
Armenia, 164
Arrian, 19
Arviragus, 151
Asclepiades, 42

Asia, 5, 24–5, 34, 38–9, 156; as theatre, 35
Atrebates, 71; see also Commius
Augustus, 6, 11, 20, 22, 65, 76–80, 84–5, 88, 96; and Cleopatra, 29–30, 119; and geographers, 81, 89; medallion, 98–9

Bath, 13, 17
Battersea Shield, 12, 13
Belgae, 50, 181
Berenice, 126
Berikos, see Verica
Birrens, 182n.8
Bithynia, 34, 42
Bodunni, see Dobunni
Bodvoc, 74
Boudica, 8, 111–12, 124, 132–46, 155, 159; Roman, 4, 134, 144
Bretannos, 66
bridges, 13, 19, 91–4
Brigantes, 125–6, 131, 145, 149
Britain, another world, 3, 5, 8, 11, 20–2, 24, 42–4, 60, 66, 97, 116, 124, 158, 177; Caesar's invasions, 41–66, 83–4; Claudius' invasion, 96–108; cold, 42; conquest of, 171, 175; Domitian's 'neglect', 175–6; Gaius' 'invasion', 89–96; and Gaul, 60, 84, 88; and Germany, 175; longevity in, 42, 149; personified, 103–4; poor, 11, 46, 84, 176; 'Roman property', 87; slaves from, 46, 48; as theatre, 3, 5; utopia, 24, 41–2; see also Augustus; Bretannos; chariots; Ocean; tides
Britanni, 125

Britannia, 103–4
Britannicus, 102, 105

Caesar, Julius, 5; and astronomy,
186n.7; and Bithynia, 34;
Commentaries, 5–6, 34, 48–66,
100; critics of, 6, 45, 50–4, 57–9,
63–5, 84, 94; crossing Rubicon, 19;
entourage, 44, 57; invades Britain,
41–66, 83–4; and *lex Iulia*, 59;
luxury of, 45, 52; 'man of letters',
44–5, 48–54; and Marius, 55–6;
Parthian campaign, 20; and Piso,
34; and poetry, 10–11; and
Pompey, 42, 53; as precedent,
78–9, 89, 91, 94, 97, 106, 107,
149–50, 196n.100; on speeches,
167; and Strabo, 81–5; triumphs
over Britain, 54
Caledonia, 8–9, 149–50, 165–71, 176
Calgacus, 8, 145, 151, 166–71, 176
Caligula, *see* Gaius
Campus Martius, 103, 110, 113
Camulodunum, 102, 103, 132, 135–6;
see also Lexden
Cantii, 65, 72, 74
Capitol, 83–5, 95, 106
Caratacus, 7, 72, 99–101, 112–16,
127–9, 131
Cartimandua, 4, 7–8, 124–32, 136,
141, 144–5
Cartivel, 75
Carvilius, 65
Cassius Dio, 7–8, 19, 52, 64, 78–9,
91–2, 96, 100–1, 106, 112–13, 139,
141–6, 148–9, 174
Cassivellaunus, 60, 64–6, 68
Castlecary, 15
Cato, Elder, 28, 30, 118
Cato, Younger, 51, 64
Catti, 74
Catullus, 34, 77, 94
Catuvellauni, 68, 72, 100–1
chains, 19, 60–1, 72, 115, 127, 134–5,
197n.23; *see also* bridges
channelling, 15–16
chariots, 46–8, 62, 78, 82, 92, 137,
151, 187n.35; *see also* Homer
cheese, 82–4

Chester, 131
Chesters, 12–13, 16
Cicero, M., 4–5, 24–48; on Caesar's
Commentaries, 53; epic on
Britain, 11, 44; as governor of
Cilicia, 34; to Lucceius, 50; to
Posidonius, 53; on his
quaestorship, 36–9; and Quintus,
24–8; on river crossing, 19
Cicero, Q., 5, 44, 46, 48; *see also*
Cicero, M.
Cimbri and Teutones, 55–6, 57
Cingetorix, 65
citizenship, 110, 125, 133
Classicianus, 139–40; criticized,
198n.57
Claudia Rufina, 162
Claudius, 7, 10, 22, 43, 65, 82, 89–90,
95, 135; and the Flavians, 147, 170,
173, 178; on Gaius, 116–17;
invasion of Britain, 96–108; at
Lyons, 108; triumph, 106;
triumphal arches, 102–6
clemency, 114–15
Cleopatra, 8, 29–30, 119–23, 126,
139, 146
Cluvius Rufus, 144
Cogidubnus, 7, 108–12, 128; name,
108–9
coins, 6, 15, 67–75, 80, 85, 95, 99,
102, 105, 133
Colosseum, 149
comedy, Athenian, 26; *see also*
satire
Commius, 60–1, 70, 72–4
Comux, 73, 74
Cor, 75
Corbulo, 173
Corieltauvi, 74–5
Corio, 74, 80
Coritani, *see* Corieltauvi
Cotta, 45, 52
Cotys, 31
Crab(os?), 74
Crassus, 19
crossing, 19, 60–3, 91–4, 97, 101–2,
106; *see also* bridges; sailing
Cunobelinus, 7, 69, 70, 74, 86, 95,
99–100, 102

Curio, 51
Cyprus, 51
Cyrenaica, 36
Cyzicus, 106, 110

Darius, 92
Decianus Catus, 136, 139
Demetrius, 12, 20, 174
Dias, 74
Didius Gallus, 109, 159
Diodorus Siculus, 15, 48, 67, 80,
    188n.60
Dionysius of Halicarnassus, 29
Dionysus, 21, 42
diplomacy, 6, 60, 76, 79–80, 83–5,
    88–9, 96, 103
Diviciacus of the Aedui, 56, 65
Diviciacus of the Suessiones, 60
Divico, 56
Dobunni, 71, 74, 80, 100–1
dogs, 82
Domitian, 8–9, 24, 40, 56, 72,
    149–52, 158, 169, 171–2, 178;
    blushes, 200n.30; on Britain and
    Germany, 173–5; Richborough
    arch, 173–4; 'sham' triumph, 171,
    175
Druids, 60, 97
Drusus, 102
Dubnovellaunus, 65, 74
Dubnovellaunus (Kent), 71
Dumnocoveros, 75
Dumnovellaunos, 75
Dumnovellaunus, 84–5
Dumnorix, 63
Durotriges, 74

Ecen, 74–5
Eisu, 74
elephants, 54, 101
emperors, 30, 89–90, 123–4, 167–8,
    172–3, 178; heads on coins, 69–70,
    85–6; control of entourage, 28, 30,
    97, 123; and rivers, 19
entourage, 28, 30, 32, 33, 44, 45, 57,
    85, 97, 123
envy, 92
Epaticu(s?)/Epaticcus, 70, 71, 74

epic, 4, 5, 11, 19, 20–1, 33, 44–5, 48,
    94, 97, 103, 174, 177; see also
    Homer
Epicharis, 132
Epicurus, 23, 26, 32, 48; see also
    Philodemus
Eppillus, 70, 72, 73
Erigone, 186n.15
Esico, 70
Eumenes, king of Pergamum, 30
Eunones, 128
eunuchs, 106
exploration, 11, 20–1, 41–54, 60, 158;
    see also geography; Mela; Strabo

Fabius Rusticus, 148, 152
Favonius, 64
Fishbourne, 111
flattery, 33
fortune, 114–15, 128
Frampton mosaic, 15
freedom, 7, 9, 113–14, 124, 127–8,
    135, 138–40, 151–2, 158–9, 168–9
Frontinus, 72–3, 159
Fronto, 173

Gabinius, 32, 119
Gaetulicus, 94
Gaius, 6–7, 65, 82, 86, 103, 155;
    Claudius on, 116–17, 178;
    influenced by kings, 30; invasion
    of Britain, 89–96; 'sham' triumph,
    95
Galba, 115, 156
Gallus, C. Cornelius, 10, 30–1, 66
geography, 3–4, 11, 19, 81, 102, 174;
    see also exploration; Mela;
    Ptolemy; Strabo
Germania, 9, 21, 129, 151, 164, 175
Germanicus, 20–1, 89
gifts, 80
governorship, 9, 24–40, 109, 156,
    159, 169, 178; as career choice,
    37–9; as test of character, 35,
    156–60; wives' presence, 200n.38
Gracchus, C., 28

Hadrian, 19
Hadrian's Wall, 12–13, 16

Helvetii, 55–6
Helvidius Priscus, 152, 172
Hercules, 21, 42, 65, 94, 122
Herodotus, 26, 93, 113, 123, 141
Hiero II, 30
Hirtius, A., 49–50
History, and archaeology, 68, 179–81; and biography, 151–2; from coins, 67–75; and monarchy, 26; place in, 5, 10–11, 34, 54; speeches, 167; truth, 2, 50, 53–4, 163, 168, 175
Homer, 11, 15, 32–4, 45, 64, 137; see also chariots; epic; Philodemus
Horace, 22, 77–80
Humanitas, 115, 161–2

Iceni, 74, 132, 135, 145; see also Boudica; Prasutagus
imperialism, 3–4, 10–12, 97; criticized, 167; and diplomacy, 80, 84–5, 88–9; and justice, 28–40, 55–66, 116, 135, 145, 161, 165
Inam, 74
Ireland, 65, 125, 164
Isocrates, 26, 158

Josephus, 147–8, 150
Jugurtha, 30
Jupiter, 77–80, 122, 149
Juvenal, 151, 163–4, 167

kings, 86, 118; and coins, 6, 67–75, 80, 85, 95, 102; as 'dynasts', 86, 89; homonymous, 6, 73; moral danger of, 30; and rivers, 19; of Rome, 29; and slavery, 109, 114, 118, 122, 128, 132, 134–5; see also monarchy; queens

Latin, 70–1, 133, 161–2
Lexden, 98–9; see also Camulodunum
Libertas, see freedom
lighthouse, 95
Lindow Man, 14
Lucilius, 28
Lucretius, 23
Lucullus, 19

Lugotorix, 65

Macedonia, 31–40
Mandubracius, 60, 64
Mardonius, 113
Marius, 55
Maroboduus, 96
Martial, 149, 162, 176
Medea, 122
Mela, 102
Mettius, 58
Mildenhall 'Great Dish', 15, 18
Mithridates VI, 81, 167
Mithridates VIII, 115, 128, 131
monarchy, 81; governorship and, 25–6, 30–1, 109, 158; issue, 3–4, 8, 24–40, 118; and knowledge/self-control, 27, 32, 118, 160; philosophy of, 3–4, 24–8; and triumph, 40; see also kings; queens; theatre
Mons Graupius, 8, 151, 166–71
Mucianus, 156
Mummius, Sp., 28
Murena, 38–9

Narcissus, 141
Neptune, see Ocean
Nero, 10, 109, 111–12, 125, 133, 139, 142–3, 147, 155–6, 164
Nerva, 151–2, 158; see also Trajan
Newcastle-upon-Tyne, 13, 16
Nicomedes of Bithynia, 34
Nitiobriges, 188n.5
Nymphidius Sabinus, 115

Obses, 201n.60
Ocean, 3–4, 6, 12–23, 41, 53, 54, 63–4, 77–8, 94, 106–8, 139, 150, 177; and Neptune, 13–14, 92, 109; and Rhine, 43, 93–4, 149–51; see also crossing; pearls; rivers; tides
Octavian, see Augustus
Omphale, 122
Oppius, 43, 48
Ordovices, 159–60
Orkneys, 106, 150, 158, 164
Ostorius Scapula, 109, 125, 132, 159
Ovid, 78–80

Pacuvius, 36
Palatine, 95, 106, 107, 171
Panegyric of Messalla, 78
Parthenius, 66
Paullus, L. Aemilius, 36, 115
Pausanias (Spartan), 13
pearls, 52, 95, 187n.56
Pedanius Secundus, 135
Penthesilea, 122
Pericles, 27, 184n.4
Petilius Cerealis, 156, 159
Petronius Turpilianus, 159
Petrus Patricius, 196n.94
Philodemus, 31–40, 41–2; *see also*
    Epicurus
Pinarius, 45
piracy, 29
Piso, 31–40, 56
Plancius, 36–8
Plato, 25–7
Plautius, A., 101–2, 106, 109, 141,
    148, 159, 173, 199n.7
Pliny, Elder, 15, 48, 103, 149, 162
Pliny, Younger, 9, 15, 151, 167
Plutarch, 12, 43, 48, 64, 174
Poenius Postumus, 139
poetry, 10, 77, 89, 106–7, 119–23,
    149–50; *see also* epic; satire;
    theatre
Pollio, 54
Polyclitus, 139
Pomerium, 107–8
Pompey, 42
Porta Viminalis, 113–14
Posides, 106
Posidonius, 53, 64, 184n.10
Prasutagus, 69–71, 75, 112, 132–4,
    144–5
Procillus, 58
Propertius, 119–23, 146
Ptolemy (geographer), 111
Ptolemy Auletes, 32
Pulcher, Ap. Claudius, 34–5
Pytheas, 41, 192n.26

queens, 4, 7–8, 24, 114–15, 118–46;
    adultery, 126, 131, 145; worse than
    slavery, 129, 132
Quintilian, 41

refugees, 60, 65, 73, 81–2, 84–5,
    95–7, 100, 128, 131
Regni/Regnenses, 111
Res Gestae, 79–80, 84–5, 96
Rex, 70–1, 86; *rex magnus*, 110–11
rivers, as allies, 31, 77–8, 92; as
    boundaries, 19; as bulls, 15; and
    cults, 12, 15, 19, 92; as fathers, 15;
    as procreators, 15; as prophets, 15,
    93–4; as protectors, 15, 92; in
    triumphs, 54, 92–3; Araxes, 19;
    Clitumnus, 93–4; Danube, 15, 77,
    182n.14, 183n.24; Euphrates, 19,
    93, 182n.14, 183n.24; Indus,
    182n.14; Nile, 31, 77, 121–2,
    182n.14; Phasis, 19, 182n.14;
    Rhine, 7, 43, 54, 57–9, 93–4, 149,
    182n.14, 183n.24; Rhône, 54;
    Rubicon, 19; Thames, 12, 64, 102;
    Tiber, 15, 19, 63–4, 107, 121;
    Tigris, 77; *see also* crossing;
    Ocean
Romanization, 6, 69, 98–9, 110–11,
    126, 133–4, 161–2; of British
    coinage, 69, 133; as corruption, 9,
    116, 161–5
Romulus, 107
Rusellae, 103

Saenu, 74
sailing, 19, 73, 94–5, 103
Sallust, 30, 55, 167
satire, 28, 167; *see also* Catullus;
    comedy; Juvenal; Lucilius
Scipio Africanus, 25–6
Sego, 74
Segovax, 65
Semiramis, 118–20, 142, 146
Seneca, 125, 147
Senecio, 152
Sextus Pompey, 193n.10
Sicily, 29, 30, 34, 36–9
silence, 56, 152–3, 156, 165, 171;
    see also slavery
Silius Italicus, 149–51, 174
Silures, 72
Sitones, 129
slavery, 7, 28, 32, 46, 95, 106, 109,
    122–3, 127–9, 132, 134–5, 139–40,

151–2, 161, 164, 175; *see also* silence
Stanwick, 126
Statius, 149–50, 174
Stoicism, 87; *see also* Helvidius Priscus; Thrasea Paetus
Strabo, 6, 41, 52, 67, 80–9; *see also* geography
subsidies, *see* gifts
Suetonius (biographer), 52, 74, 91–2, 95, 97, 106, 148; grandfather of, 91
Suetonius Paulinus, 109, 136–7, 138, 139, 155, 159–61
Sulis Minerva, 13, 17
Sulla, 29, 187n.46

Tasciovanus, 69, 71, 74, 86
Taximagulus, 65
Tethys, 12
theatre, 3, 5, 35, 36, 39–40, 103; *see also* tragedy
Thrasea Paetus, 139, 152, 172
Thucydides, 27
Thule, 149–50, 158
Tiberius, 6, 11, 41, 69, 84–6, 89, 96
Tides, 62, 64, 73, 84
Tigirseno, 75
Tigurini, 55–6
Tincommius, 65, 72, 84–5, 110
Titus, 126, 148–50, 173
Togodumnus, 99–101, 112
tragedy, Athenian, 26–7, 36, 44; on campaign, 44
Trajan, 8–9, 10, 148, 151–3, 158, 172–3, 175–6, 178
Trebatius, 45–7
Trebellius Maximus, 163
tribes, 72
Trinovantes, 60, 63, 64, 71–2, 74, 75, 135

Ulysses, 42
Usipetes and Tencteri, 51

Valerius Flaccus, 150
Varro Atacinus, 44–5
Vectis, 148, 150
Vellocatus, 126–7, 130
Veneti, 60
Venutius, 126–7, 129–30
Vepocomes, 74–5
Veranius, 109, 159
Verica, 65, 69–70, 71, 72, 73, 85, 96–7, 110
Verres, 29, 35
Vespasian, 8, 73, 117, 126, 128, 147–51, 159; and Claudius, 147–51, 170, 173, 178; and Julius Caesar, 149
Vettius Bolanus, 149–50, 156
Vindolanda, 186n.25, 200n.38
Virgil, 19, 80
Vitellius, L., 93
Volisios, 75
Volusenus, 61
Vosenos, 74

Waterloo helmet, 12, 14
Welwyn, 98–9
wills, 112, 133–4, 144–5
Withington mosaic, 15, 17

Xenophon, 25–8, 158
Xerxes, 92–3, 183n.17

Zalaces, 164
Zenobia, wife of Radamistus, 198n.40
Zonaras, 112–13